C000134091

THE
INVE$TOR'S
SOLUTION

STOCK MARKET
WEALTH CREATION,
SIMPLIFIED

RICHARD WORNER

WHICHWAYHOME LIMITED

Copyright © 2020 WhichWayHome Limited

All rights reserved. No part of this publication may be reproduced, stored in a retrieval system or transmitted in any form or by any means electronic, mechanical, photocopying, recording or otherwise, without written permission of the publisher in advance.

Published by Whichwayhome Limited.

ISBN: 9798597472041

For Cami

ACKNOWLEDGEMENTS

The publisher and its employees would like to thank the following copyright holders for their permission to reproduce copyright material in this book: WNET for sharing "Adam Smith's Money World: Episode #112: Money Managers: Meet The Man Who Bats 1000;" The BBC for sharing "The World's Greatest Money Maker: Evan Davis meets Warren Buffett – A Modest Man.

I've never met Warren Buffett but having immersed myself so deeply in his words I feel like I know him. Mr. Buffett, thank you for your teachings. I have learned a lot from you. Your wisdom has helped me grow to become a better person. I intend to pay it forward.

Jodie Stapleton, thank you for being you, for pushing me, for your infinite creativity and absolute clarity. Our time together is characteristically "*unique and fun*".

RESOURCES

For more resources from THE INVE$TOR'S SOLUTION, please visit: www.theinvestorssolution.com

There you'll find the free Goal Planner & Stock Screen spreadsheet along with recommended stock screen tools and services.

Stay up to date with the latest thinking and developments by following THE INVE$TOR'S SOLUTION on social media.

Instagram: @theinvestorssolution
Facebook: @theinvestorssolution
Twitter: @investssolution

DISCLAIMER

The information in this book does not constitute financial or other professional advice and is general in nature. It is not intended to provide specific guidance, does not take into account your specific circumstances and should not be acted on without professional advice from a fully qualified and independent financial advisor who should have a full understanding of your current situation, future goals and objectives.

Although the publisher and its employees have made every effort to ensure that the information in this book was correct at the time of printing, the publisher and its employees do not assume, and hereby disclaim any liability to any party for any loss, damage or disruption caused by errors or omissions, whether such errors or omissions result from negligence, accident or any other cause.

CONTENTS

INTRODUCTION

People with lots of money didn't always start out that way, and there's no reason you can't join them! Their methods of making money can be studied, understood and replicated. That's what we are going to do here. We're going to peer into the mind of one of the greatest investors of all time, Warren Buffett, distilling his approach right down to its core essence. With these insights fresh in our minds we will then take action, following a set of simple steps towards wealth and freedom. This is the book I wish I'd been given 20 years ago!

WHAT IS YOUR DREAM?

What would it feel like to be wealthy?

How would it feel to have substantial reserves of cash that enable you to do all of the things you want to do, and to be all the things you want to be? How would it feel to be able to chase your dreams? How satisfying would it feel to be filled with the sense of excitement and empowerment that money affords you?

How would it feel to be free, to live life on your own terms?

Perhaps you're more interested in financial freedom - providing security, certainty and safety for yourself and your family. What would it be like to enjoy the freedom and peace of mind that financial security brings? Perhaps you'd buy your own home, pay off your mortgage, retire early or take some time out to travel around the world.

How would it feel to eliminate much of the uncertainty from life?

Imagine not having to worry about going into work each day, or paying the bills. Perhaps you'd like to secure a comfortable retirement, which promises you the quality of life you desire, safe in the knowledge that you won't outlive your savings.

How would it feel to help and support others - those you love and those in need?

How would you contribute to the world, making it a better place? Imagine what things you might discover, new things that excite and reward you, providing you with a clear sense of purpose. How would you use those passions to give back? How would you improve the lives of your family and friends? What opportunities would you give them that you never had?

How would money help you grow as a person?

What would you learn? What new hobbies would you take up? What have you always wanted to do but have never had time for? Perhaps you'd take the opportunity to start your own business and become your own boss.

YET SUCCESS DOESN'T COME EASILY

"There are a million ways to make money in the markets. The irony is that they are all very difficult to find."[1]

Jack D. Schwager, The New Market Wizards

Despite the lure of the financial markets and the promise of untold riches, starting your investing journey can seem like a very daunting prospect. The scale and complexity of the markets, accompanied by the constant bombardment of market and media information, can prove overwhelming. Add to the mix the high levels of volatility we've experienced in recent years and you'd be forgiven for electing to watch from the sidelines instead.

As humans, there are two key challenges we face when investing.

1. MENTAL CHALLENGES

The first of these is mental, concerning our ability to assimilate high volumes of information, focus on the right information, think rationally and make sound judgments.

INFORMATION OVERLOAD

The scope of the financial markets is vast. Every day, tens of thousands of stocks and bonds are traded on exchanges all over the world. There are over 122,000 mutual funds globally, with a combined value exceeding $17.7 Trillion,[2] and over 7,000 ETFs (Exchange-Traded Funds).[3] Add to this list all of the currencies, precious metals, commodities, futures, derivatives and so on, and we're faced with a bewildering array of investment securities to wrap our heads around.

Furthermore, we are continuously being bombarded with new information. Amplified by the speed and reach of the Internet, we have millions of fragments of information coming at us every second. At the current rate, available information doubles every year. Even under ideal conditions, the conscious mind has a limited capacity to process information. So how do we cope?

FOCUSING ON THE RIGHT INFORMATION

In his book, *Trade Your Way to Financial Freedom*, psychologist and trading coach Dr. Van K. Tharp, reveals that our brains have to use 'shortcuts' to generalise and delete most of the information to which we are exposed. This is the only way we can sift and sort vast volumes of data. *"We could never make market decisions without them, but they are also very dangerous to people who are not aware that they exist."*[4] As investors, we must work out whether we're focusing on the right information and not ignoring something important.

In order to distil tens of thousands of stocks, 122,000 mutual funds and 7,000 ETFs, down to a handful of suitable investment candidates, we must determine what criteria we will use to filter them. We must cut through the noise and focus on the things that matter most. But what factors do matter most? Should we examine fundamentals, technicals, or a combination of the two? What metrics and ratios are important predictors of future performance? What about the P/E, P/B, EV, ROA, ROE, ROCE, EPS, DPS, EBITDA, FCF?

To become successful investors, we must decide *what* securities to invest in, and *what* information we will examine to make investment decisions.

FORMING A RATIONAL APPROACH

Once we have decided 'what' we will focus on, we must

consider 'how' we will invest.

Should we go long or short? Should we look for value or use technical charting analysis? Should we follow trends, identify breakouts, trade volatility, identify long-tail events, use arbitrage, trade pairs? There are as many ways to trade as there are securities to trade, so to be successful we must create a rational 'trading system' – our overall approach to investing – and define it very clearly.

Let's say that we have decided to embark on a 'value investing' strategy in which we attempt to profit from a discrepancy between the price of a particular company and the value of its underlying business. To execute that relatively simple approach we'd still need to define what value is, when a security is undervalued, our criteria for buying it when it is undervalued, our criteria for selling it when it is at fair value or overvalued, the size of our position relative to our portfolio equity, our approach in the case that the company announces a merger, and so on.

TIMING INVESTMENTS

Finally, we need to consider 'when' we will invest – the timing of our investments. What are your current views on global macroeconomic trends? Are we heading into a period of growth, recession, or depression? Will inflation rates accelerate due to the high volume of government money printing? What do negative interest rates mean for asset valuations? How will the COVID-19 pandemic stunt economic growth and when will things return to 'normal'?

There are so many interrelated factors impacting the markets that it is impossible to fathom exactly what will happen next. Correlations between different asset classes are highly variable and depend on prevailing circumstances. For example, typically, gold and bond prices are inversely related (move in opposite directions) because increasing inflation will be positive for gold and negative for bonds. However, in the first half of 2020, aggressive monetary easing has lowered interest rates, increasing bond prices, while at the same time surfacing concerns about a possible dollar devaluation further down the road, raising the gold price. In this environment, bond and gold prices have been positively correlated (have moved in the same direction), the exact opposite of their normal relationship.

Given the massive complexity of the financial markets and the impossibility of predicting the future, we must form a practical approach to timing our investments, a rational approach that works in any environment.

2. EMOTIONAL CHALLENGES

The second key challenge humans face when investing is emotional.

*"I believe that uncontrolled basic emotions are the true
and deadly enemy of the speculator; hope,
fear and greed are always present."*[5]

Jesse Livermore, How to Trade in Stocks

For most people, the emotional side of investing is the hardest part to master. First and foremost, investing often becomes dominated by our ego. In the investing process, everything leading up to the point that we invest is in our control - the idea generation, the strategy, the research, the selection of securities, the timing. But as soon as we pull the trigger, we are no longer in control. We are at the mercy of market forces. As market prices swing up and down our emotions have the tendency to swing with them.

The market doesn't care that we have a new position. The market doesn't care whether our wealth is increasing or decreasing. Yet, to the average investor, it sure doesn't feel that way. The negative emotions we experience originate from our ego's perception of the world – it likes little boxes it is familiar with. So if something happens to contradict us, we'll consider that we have suffered in some way. What we call misfortune, or a negative experience, is simply a contradiction of our ego's opinion. When entering the financial markets, the first thing we have to do is to remove our ego.

Investing surfaces several behavioural quirks that result from the way our brains are wired - emotional biases that creep in and affect our decision-making. Examples include:

- Seeing patterns where none exist
- Avoiding evidence that contradicts our views
- Assuming the probability of a win goes up after a long losing streak

Management of our emotional state is no easy task. The truly exceptional investors can remain calm when things aren't going their way, continuing to make rational decisions in accordance with their trading system. But for most of us, a period of poor performance can cause our confidence to wane, leading to sub-optimal decision making, often at exactly the wrong time. We'll always have that little voice in the back of our heads saying, "*What if I'm wrong?*" "*What if I fail?*" "*What if I lose it all?*"

BEEN THERE, OVERCOME THAT

Well, I've experienced all of that, and more! I've been on my investing journey for over 20 years. I made lot of mistakes along the way. You don't have to. You can benefit directly from the things I've learned, accelerating your own journey. Your path will be quicker, easier and more enjoyable.

I started investing while in university and was keen to find investment opportunities that would unlock my dreams. I imagined my wealth growing at a magnificent rate, enabling me to become happy, comfortable and free.

This vision was very appealing as the thought of getting a graduate job was scary and full of uncertainty. I didn't like uncertainty. Yet, for some reason, I believed that the uncertainty that is an inherent part of investing wouldn't bother me. On reflection, this belief probably stemmed from the fact that, through investing, I was taking control of my own life. I preferred making my own decisions and living with the consequences, rather than being told what to do.

Despite having no idea what I was doing, I decided to jump in. I chuckle when I remember the first question that I asked myself: "*How do I invest?*". I was a complete newbie. That first question was quickly followed by "*What should I buy?*", "*When should I buy it?*", "*Why am I buying it?*", "*When should I sell?*", "*How much should I invest?*" and "*How much do I actually have available to invest?*"

I didn't find investing as easy as I had first imagined. I was often nervous and lacked confidence. I was struck by every emotional pitfall that afflicts an investor, every single one. I wondered what I had got myself into. I had trouble with three things in particular.

First, there was the empty, hollow, bottomless-pit-like feeling I got whenever I bought something that immediately went down in price. Everything I bought had the knack of falling 4-5% the instant I clicked the 'Buy' button. I hated that initial feeling of helplessness. It was as though my dreams were being forcibly taken from me.

Second, I was a prisoner of the computer screen for hour upon hour every day. My prison sentence commenced at the instant I bought a stock. Since each second-to-second price change was inextricably linked with my freedom and fortune, how could I look away? On a beautifully sunny day, I'd be on the computer, indoors. Worse still, I was sacrificing time with family and friends.

Third, when a stock I bought actually did go up, I hated the stress of not knowing when to sell. Should I sell quickly and secure a small profit, or hold with the hope of bigger gains, only to endure days and weeks of more volatility and stress?

There had to be a better way. And there was – it may have taken me a while, but I found one!

If you're starting your own investment journey, working out how to invest so that you can provide yourself and your family with financial freedom and wealth, don't worry - I've been there, I've done that, and I have a solution for you.

THE INVESTOR'S SOLUTION

This investment approach is designed to create high levels of compound growth, which, over long periods of time, will afford you all the money and freedom you need to thrive. It is a simple and effective approach. I explain it in clear language and believe, once you have read it and understood it, that you will find it to be sensible and common sense. It is on the low-stress end of the scale. It doesn't require much time to execute or to maintain, leaving you with plenty of time to enjoy life and spend time with family and friends. Plus, anyone can follow it, regardless of IQ level or financial means. I am excited to share it with you.

RICHARD WORNER

CHAPTER 1: THE STUDENT

1998: THE BOOM AND THE BUST

My interest in investing began in 1998, during my final year of university in London. I had no idea what I wanted to pursue as a career, so I began reading the daily newspapers to expand my horizons and become more worldly. I tended to favour financial stories over political and other news, and my attention was drawn towards the abundant share tips, prominently positioned within the financial pages of all leading newspapers. Lured by the temptation of easy riches I began making speculative investments with £3,000 of savings.

Let me share with you the first investment I made, and the pitfalls it created subsequently. Early one morning I bought £1,000 of SmithKline Beecham; a large U.K. pharmaceutical company that the newspapers unanimously concluded was destined for growth. From the instant I clicked 'Buy' I watched the share price tick downwards. Despite having plans to the contrary, I spent the first day of my investment career staring at the computer screen, watching continuously until the market closed.

In the seven hours between purchase and the close, my investment had fallen 2%; I was in the red before my cheque had even cleared. A restless night followed, as I waited for the market to reopen the next morning. On the second day SmithKline opened down further and I felt horrendous. I kept picturing the worst-case scenario; losing the entire £1,000 investment. Yet, I was frozen, unable or perhaps unwilling to sell. Selling would mean taking a loss. Which would mean I was wrong. Which would mean that I had failed. Which would mean that my dream of financial freedom had disappeared. For the second day in a row, I watched the screen all day, feeling like a prisoner of my own making.

I hung on to my position for dear life. After a few more weeks of nerve-wracking fluctuations, the price reversed course and I eventually found myself up about 7%. Reluctant to endure any more stress, I sold out, securing a gain of £70. Relative to the size of my savings, that seemed like a huge win for a few weeks of work, possibly even worth the stress.

What I didn't know then, but do know now, and pass on to you, is that having your first investment go in your favour is possibly the worst thing that can happen as a beginner. It paved the way for huge, painful losses further down the line.

When you're an amateur investor and your first trade goes in your favour, you don't feel the pain of loss. Carried away by hope, it is common to believe that you are somehow a natural at this game. If your first trade is a winner you don't fear the risk of loss as much, and you don't respect your capital as much as you should. Often, this course of events leads to greater risk taking over time, lengthening the learning process as complacency sets in.

Investing is unique in that a complete beginner has a 50/50 chance of being right. You can't simply decide to walk into a courtroom and start practicing law. You have to work hard and undertake strict examinations of your knowledge and skill. It is the same for accountants, doctors, and so on.

In no other profession can you simply just begin and expect to know what you are doing. However, in investing, half of the people will start, and be right the very first time they try. If the entire market were made up of beginners, each betting their entire stake once per day on the outcome of a coin toss, on the first day 50% would be wrong and be out of the game. The remaining 50% would progress to the second day and repeat the process. After a month and 30 trades, some investors would still be in the game and would have won every single day. That winning streak may be attributed to 'skill', but it is simply a matter of luck. Such luck can lead to overconfidence.

Naturally, I thought I was in the 'skilled' camp! It was like that feeling you get when you buy a lottery ticket for the first time, an air of infinite positivity; *"I think I'm actually going to win this thing tonight!"* I continued trading, relying on the newspapers for a never-ending stream of stock tips. I still had some bumps along the way; buying a gaming company at 9 a.m. and seeing it drop 30% at 10 a.m. following a scheduled news announcement that I was blissfully unaware was due; selling a very stable mining stock so that I could immediately re-buy it in a tax-efficient trading account, only to see it rise 10% in the five minutes between me selling it and rebuying it; buying an oil company the day before it experienced a devastating oil spill. There were some priceless, and frustrating moments. But, on balance, I was making money and my wealth was growing at a good rate.

1999

In 1999 I started training as a Chartered Accountant in the Banking & Capital Markets division of PricewaterhouseCoopers, based in London. I continued reading, learning and investing at a furious pace. Stock prices continued to rise, and I was literally experiencing my dream. My capital had grown so much that, on a good day, I would be up £10,000, and gains like that were not uncommon for me. There was one particular instance in which I made over £30,000 in a day. I was experiencing the financial freedom that I had craved. I started looking at flats to buy in Notting Hill and visiting the nearby Ferrari showroom. What I didn't realise was that I was being swept along by one of the biggest manias in history – the Dot-com bubble.

2000

From March 2000 onwards my fortunes reversed. My wealth fell much, much faster than it had grown. I didn't lose everything I had made; my assets fell around 90% from the peak. Compounding my naivety, I bought more stocks as the market plunged, absolutely convinced that I was purchasing bargains. Wrong again! Most of the companies I bought went into administration.

Many of my colleagues suffered the same sudden reversal of fortune that I did. Usually the losses commenced with sharp falls from the market highs, then a long, slow, painful trudge right down to the bottom of the market in March 2003. Three years of losses, that dragged on day after day and month after month, with little sign of recovery. I think it is fair to say that most people lost most, if not all, of the money they had made before the crash.

Now, you might think that this fall from grace hurt me deeply. I would expect the same thing too if I were on the outside looking in, especially given my proclivity for stress in my early trades. However, the more prices fell, the more fascinated I became. I thought to myself, "*Stocks rose at a fantastic rate, the whole world was buying, everyone was happy, and yet, there was this big crash that nobody saw coming - how can this possibly be the case?"*

It was at this point that I noticed a difference between my colleagues and myself. Scarred by losses, they threw in the towel. No more over-the-desk banter about the market. No more inter-office competitions to see who could engineer the best performance over a certain month. They had lost their appetite for investment. It was now a painful topic, dismissed as gambling.

My perspective was different - I was just plain fascinated by the market's capitulation. The losses I experienced had ignited my curiosity. I simply had to know why the market acted like it did. How was it possible to make so much money so quickly and then lose it even quicker? Was it possible to make that money and then just keep it? Are there people out there who anticipated the market's swift demise and capitalised on it? How did they know? How did they do it?

Since I was still training to be an accountant at PricewaterhouseCoopers, I was exposed to a range of companies in the financial sector. My clients included hedge funds that, as I had suspected, knew exactly what was happening and had timed their market exit perfectly. That was all the proof I needed - the markets could be mastered!

2000-2005:
JUST THE BOOM THIS TIME

Between 2000 and 2005 I sought to learn from my previous mistakes. I read as many investment books as I could get my hands on. I undertook investigations to verify the lessons I learned and undertook tests of my ideas. I scribbled down all of my thoughts and revelations and spent hour upon hour reviewing stock charts, company financial statements and news articles. Over time I developed my own investment methodology, designed to foster intelligent capital appreciation, accompanied by low levels of risk.

I formed views top-down, starting with a helicopter view of the entire market. Understanding the market dynamic in that way gave me insights into the stability of the prevailing environment as well as the opportunity to identify market anomalies. My objective was to use those anomalies, and the mispricing they created, to construct trades with valuable asymmetrical risk/reward characteristics. I used fundamentals to determine the relative valuation of asset classes and used technical analysis to estimate price trends and to assist with the timing of investments.

In summary, I was looking for opportunities in which the reward significantly outweighed the risk. The biggest, most successful demonstration of that approach was the prediction of the 2007 Credit Crisis, which as you will see next, was lurking just around the corner.

Please note, this isn't my approach now. I'm simply providing you with an overview of my background so that you can understand the journey I have been on and how I subsequently came to create The Investor's Solution.

2006

In 2006 I felt my understanding shift up a gear. Pieces of the market puzzle began slotting into place. I was able to make key connections between subject matter in different books, leading to an interconnected web of ideas and a world market view. As I read more books my 'bullshit meter' became first class - I could tell from the first couple of chapters, and sometimes from the solely the contents, who knew what they were talking about and who didn't. More importantly, I could tell who was 'right' given prevailing market conditions. I wasn't reading books and forming views from a place of judgment, instead I examined all pieces of information very openly. Some elements simply made rational sense, and fitted neatly with my evolving worldview, while other elements didn't fit whatsoever. Let me give you a specific example to help illustrate my thought process at the time. Back in 2006, there were a number of books warning of a coming deflation, a contraction in the supply of money, and an economic depression. That just wasn't going to happen; there was no way that politicians were going to let us fall into deflation, which would have meant that debt, including government debt, became more expensive to pay off. The U.S. government in particular had a massive debt burden. When they have the option of printing as much money as they wish, stoking inflation, why on earth would they opt for deflation? I became adept at identifying which authors had their finger on the pulse and which didn't.

Crucially, as new information came in, I was able to hold it up and examine it, to compare it against my view of the world, and either enhance that view with the new information so that it made even more sense, or discard the information as 'noise'. That macroeconomic view was reinforced and refined with every passing day.

We were experiencing rapid growth in asset prices, fuelled by low interest rates, money printing and easy credit. House prices had climbed in line with the rapid expansion of credit, creating a feedback loop in which banks loaned money to homebuyers because house prices were rising, but the more the banks loaned, the more that money was used to chase house prices higher still. This had all the hallmarks of a bubble, a flashback to the Dot-com bubble I had experienced in 1999-2000.

In an attempt to help people understand what was happening, to help them avoid the coming crash, and to help them avoid the mistakes I had made previously, I decided to launch a free website to explain my views.

WHICHWAYHOME.COM

In the latter-half of 2006 I wrote the content for the new website, which I named whichwayhome.com. Its mission was to explain the complex, volatile world of investments in a straightforward way. Seeking to identify winning investment themes ahead of time and to position readers to profit from its 'big picture' views, it published unwavering medium- to long-term views and refused to get swayed by short-term volatility or pushed media noise.

At the time, buying a home seemed like a daunting task. Even if you found a property that met your requirements, the financial commitment was colossal. Given the high valuation of property, many readers found themselves asking the difficult question "*Should I buy a house or not?*" hence the origin of the website's name 'Which Way Home'.

The first thing I wrote was what I called '*The Essentials*', eight key facts that readers needed to know in order to make sense of the market and to inform their decision making. Following $640 billion of new 'subprime' loans made in the U.S.A., such loans amounted to a massive 17% of all home purchases that year. Substantially owned by financial institutions and hedge funds, 13% of these loans were delinquent and 2% were in foreclosure.6 And this was the picture while the economy was supposedly healthy! It didn't take much imagination to realise that further deterioration of these loans would have widespread implications for the financial markets.

2007/08: PREDICTING THE CREDIT CRISIS AND AVOIDING THE BUST

As 2007 progressed I published more detailed views on the markets. The economy was beginning to turn, and it was likely that easy money would disappear from the table. I concluded that the increase in loan defaults would accelerate, forcing banks to become more conservative, bringing about a collapse in credit. As credit contracted, high stock prices and house prices would be unsustainable, leading to a massive dislocation in both markets.

Whichwayhome.com was among the tiny number of publications worldwide which successfully predicted the 2007/08 Credit Crisis, the 60% stock market dislocation, the real estate crash (prices fell 33% in the U.S. and 21% in the U.K.), plummeting interest rates, and major blue-chip and Wall Street bankruptcies. The site described how these events would unfold and documented the collapse in real time.

FIGURE 1: WHICHWAYHOME.COM TIMELINE[6]

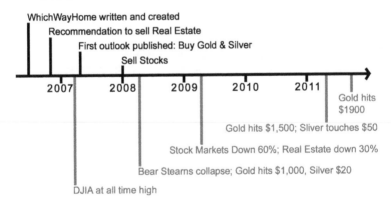

FIGURE 2: WHICHWAYHOME.COM
RECOMMENDATION TO SELL REAL ESTATE[7]

FIGURE 3: WHICHWAYHOME.COM
RECOMMENDATION TO SELL STOCKS[8]

2008: A FORECASTER'S JOB IS NEVER DONE

A year after whichwayhome.com was launched, Wall Street collapsed, house prices crashed, global stock markets crumbled and governments around the world began to bail out disintegrating financial institutions. Despite successfully predicting one of the biggest bubbles and collapses of all time, and despite many of my readers benefiting from those predictions, there was no rest for the wicked. All my readers wanted to know was… *"What's next?"* Back to work for me then!

I had already recommended that my readers buy precious metals in the first quarter of 2007 in order to protect their wealth from inflationary pressures. In 2008 I began shifting more of my focus towards metals.

Money printing had become even more prevalent in response to the global credit crisis, as the monetary powers focused on bailing out the financial system. Central banks were pumping truly vast sums of money into the economy. They were trying their best to provide a financial fix; however, the problem was too much debt, and by focusing very intently on adding more debt they were inadvertently creating bigger problems for themselves further down the line.

I could foresee an increase in inflation in the years ahead and believed that the price of gold and silver would increase as a safe haven, a store of wealth and a hedge against that inflation. While the precious metals were likely to suffer from market volatility over the short term, I believed that their long-term destiny had already been set out by the actions of governments and central banks. From the point I recommended buying precious metals until their peak in 2011, both gold and silver tripled in value.

FIGURE 4: WHICHWAYHOME.COM
RECOMMENDATION TO BUY GOLD[9]

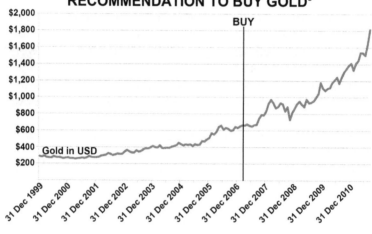

FIGURE 5: WHICHWAYHOME.COM
RECOMMENDATION TO BUY SILVER[10]

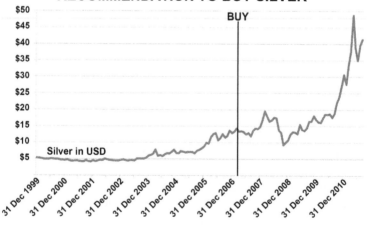

2009-2019: CLARITY

After just over 10 years of intensive immersion in the financial markets, with some big successes along the way, I was exhausted. I felt a lot of pressure to deliver the best insights to my readers and to continue to work out big market moves. I was fatigued, and some of the passion I once felt had started to fade.

I mirror Ray Dalio's sentiment that market relationships operate in a certain way for long periods of time, and that big shifts in behaviour, which he calls "*paradigm shifts*" happen in roughly 10-year cycles.[11] The 1990s built towards the top of the Dot-com bubble, which burst in 2000. In the 2000s we built towards the bursting of the Credit Crisis, which finished unraveling in 2009. I decided to take a decade off. I needed to recharge and to clear my head. I wanted to allow the insights and knowledge I had accumulated to sink in. I also wanted to go through a filtering process, allowing certain rationales, thoughts and beliefs to drop away over time, leaving me with a better, simpler, purer approach to the markets.

For a long time, I didn't read a single new book, look at a chart or read a financial headline. I knew the time would come when I would instinctively resume my studies. Then, in 2019, I started reading in earnest once again. Knowledge gained from previous experiences combined with a more mature, steady and patient mindset. It occurred to me that this fresh start provided a great opportunity to revisit the life and works of the world's greatest investors. Warren Buffett was top of mind. His relaxed approach and quiet demeanour, yet stellar track record, were traits worthy of emulation.

I read his annual reports, I watched footage of his shareholder meetings, I watched interviews with him and read articles he'd published in the past. The true essence of his approach became clearer to me every time I read his words or heard him speak. It was so simple. And it was clearly very effective – he is one of the richest men in the world. A sense of serenity washed over me when, once again in life, I felt like I had reached a higher level of understanding.

Previously, I had read tens of books about Buffett, his life and his approach. As I outlined the concept for this book, I continued to conduct more research, reading another thirty or so. While each was very interesting, and I learned something from every single one of them, none of them appeared to convey the simplicity of his approach. In some cases, I might even suggest that that the authors *over-complicated* his approach. Few contained specifics on how to replicate his performance, and many attributed Buffett's performance to his own particular and unique skills as an investor.

When you listen to the man himself, however, he tells a different story. He insists that he uses a simple approach and that anyone can do it. What's more, he has been telling us the same thing over and over again for decades!

I believe this book is a great combination of Buffett's core investment philosophies, and my ability to simplify complex information into practical investment approaches. I believe it will help you to create wealth and freedom in a smart, efficient and effective manner.

CHAPTER 2 : INVESTORS, OBSTACLES & SOLUTIONS

CHAPTER SUMMARY
2.1 INVESTOR PROFILES
2.2 INVESTOR NEEDS
2.3 INVESTOR OBSTACLES & SOLUTIONS

By far, the biggest challenge I faced when writing this book was to create an investment approach that was broad enough to cater to a very wide investor audience, yet tailorable and actionable enough to satisfy an individual investor's unique requirements. I wanted anyone to be able to pick up *The Investor's Solution* and to be able to employ its methods. This required an approach built using simple, universal principles.

As readers, you will study the pages of this book at different points in time and in different parts of the world. You will be experiencing different economic conditions, transacting in different currencies, and abiding by different tax laws. Furthermore, each of you will be in different life stages, have different needs, motivations, ambitions and timeframes. You will have different concerns and face different obstacles.

Fortunately, whenever you pick up this book, wherever you are in the world, and whatever your particular set of requirements might be, core commonalities exist among all of you. I have sought to create a solution that addresses those commonalities.

To demonstrate this, we will step into the shoes of four different investors. Each has a different background, is situated within a different life stage, possesses different goals, and uses different criteria to drive their decision-making. Despite these differences, you will notice that they possess consistent needs, face common obstacles and ask similar questions. *The Investor's Solution* aims to fulfil those needs, address those obstacles and answer those questions.

2.1
INVESTOR PROFILES

INVESTOR A
NEW TO INVESTING, WANTS CASH RESERVES TO PROVIDE FREEDOM AND FLEXIBILITY, WANTS TO LEARN FROM A TRUSTED GUIDE

"I am a beginner investor. I have a proactive personality and am keen to learn. I'd like to learn how to invest so that I can build some cash reserves and one day be wealthy."

"I want to live life on my own terms, with plenty of freedom and flexibility. I'd like to enjoy life in the moment, with the ability to travel often, for fun and adventure."

"I am early in my career, so I have plenty of time before I need to think about retirement. My aspiration would be to retire as early as possible. At the very least I'd like to generate a stream of income, independent of my job, that provides me with the option of retiring early."

"I am an independent thinker who does not follow tips or advice blindly. I like to have all the facts so that I can make my own decisions. While I am excited to learn, I have zero idea where to start. Every day I am bombarded by conflicting opinions in the media. I am blinded by information and don't know what to do!"

"I like the idea of learning from great investors who have already achieved success and can accelerate my learning. I'd prefer a step-by-step approach that I can learn a bit at a time. It must be simple and easy to action."

KEY OUTCOMES:
- An effective approach that ensures my wealth will grow
- Financial freedom and flexibility
- To travel often and experience the world
- To create an independent income stream
- To retire early

WHAT WOULD BE USEFUL IS:
- A trusted guide to learn from
- To know what stocks to buy
- To know why I am buying so that I can understand more clearly and learn faster
- An effective, step-by-step process that anyone can follow
- An approach that doesn't require too much money
- A way of using market crashes to my advantage, making them work for me

INVESTOR B
FAMILY SECURITY AND PEACE OF MIND

"I am the parent of two young kids. Spending time with them is my favourite thing to do. I love to laugh with them, to play and to watch them grow. I want to give my kids a wide variety of experiences, like clubs, sports, travels, and I want to be able to put them through college."

"I enjoy my job, but it doesn't rock my world and it isn't going to make me super rich. I'd like to provide a comfortable future for my family, but I don't want to sacrifice our time together or our quality of life. I want to secure financial freedom so that we can enjoy experiences without having to worry about money."

"I'm frustrated because the current low interest rates mean that my pension and modest savings aren't growing. I have no certainty over the size of my pension pot on retirement or the income stream it will provide. As a result, I'd like to take more proactive control of my finances."

"Being a parent of young kids, I don't have a lot of free time, and when I do, I'm often exhausted. At the moment I feel overwhelmed by the thought of investing on my own. I haven't done anything like this before, so I lack the confidence required to start and I have procrastinated until now. I'd like a practical, no-fuss way of investing for the long-term."

"I plan to put aside 10% of my income for investment each month. I'd like to generate meaningful returns from my money but need some assurance that the approach will work – I do not want to gamble with our futures by taking on too much risk. It seems sensible to make the most of tax efficiencies so that I have as much money working for me

over the long-term as possible."

KEY OUTCOMES:
- To secure financial freedom for myself and my family
- To avoid unnecessary stress and achieve peace of mind
- An effective way of investing 10% of my income each month
- To know why I am buying so I have the courage to sit through price fluctuations
- A way to gauge whether I am likely to achieve my goals

WHAT WOULD BE USEFUL IS:
- Having the complex world of investing simplified for me
- Learning in digestible chunks and in plain language
- An approach that is easy to action
- An approach that doesn't take much time
- An approach that works for any income level

INVESTOR C
SEEKING CERTAINTY OVER PENSION INCOME AND RETIREMENT TIMEFRAME

"I am a successful businessperson, around halfway through my career. I have progressed quickly at work and have a good salary that enables me to save money and contribute to my pension each month. I also have a lump sum available that I could invest if the right opportunity came along. My family lives comfortably and we have a high quality of life."

"Being able to retire early is very appealing to me but I need to balance that desire with the ability to maintain our standard of living. I want the peace of mind of knowing that, by the time I retire, I will be debt-free and have paid off the mortgage."

"I feel concerned that, despite the savings I have built up over the last twenty years, historically low interest rates mean that the income I'll earn on my investments won't be enough to cover our living expenses when I retire. At the current interest rate of 0.5%, a $1 million pension pot would only provide me with $5,000 of interest income - hardly adequate."

"I'd like more certainty so that I can plan ahead. I'd like to know what returns are possible in order to retire comfortably, and when retirement is likely to happen. I need a clear approach that will generate compelling returns and will make my money work for me."

"Between my job, my family and friends and my hobbies, I don't have a lot of free time to do endless reading or research. But I want to take control of my future – now is the time to make it happen."

KEY OUTCOMES:
- To retire early and enjoy the freedom I've worked hard to achieve
- To have sufficient income in retirement so that I can maintain our quality of life
- To sense check the expected value of my investments on retirement
- To know what to buy in order to bridge any shortfall
- To meet those financial goals without taking on too much risk

WHAT WOULD BE USEFUL IS:
- Knowing the most effective way of putting my money to work
- A way to project my returns into the future so I can course-correct my investments or add more savings over time if required

- A way of experimenting with different retirement dates to work out different retirement scenarios
- An approach that isn't overly complex and doesn't take up too much time

INVESTOR D
LANDLORD SEEKING DIVERSIFICATION WITHOUT SACRIFICING RETURNS

"I am a landlord with an established property portfolio. The properties are financed with mortgages that are paid off by the tenants over time. There is a high degree of leverage employed in the portfolio – I put in 20% and loans make up the remaining 80%, resulting in portfolio leverage of 5x my equity."

"By its nature, my portfolio is illiquid. Substantial transaction costs would be required in order to liquidate. The size of the mortgage payments and the value of the properties are both exposed to a rise in interest rates from the current historic lows. The leverage amplifies the risk of a fall in property prices."

"Recent tax changes have eaten into the returns achievable. I have additional money available to invest and would like to do so in a tax efficient manner."

"It is crucial for me to maintain an independent source of income in order to remain self-employed, managing the portfolio. I enjoy working for myself and find managing my assets stimulating and engaging. Longer-term I intend for the portfolio to act as my pension."

"I would like to reduce the concentration of risk in a single investment sector, gradually re-balancing the portfolio to incorporate other asset types. By purchasing stocks, I may

be able to create returns in excess of those possible within the property portfolio, while simultaneously reducing risk and leverage."

"I have learned how to invest in property, but that knowledge doesn't translate directly to the stock market. I lack the confidence to jump in without a robust approach."

KEY OUTCOMES:
- To maintain or enhance my independent source of income
- To diversify my holdings while maintaining or exceeding the long-term expected return
- To reduce the leverage inherent in a property portfolio
- To reduce exposure to a single investment sector (real estate)
- To take advantage of tax efficient vehicles

WHAT WOULD BE USEFUL IS:
- An investment approach that is transparent so that I can fully understand it
- To understand what returns will be generated and whether these are comparable to leveraged property investment
- Having stock market investing simplified for me
- New and effective ways of putting my money to work

INVESTOR PROFILE SUMMARY

While each investor's requirements reflect different sets of circumstances, clear commonalities exist between each of them. These commonalities have their roots in our evolutionary past and are driven by human nature. The five key needs we will examine on our investment journey are: the need for *Freedom*, the need for *Independence*, the need for *Security*, the need for *Knowledge*, and the need to *Give Back*.

2.2
INVESTOR NEEDS

THE NEED FOR FREEDOM

How would it feel to be free, not burdened by anything?

Imagine a life that isn't governed by calendars and alarm clocks, one in which you have all the time in the world. Imagine being able to change your plans at the drop of a hat and travel the world. Take a moment to imagine yourself in that situation. Perhaps you'll bring to mind the feelings associated with arriving at an exotic destination; stepping outside an air-conditioned airport to feel the warm air hit your body. Or that moment you get to the beach, wiggle and bury your toes into the sand, and let all the stress and tension release in one big exhale as the waves roll in gently around your feet.

THE NEED FOR INDEPENDENCE

How would it feel if you only had to answer to yourself?

While, on the surface, many claim to want to be *wealthy*, what they're really looking for is the sense of *Independence*, which is the empowerment that money affords them. After all, it's not the money that matters; it's what you do with that money that counts! Having cash reserves enables you to do all of the things you want to do, without having to answer to anybody. Imagine no longer having to worry about going into work each day, instead being able to support yourself.

Achieving *Independence* requires that the return you receive from your savings and investments is sufficient to provide you with all of the income you need to live comfortably. In effect, the money works for you, you don't work for it.

THE NEED FOR SECURITY

How would it feel to be more certain of outcomes?

What prevents us from feeling *Freedom* and *Independence* is a lack of *Security* in life. The need for *Security* might be tangible, such as guaranteeing safety for yourself and for your family. It might come from the knowledge that you can buy a home, pay off the mortgage, pay the bills, and put your kids through college. It might also be aspirational - the desire to know what the future holds. I'm sure we'd all like to flash forward to know how much money we'll make through investing, and when we'll reach a certain monetary goal. Wouldn't this immediately reduce your stress and enable you to plan better? Perhaps you'd like to secure a comfortable retirement, certain that you won't outlive your savings. Perhaps you'd like to retire early, or young. If you knew the future, you wouldn't have to worry in the present, and life would be significantly more enjoyable.

THE NEED FOR KNOWLEDGE

How would money help you learn and grow as a person?

Learning and growth equal happiness. Success in investing is a worthy goal, but it is worthless if it is not accompanied by success in your life. It is important in life to learn, to improve yourself, to expand your horizons and experience new things. Think about the things you have always wanted to do but have never had time for. Where would you travel? What language would you learn? What hobbies would you take up? If you were entrepreneurial, what business would you start?

"By far the best investment you can make is in yourself."[12]

Warren Buffett

THE NEED TO GIVE BACK

How would it feel if you could help and support others - those you love and those in need?

There is also the need to give back - to love, help and support others. How would you make the world a better place? What is your true purpose in life? How would you use your passions to contribute? How would you improve the lives of your family and friends? What opportunities would you give them that you never had? My hope is that *The Investor's Solution* will enable you to reach your goals, creating financial *Freedom*, *Independence*, *Security* and *Knowledge*. Its impact will be amplified if you then take some of that money and do good things in this world of ours by *Giving Back*.

"The best armour of old age is a well spent life preceding it; a life employed in the pursuit of useful knowledge, in honourable actions and the practice of virtue; in which he who labours to improve himself from his youth will in age reap the happiest fruits of them; not only because these never leave a man, not even in the extreamest old age; but because a conscience bearing witness that our life was well spent, together with the remembrance of past good actions, yields an unspeakable comfort to the soul."[13]

Cicero

I'm sure you will be able to relate to all five needs, and to some needs more than others. To satisfy those needs we must overcome four principle obstacles that stand in our way: A *Lack of Confidence*, a *Lack of Knowledge*, a *Lack of Money*, and a *Lack of Time*.

These obstacles give rise to questions. A lack of confidence, for example, generally arises from the need to know "*Why am I doing it?*" and "*Will it work?*" A lack of knowledge gives rise to the questions "*What do I need to do?*" and "*Can you show me how?*" A lack of money gives rise to the question "*How much do I need to invest?*" and a lack of time gives rise to the questions, "*How long will it take to learn?*" and "*How long will it take to get a return?*"

Figure 6 illustrates how *The Investor's Solution* overcomes these obstacles and addresses these questions.

FIGURE 6: INVESTOR NEEDS, OBSTACLES, QUESTIONS AND SOLUTIONS

INVESTOR NEEDS	OBSTACLES	QUESTIONS	SOLUTIONS
Freedom	A. Lack of Confidence	A1. Why am I doing it?	A1. Transparent & common sense
Independence		A2. Will it work?	A2. Demonstrated to work
Security	B. Lack of Knowledge	B1. What do I need to do?	B1. Simple
Knowledge		B2. Can you show me how?	B2. Actionable
Giving Back	C. Lack of Money	C. How much do I need to invest?	C. Scalable
	D. Lack of Time	D. How long will it take to learn and return?	D1. Efficient
			D2. Incremental

2.3
INVESTOR OBSTACLES & SOLUTIONS

OBSTACLE A: LACK OF CONFIDENCE

QUESTION A.1: WHY AM I DOING IT?
"I am an independent thinker who does not follow tips or advice blindly. I like to have all the facts so that I can make my own decisions."

Investor A

"I'd like to know why I am buying so that I can understand more clearly and learn faster."

Investor A

"I'd like to know why I am buying so I have the courage to sit through price fluctuations."

Investor B

SOLUTION A.1: IT'S A TRANSPARENT, COMMON SENSE APPROACH
In any investing endeavor, it is crucially important to understand why you are doing what you are doing. When writing this book, and describing *The Investor's Solution*, I chose to be as clear and transparent as possible so that you can understand the why. By truly understanding the underlying idea, I was able to express it so that others can understand and utilise it. I believe this book successfully combines timeless investment philosophies with a clear, common sense investment approach.

QUESTION A.2: WILL IT WORK?

"I like the idea of learning from great investors who have already achieved success and can accelerate my learning."
Investor A

"I'd like to generate meaningful returns from my money but need some assurance that the approach will work – I do not want to gamble with our futures by taking on too much risk."
Investor B

"I'd like more certainty so that I can plan ahead. I'd like to know what returns are possible in order to retire comfortably."
Investor C

SOLUTION A.2: IT'S DEMONSTRATED TO WORK

The best way to demonstrate that an approach works is to find someone who has already achieved what you want; a trusted guide you can follow. I selected one of the greatest investors of all time, Warren Buffett, as our trusted guide for three key reasons. First, his track record is unparalleled, and thus his investment approach is highly effective. Second, his record spans decades, it is not the result of luck. Third, he uses timeless principles that don't change over time and remain consistent regardless of the market environment. *The Investor's Solution* utilises the core of Buffett's approach to make above-average returns available to all.

OBSTACLE B: LACK OF KNOWLEDGE

QUESTION B.1: WHAT DO I NEED TO DO?

"While I am excited to learn, I have zero idea where to start.

Every day I am bombarded by conflicting opinions in the media. I am blinded by information and don't know what to do!"

Investor A

"I need a clear approach that will generate compelling returns and will make my money work for me."

Investor C

SOLUTION B.1: IT'S A SIMPLE APPROACH

When you first start out on your investment journey you are bombarded by different ticker symbols, metrics, tips, advice and jargon. It is a nightmare! *The Investor's Solution*, by contrast, is a simple distillation of a few key principles, mechanisms and metrics. I will show you a straightforward way to achieve above-average returns.

The lessons start with the absolute basics and we build from there. In the next chapter you will discover four of Warren Buffett's high-level investment principles. You will then learn four key investment mechanisms that he uses to achieve superior returns. You will find his approach sensible and understandable. Next, using only a few key metrics, you will learn how to estimate the theoretical short- and long-term returns you can expect to achieve with a particular stock investment. You'll learn how to connect the two, giving you the ability to estimate your theoretical return at any point in time. In Chapter 8 you'll learn how to optimise those returns, and by the time we reach Chapter 12 you'll be screening for your own investment opportunities and making your own investment decisions.

QUESTION B.2: CAN YOU SHOW ME HOW TO DO IT?

"What would be useful is having the complex world of investing simplified for me."

Investor B

"I'd like an effective, step-by-step process that anyone can follow...it must be simple and easy to action."

Investor A

SOLUTION B.2: IT'S AN ACTIONABLE APPROACH

It's not my job to change people; my job is to lead by example. I will provide the background, context and approach, but it is up to you to take the action - nobody is going to do that for you. The great news is that the actions you need to take are straightforward and easy to follow.

We have already discovered that *The Investor's Solution* is transparent and common sense, so you will know *why* you are doing it. Buffett has demonstrated that these concepts work, so you can have confidence in the long-term results. It's a simple approach, requiring knowledge of only a few key principles, mechanisms and metrics. The barriers to action are truly minimal. I'll take you through the process step-by-step and you can immediately take what you have learned and screen the market for stocks matching your particular investment criteria.

OBSTACLE C: LACK OF MONEY

QUESTION C: HOW MUCH DO I NEED TO INVEST?

"What would be useful is an approach that doesn't require too much money."

Investor A

"What would be useful is an approach that works for any income level...an effective way of investing 10% of my income each month."

Investor B

"I'd like a way to project my returns into the future so I can course-correct my investments or add more savings over time if required."

Investor C

SOLUTION C: IT'S SCALABLE

Anyone can follow this approach, regardless of financial means. If you have a lump sum to invest you can screen for stocks that meet your criteria and add several holdings to your portfolio immediately. If you are adding to your investments on a regular basis, you can add a new holding with each new installment or top up existing holdings. If you can only invest a small amount, perhaps on an irregular basis, you can drip-feed that money into a low-cost index fund or save up your installments to make a larger investment at a later date. Rest assured, having a small amount of money to invest does not preclude you from following *The Investor's Solution*. In fact, it might be the most suitable approach for the small investor to take.

"It's a huge structural advantage not to have a lot of money."[14]

Warren Buffett - The Warren Buffett You Don't Know, Business Week

OBSTACLE D: LACK OF TIME

QUESTION D: HOW LONG WILL IT TAKE TO LEARN AND RETURN?

So, how long will it take to get a good return? *The*

Investor's Solution provides you with a range of options to balance short- and long-term performance to suit your individual needs. If you are planning to retire within 10 years, there are particular stock characteristics that you would look for to maximise your chance of generating high returns during that period of time. Such stocks are likely to offer lower returns over the longer-term, however. Alternatively, if you have a long-term view you could look for stocks that offer lower returns in the early years but experience substantial growth as time passes.

For example, an investor with a long-term horizon and the ambition to exceed Warren Buffett's track record of 20% per annum might select a stock that returns only 5% in the first year of investment, but grows to achieve a cumulative return of 12% per annum by Year 10, 19% by Year 20, and 22.5% by Year 30.

It is a balancing act, based on your own personal circumstances.

SOLUTION D.1: IT'S AN EFFICIENT APPROACH

"Being a parent of young kids, I don't have a lot of free time, and when I do, I'm often exhausted...I'd like a practical, no-fuss way of investing for the long-term."

Investor B

"Between my job, my family and friends, and my hobbies, I don't have a lot of free time to do endless reading or research."

Investor C

"I'd like an approach that isn't overly complex and doesn't take up too much time."

Investor C

The Investor's Solution doesn't require much time to read, understand, action or maintain, leaving you with plenty of time to enjoy life. Since the approach is based on timeless principles and mechanisms, once you've learned them, they will remain in place throughout your entire investing career. Once you have made an investment, you only need to check on its performance once per year, following the release of that company's annual results.

SOLUTION D.2: IT'S AN INCREMENTAL APPROACH

"I'd prefer a step-by-step approach that I can learn a bit at a time."

Investor A

"What would be useful is learning in digestible chunks and in plain language."

Investor B

Learning a small amount each day really adds up. If you can improve a capability just 1% per day, after one year you will have improved that capability 36-fold. This is the beauty of compounding, which we will examine in the next chapter. Any task or topic can be broken down and conquered in this way, irrespective of how daunting the initial task may seem. This book may itself seem daunting at first, but I talk you through *The Investor's Solution* step-by-step. Read one page a day, taking time to fully absorb it, and before you know it you'll have mastered an investment approach that will serve you for the rest of your life.

For an investment approach to be truly successful it must be accessible to all types of investor. This book seeks to provide universal solutions to common investor obstacles, providing everybody with the opportunity to achieve above-average returns.

Later in the book we will revisit these four investor profiles, establishing their particular investment time horizons and return goals, before going on to identify stocks that meet their unique investment requirements.

In the meantime, it's time to start discovering some investment basics. Let's turn to Chapter 3 and discover how Warren Buffett became one of the greatest investors of all time, and one of the richest men in the world.

RICHARD WORNER

CHAPTER 3:
THE MASTER

CHAPTER SUMMARY
3.1 WARREN BUFFETT'S TRACK RECORD
3.2 INVESTMENT PRINCIPLES
    1: SIMPLE IS BETTER
    2: ANYONE CAN DO IT
    3: OWN PART OF A BUSINESS, NOT A STOCK
    4: HOLD FOR A LONG TIME
3.3 INVESTMENT MECHANISMS
    1: RETURN ON EQUITY
    2: PRICE
    3: COMPOUND GROWTH
    4: CAPITAL ALLOCATION
3.4 CHAPTER RECAP

3.1
WARREN BUFFETT'S TRACK RECORD

If we want a highly successful, trusted financial guide to imitate, one investor stands head and shoulders above all others, Warren Buffett.

THE EARLY YEARS

Warren Buffett began investing at an early age. By the time he was 26 he had already created his own investment firm, the Buffett Partnership. The partnership started with $105,100. Buffett, acting as the general partner put up $100, and a mix of family members and friends put up the remaining $100,000, participating as limited partners.

Over the next 13 years Buffett achieved extraordinary results, materially beating the S&P every single year, and without employing leverage. Between 1957 and 1969 the Buffett Partnership achieved an average annual return of 30.4%.[15]

THE BERKSHIRE YEARS

Buffett dissolved the Buffett Partnership 1969, but before doing so he started to buy shares in an undervalued company called Berkshire Hathaway. Berkshire was a textile business that was in terrible condition and was destined to become extinct eventually.

Buffett started buying shares in 1962 and by 1965 had acquired enough shares to establish control of the company. Once in control, he made the decision not to make any further investments in the low-return textile business. Berkshire was closing mills, and as it closed mills it would free up some capital. Buffett used the capital thrown off by Berkshire to buy businesses with much more favourable economics, starting with the insurance company

Northern Indemnity. Using NI's vast insurance float, he bought additional publicly traded securities and wholly owned businesses. In short order, through these acquisitions, Buffett turned an ailing Berkshire into a profitable, cash-generating business.

Since then, by investing in stocks and buying entire businesses, Buffett has grown the market capitalisation of Berkshire Hathaway from around $18 million to an astounding $420 billion today. On a per-share basis, the share price has grown from $7 to $340,000. Nobody else has a track record as impressive. In 2019 Berkshire ranked fourth on the Fortune 500 list of largest U.S. companies, trailing only Walmart, Exxon Mobil, and Apple.[16]

To reinforce the spectacular nature of these results, the second page of the 2019 Berkshire Hathaway Annual Report sets out his track record relative to the S&P500 for the last 55 years.[17] Over that timeframe Buffett grew the per-share market value of Berkshire at an annual compound rate of 20.3%, trouncing the 10.0% delivered by the S&P 500 (with dividends included). To put that performance into perspective, the overall gain in Berkshire's value over that period was 2,744,062%, versus 19,784% for the S&P 500. 20% is an excellent return for a single year; but 20% per year over several decades is unheard of.

FIGURE 7: BERKSHIRE HATHAWAY PERFORMANCE VERSUS THE S&P 500 WITH DIVIDENDS INCLUDED[17]

	Annual Percentage Change in Per-Share Market Value of Berkshire Hathaway	Annual Percentage Change in S&P500 with Dividends Included
Compound Annual Gain 1965-2019	20.3%	10.0%
Overall Gain 1964-2019	2,744,062%	19,784%

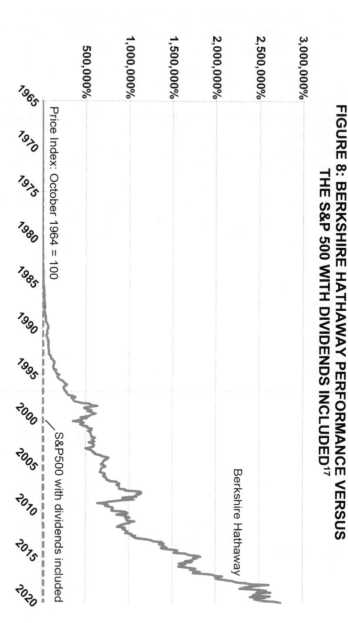

FIGURE 8: BERKSHIRE HATHAWAY PERFORMANCE VERSUS THE S&P 500 WITH DIVIDENDS INCLUDED[17]

Buffett's investment approach has made him one of the richest people on earth. According to Bloomberg's Billionaire Index, at the time of writing, Buffett has a net worth of $80.8 billion.[18] Every year, over 40,000 investors flock to Omaha to see Buffett at the Berkshire Hathaway Annual Meeting where he discusses the results of the company, imparts wisdom to the audience and answers their questions for several hours.

Yet, despite his enormous wealth and success, Buffett is quiet, down to earth, witty and unassuming. He still lives in the same modest house he bought for $31,000 over 60 years ago - and it's not even the biggest house on his street. Berkshire Hathaway's head office has been based in the same office building, located in Omaha, Nebraska, for over 58 years. Buffett likes to keep things quiet there, shutting the door to his office and reading for 5 or 6 hours a day.[19] He only has 26 people at head office, despite the fact that Berkshire and its consolidated subsidiaries employ over 390,000 people worldwide.[20]

In 2006 Buffett pledged to give away over 99% of his fortune to charity, much of it to the foundation of his friends Bill and Melinda Gates. It is the largest philanthropic gift in history.[21]

3.2
INVESTMENT PRINCIPLES

INVESTMENT PRINCIPLE 1:
SIMPLE IS BETTER

"Business schools reward complex behavior more than simple behavior, but simple behavior is more effective."[22]

Warren Buffett - The Convictions of a Long Distance Investor, Channels

"There seems to be some perverse human characteristic that likes to make easy things difficult."[23]

Warren Buffett - The Superinvestors of Graham-and-Doddsville

Ever on the lookout for great businesses to buy, in his 1982 Letter to Shareholders, Buffett ran an advert to encourage acquisition candidates to contact him.[24] His requirements were very simple:

- Large businesses with at least $5m in after-tax earnings
- A historical record of consistent earnings power, noting he was not interested in projections of future earnings or turn-around situations
- Good returns on equity while employing little or no debt
- A simple business that he can understand
- Management to remain in place, so that Buffett doesn't have to manage the new business himself
- An offering price that makes sense

In his 2014 Letter to Shareholders, some 32 years after the original, Buffett's re-published the advert.[25] Other than a single amendment to the after-tax earnings requirement, adjusted upwards to $75m to take into account Berkshire's greater size, Buffett's purchase criteria remained unchanged, and consistently simple.

In both instances he also proclaimed that he could provide a very fast answer, customarily within five minutes![24,25,26] There is *no* complex financial modelling here. Yes, his speed is partly the result of his vast experience, but it is equally the result of his simple approach.

In a 1985 TV interview on *Adam Smith's Money World*, Buffett was asked, if it really is so simple, why doesn't everybody adopt his approach? "*I think, partly, because it is so simple*,"[27] Buffett said. He noted that the academics delve into all sorts of variables, just because the data exists. They might analyse the data a thousand different ways and come up with elaborate patterns and predictions. When you've learned how to manipulate data, and specialise in manipulating that data, there is a human tendency to make data manipulation the centre of your universe; to a man with a hammer, every problem looks like a nail.

People like to make predictions about the future of the market, but conditions are constantly changing, rendering forecasts ineffective. In all the years that Buffett has invested at Berkshire Hathaway, he has never made a decision based on a prediction of what the economy will do in the future.[28] If you can adopt Buffett's simple approach, one that has made him extraordinarily rich, why seek to make things any more complicated than that?

This line of thinking extends to his selection of companies that he 'understands'. After all, why should we expect to make money on things we don't understand?[29] Buffett believes that we must only invest in businesses that we understand and can reasonably conclude will still be doing well 10, 15 or 20 years from now.[30] In a 1998 Fortune article he provided a great example of this thinking, "*Take Wrigley's chewing gum,*" he said, "*I don't think the Internet is going to change how people are going to chew gum.*"[31]

Buffett believes that Coca-Cola will still be the drink of preference 15 or 20 years from now. He owns 9.3% of the company, the largest manufacturer and distributor of carbonated soft drink concentrates and syrups in the world. Arguably the world's favourite drink, Coca-Cola has been enjoyed since 1886. We humans require between 70-100 ounces of water a day just to survive, and there are over 7 billion of us on the planet. By creating a refreshing drink with a satisfying flavor, Coca-Cola has established universal appeal, making the ingestion of water a more pleasurable experience. The result has been market domination; Coca-Cola sells 2 billion servings per day across 200 countries.

Prior to its acquisition by Proctor & Gamble in 2005, Buffett also held a large investment in Gillette. Shaving has been around for a very long time and this activity is unlikely to change in the future. Every night, 3.5 billion males around the planet go to bed and their hair grows while they sleep. Every morning Gillette has 3.5 billion potential new customers who need to shave and must buy razors in order to do so. Of the 20-21 billion razor blades consumed at the time of the P&G acquisition, 30% of those were Gillette's, representing 60% of sales by value. Gillette had 90% market share in some countries. Here's something you need to do every day, and for only $20 a year Gillette gives you a terrific shaving experience. Gillette's position, both in the market and in the minds of consumers, was incredibly strong and durable.

"I can understand Gillette, I can understand Coca-Cola and I can understand Wrigley's Chewing Gum...and I have a pretty good idea of what they're going to look like 10-15 years from now."[30]

Buffett's partner at Berkshire Hathaway, Charlie Munger, sums all of this up for us: *"We have to deal in things that we're capable of understanding. And then, once we're over* that filter we have to have a business with some intrinsic characteristics that give it a durable competitive advantage. And then, of course, we vastly prefer a management in place with a lot of integrity and talent. And finally, no matter how wonderful it is, it's not worth an infinite price, so we have to have a price that makes sense. It's a very simple set of ideas."[32]

INVESTMENT PRINCIPLE 2:
ANYONE CAN DO IT

"*You don't need to be a rocket scientist. Investing is not a game where the guy with the 160 IQ guy beats the guy with the 130 IQ.*"[33]

Warren Buffett – Tap Dancing to Work: Warren Buffett on Practically Everything

"*What we do is not beyond anyone else's competence...it is just not necessary to do extraordinary things to get extraordinary results.*"[34]

Warren Buffett – Fortune, April 1988

Buffett's success as an investor has led amateur investors, and investment professionals alike, to emulate his strategies. His approach is hidden in plain sight. Countless times he has talked about it openly in interviews, in the media, at his annual shareholder meetings and in his letters to Berkshire Hathaway shareholders.

He insists that you don't need to be a genius. "*It's a temperamental quality not an intellectual quality. You don't need tons of IQ in this business...you do not have to be able to play three-dimensional chess.*"[35]

Buffett doesn't have a computer in his office, a calculator

or a stock ticker.[36] Sitting in his Omaha office, reading quietly, is a world away from the Wall Street stereotype of frantic trading rooms and high-stress day trading. Most investors monitor the market constantly, following fleeting price movements, jumping in and out of stocks and chasing quick profits. Yet, despite all of that activity, not one of them is as successful as Buffett.

Buffett's secret to investment success is not finding hidden gems, unseen or overlooked by amateur investors, professional traders and hedge funds. His biggest stock market investments are currently Apple, of which he owns 5.7% of the company, worth $73.3 billion, Bank of America (10.7%, $33.4 billion), Coca-Cola (9.3%, $22.1 billion), American Express (18.7%, $18.9 billion), and Wells Fargo (8.4%, $38.2 billion).[37] These are household names, of which we are all aware. After examining his investment track record, one might easily conclude that the average investor could have easily replicated a large number of Buffett's purchases. His secret to success is not hidden - wealth and financial freedom are available to all of us.

INVESTMENT PRINCIPLE 3: OWN PART OF A BUSINESS, NOT A STOCK

"We own [5.7%] of Apple and it's probably the best business I know in the world...I don't think of Apple as a stock, I think it's our third largest business."[38]

Warren Buffett – Interview with Becky Quick, CNBC

A key element of Buffett's approach is that he sees every stock he buys as being part of a business.[39] Most investors focus on the *price* of a stock, seeking to capture short-term gains by selling to somebody else the next day, week, month or year. Some financial markets are open 24 hours a day, 7 days a week, making the inclination to buy and sell persistent and pervasive. Just because we can trade 24/7, however, doesn't mean that we should. This isn't the mindset you would have if you were buying a farm or a home, and it isn't the mindset you should have when buying a business.

Buffett believes we'd be better off if we said, "*I bought a business today,*" rather than, "*I bought a stock today*" because that gives a crucially different perspective on our investment. Instead of relying on price fluctuations to generate your return, look to the asset itself.

Take the example of $1,000 in a bank account, earning interest at 20% per annum. If you focused on *price*, you may start to look around for someone to buy the account from you. On the day you open the account you could reasonably expect someone to pay $1,000, since that is what the account is worth at that point in time. A year later you would have earned 20% of interest income, or $200, and your account would be worth $1,200. Would you look to sell it then? At what price? Imagine how you'd react if one day someone came to you with a quote for your account and they offered you 10% less than it was worth. Would you panic? If the account is still generating a 20% return, the arbitrary change in price makes no difference.

Investing in a stock is no different and we must look to the business itself to determine whether our investment is a good one. If you buy a company at fair value that earns a 20% return through its operations, let that company rack up 20% returns year after year and watch your investment grow over time. As the business grows the stock price will follow it higher, and fleeting price fluctuations will seem inconsequential.

INVESTMENT PRINCIPLE 4:
HOLD FOR A LONG TIME

"Wall Street makes its money on activity. You make your money on inactivity."[40]

"In the short run, the market is a voting machine but in the long run it is a weighing machine."[41]

Warren Buffett

You can achieve fantastic returns over long timeframes, even when starting small. The longer you hold, the bigger the payoff, and Buffett uses the power of compounding to let his investments grow and grow. Instead of thinking about small gains you might be able to extract from short-term stock price fluctuations, think about the returns you will generate in terms of the earning power of the businesses you are buying over the next 10, 20 or 30 years. Buffett has owned American Express for 20 years and Coca-Cola for 40 years. He considers them businesses that aren't to be sold based on media headlines.[42] The ultimate test, in Buffett's view, is whether you care if the stock market were to close tomorrow. If you're making a sound investment in a high-quality business, it shouldn't bother you if the market were to close down for five years.[43]

The future is unknowable. We don't have the faintest idea what the market will be doing 6 or 12 months from now. But we do know that the stock market tends to rise over the long-term. Buffett believes that, while we can't predict what the stock market will do 10 minutes from now, 10 days from now or 10 months from now, we can predict improvements and growth over the long-term and that 20 or 30 years from now, stock markets all over the world will be higher than they are today.

Buffett regularly reiterates that he has zero intention of

selling any of his wholly owned businesses, no matter how much he is offered.[44] In terms of his marketable securities, such as his stock investments, he refuses to sell a business just because the price looks high[45] and will only sell positions if he gets really discouraged with the management, or he thinks the economics of the business have fundamentally changed, such that the returns he anticipated are no longer expected to materialise.[45] Other than that, his favourite holding period is *"forever."*[46]

3.3
INVESTMENT MECHANISMS

INVESTMENT MECHANISM 1:
RETURN ON EQUITY

"If a business does well, the stock eventually follows."[47]

Warren Buffett

Earlier, in INVESTMENT PRINCIPLE 1: SIMPLE IS BETTER, we learned about Buffett's criteria for acquisition candidates, which has remained unchanged for over 30 years. He requires his acquisitions to demonstrate a historical record of consistent earnings power and *"good returns on equity while employing little or no debt."* But what is 'Return on Equity' and why should we care? Let's start with an explanation of 'Equity'.

UNDERSTANDING EQUITY

Equity = Assets - Debts

If a business has $1,000 of cash in the bank, and a $400 loan outstanding, its Equity would be calculated simply as follows:

$$Equity = Assets - Debts$$

$$Equity = \$1,000 - \$400$$

$$Equity = \$600$$

Equity is the sum that is actually owned by the shareholders of that company - it is what they could walk away with if all of the assets were liquidated and all of the company's debt was paid off. So, the business could take the $1,000 in cash, pay off the $400 loan, and distribute the remaining $600 to shareholders.

There is a little bit of jargon and duplication here, because you will also see 'Equity' referred to interchangeably in the market as 'Shareholders Equity' or as 'Book Value'. These different names are used in different circumstances, but they mean the same thing.

$$Equity = Shareholders\ Equity = Book\ Value$$

Don't worry, there's a little more jargon coming your way, but I've kept it to the absolute minimum.

UNDERSTANDING CAPITAL

While on the subject of Equity, and to help understand some of Buffett's other investment criteria, we will also define 'Capital'.

Capital takes into account the $400, which, despite being a loan, are actual dollars the company has available to use within the business.

$$\text{Capital} = \text{Equity} + \text{Debt}$$

$$\text{Capital} = \$600 + \$400$$

$$\text{Capital} = \$1,000$$

So, while the business may only have $600 of Equity, in reality it has $1,000 of cash (Capital) to utilise as it wishes.

CAPITAL VERSUS EQUITY

In June 1996, Buffett issued a booklet to Berkshire Hathaway shareholders in order to explain his broad economic principles of operation. In it he laid out his approach to investment, stating a preference for owning businesses that "*consistently earn above-average returns on capital.*"[48] Buffett references 'returns on capital' here, versus 'returns on equity' in his 1983 and 2014 advertisements. Why the inconsistency?

There is actually no inconsistency. Buffett's full advertisement sentence read "*good returns on equity while employing little or no debt.*"[24] A great quality business will be able to produce quite satisfactory results without the need to employ high levels of debt. As investors, we much prefer to earn a return from a business that has low debt rather than achieve that same return from a business saddled with debt, since the low debt candidate poses less risk.

So, if Capital = Equity + Debt, but Buffett tends to avoid debt we can simply say:

$$\text{Capital} = \text{Equity} + \text{Debt}$$

$$\text{Capital} = \text{Equity} + \text{Debt}$$

$$\text{Capital} = \text{Equity}$$

There are a number of additional advantages to using

Return on Equity in our approach versus Return on Capital. Return on Equity is a much more widely accessible metric and can be found on all good financial websites. This makes it easier to assess the performance of companies and compare them side-by-side. It is also commonly quoted for ETF funds, which are collections of many stocks, enabling us to form a view on the overall performance of an index too. These factors will help significantly when we begin to screen for investment opportunities. However, we must remember to screen for companies with *low debt* in order for our approach to hold true.

UNDERSTANDING RETURN ON EQUITY (ROE)

Return on Equity, or 'ROE' for short, has two components. These are, unsurprisingly, the 'Return' and the 'Equity'. It is represented as a percentage, for example "*The ROE of the company for 2019 was 15.3%*".

We have already defined the 'Equity' element above so let's turn our attention now to the 'Return'.

RETURN

'Return' describes the earnings that are generated by a business after all expenses and taxes are deducted.

Consider *Company X*, which makes money by selling widgets to customers. From its sales, *Company X* must deduct the cost of doing business, such as raw materials, salary costs, office costs, utilities etc. It must also deduct any finance costs such as interest paid, and, finally, it must deduct any taxes paid. The net of all such items is the 'Return' of the company. You will sometimes see this called 'Earnings', and in financial statements it will be sometimes be referred to as 'Net Income After Taxes'. Again, we find ourselves bamboozled by jargon...three names for the same thing. The important thing to remember is the principle...whether you call it 'Return', or 'Earnings', or 'Net Income After Taxes', it is the sales of the business minus all of the deductions it is required to make.

At the start of 2019, *Company X* has $1,000 of cash in the bank, and a $400 loan outstanding. During 2019 it uses the $1,000 of cash that it has available to purchase raw materials, which it subsequently converts into widgets It is able to sell all the widgets for $1,100 It incurs an interest charge on the $400 loan equivalent to 5% per annum, or 5% x $400 = $20 It also pays a storage fee to house the raw materials and widgets of $20.

FIGURE 9: COMPANY X: INCOME STATEMENT FOR THE YEAR ENDED 31 DECEMBER 2019

Sales generated	$1,100
Cost of raw materials	($1,000)
Interest expense on the loan (5% x $400)	($20)
Storage fee	($20)
Net income before taxes ($1,100-$1,000-$20-$20)	**$60**
Tax charge at 30% (30% x $60)	($18)
Net income after taxes (or 'Earnings' or 'Return')	**$42**

In simple terms, the Return is the money the business generates that it actually gets to keep.

EQUITY

We know that Equity represents the amount of money that would be returned to a company's shareholders if all of the assets were liquidated and all of the company's debt was paid off.

In our example, at the start of the year *Company X* has $1,000 of cash in the bank, and a $400 loan outstanding. It's Equity or Shareholder's Equity or Book Value was therefore $600.

$$Equity = Shareholder's\ Equity = Book\ Value$$

$$Equity = (Assets - Liabilities)$$

$$Equity = (\$1,000 - \$400)$$

$$Equity = \$600$$

RETURN ON EQUITY

Pulling these two elements together, our Return on Equity for 2019 is simply the Return divided by the Equity, presented as a percentage value:

$$Return\ on\ Equity\ (ROE) = (Return\ /\ Equity)\ x\ 100$$

$$Return\ on\ Equity\ (ROE) = (\$42\ /\ \$600)\ x\ 100$$

$$Return\ on\ Equity\ (ROE) = 0.07\ x\ 100$$

$$Return\ on\ Equity\ (ROE) = 7.0\%$$

SEEK ABOVE-AVERAGE RETURNS ON EQUITY

In our search for investments we will seek companies with above-average returns on equity. The higher the return a company earns on equity, the more earnings it is generating and the more value it is creating. In Roger Lowenstein's book, *Buffett: The Making of An American Capitalist*, Buffett reveals, "*I would rather have a $10 million business making 15% than a $100 million business making 4%.*"[49] At a growth rate of 15%, the smaller $10 million business will quickly outgrow and overtake the $100 million business. *Company X* may have generated a good ROE of 7%, but we will be searching for companies with ROEs of 20% or more.

INVESTMENT MECHANISM 2: PRICE

"Price is what you pay; value is what you get."[50]

"It's far better to buy a wonderful company at a fair price than a fair company at a wonderful price."[51]

Warren Buffett

You cannot simply look for companies that generate above-average returns on equity. Any stock could be a good buy or a bad buy, it very much depends on the price you pay. It was a watershed moment in Buffett's investing career when he read the book *The Intelligent Investor*, written by his college tutor Benjamin Graham. In Chapter 8, Graham personifies the stock market as a volatile character named 'Mr. Market'. Some days Mr. Market offers you stocks at exorbitant prices, while on other days he slashes prices. Buffett says that it is probably the most important thing he has read in his life, enabling him to come to the realisation that the market is there to serve us, not to instruct us.[52] At no point in time are we *"forced"* to buy stocks from Mr. Market. We can simply sit there and wait for prices to come to us.

Every day, thousands of stocks are offered to you at prices that change daily, but you don't have to make decisions every day. You must see yourself as the master of the market rather than its servant. Sometimes Mr. Market's unpredictable mood swings can become extreme, during which times he offers you stocks at prices that are much too low. This might apply to one particular stock, or to the market as a whole. In either case, this is a great opportunity to make money, by purchasing stocks that are significantly more valuable than the price you pay for them.

INVESTMENT MECHANISM 3: COMPOUND GROWTH

"What is the most powerful force in the universe?...Compound interest."

Albert Einstein

"I don't know what the seven wonders of the world are, but I do know the eighth - compound interest."

Baron Rothschild

Compound growth is the mechanism by which our annual returns grow in size over time. It is creative and constructive and can lead to astonishing growth in wealth. Such growth is possible because, when we *reinvest* our returns back into our investment, future returns are generated on an ever-enlarging base. Such growth is exponential, accelerating over time.

Consider the example of a bank account containing $1,000 that offers you an interest rate of 20% per annum. You have two options: either *reinvest* your interest income by keeping it in the account, or *withdraw* it from the account and set it aside at the end of each year.

OPTION 1: REINVEST THE INTEREST EARNED

At the end of Year 1 your investment would be worth $1,200, of which, $1,000 relates to the original investment and $200 is the interest income you earned.

Interest Income = $1,000 x 20% = $200

End of Year 1 Balance = $1,000 + $200 = $1,200

Total Income to Date = $200

You start Year 2, not with your original starting capital of $1,000, but with a new, enlarged balance of $1,200. In the second year you will again earn the same 20% rate that you did in the first year, but you'll earn that 20% on the larger account balance. Your Year 2 interest won't be $200 anymore; it will now have grown to $240.

Year 2 Interest Income = $1,200 x 20% = $240

End of Year 2 Balance = $1,200 + $240 = $1,440

Total Income to Date = $200 + $240 = $440

If you kept the cash in the account for another 28 years, earning the same interest rate of 20% per annum, by the end of Year 30 your original balance of $1,000 would have grown to an outstanding $237,376. This is not *linear* growth, it is *exponential* growth, and this is what we will seek to capitalise on.

OPTION 2: WITHDRAW THE INTEREST EARNED

At the end of Year 1 your investment will be worth $1,200, of which, $1,000 relates to the original investment and $200 is the interest income you earned.

Interest Income = $1,000 x 20% = $200

However, this time you have decided to withdraw the $200 interest from our account and to set it aside.

End of Year 1 Balance = $1,000 + $200 - $200 = $1,000

You start Year 2 with the same $1,000 you had at the start of Year 1, and have $200 set aside, not earning anything.

In the second year you earn the same 20% return that

you did in the first year, generating interest income of $200, identical to that earned in Year 1.

Year 2 Interest Income = $1,000 x 20% = $200

End of Year 2 Balance = $1,000 + $200 - $200 = $1,000

Total Income to Date, set aside = $200 + $200 = $400

If you continued this approach for another 28 years, earning the same interest rate of 20% per annum, by the end of Year 30 your original balance of $1,000 would have remained unchanged at $1,000. In addition, you would have extracted 30 years of income from the account, being 30 x $200 = $6,000. This is *linear* growth and is unimpressive. The combined value of the account and the cumulative income is $1,000 + $6,000 = $7,000, quite a way below the $237,376 generated in Option 1.

Figure 10 shows the result of these options side-by-side.

FIGURE 10: BANK ACCOUNT BALANCES FOR OPTION 1 (INCOME REINVESTMENT) AND OPTION 2 (INCOME WITHDRAWAL)

End of Year...	Option 1: Reinvest Interest Earned	Option 2: Withdraw Interest Earned
Start	$1,000	$1,000
1	$1,200	$1,200
2	$1,440	$1,400
3	$1,728	$1,600
4	$2,074	$1,800
5	$2,488	$2,000
6	$2,986	$2,200
7	$3,583	$2,400
8	$4,300	$2,600
9	$5,160	$2,800
10	$6,192	$3,000
11	$7,430	$3,200
12	$8,916	$3,400
13	$10,699	$3,600
14	$12,839	$3,800
15	$15,407	$4,000
16	$18,488	$4,200
17	$22,186	$4,400
18	$26,623	$4,600
19	$31,948	$4,800
20	$38,338	$5,000
21	$46,005	$5,200
22	$55,206	$5,400
23	$66,247	$5,600
24	$79,497	$5,800
25	$95,396	$6,000
26	$114,475	$6,200
27	$137,371	$6,400
28	$164,845	$6,600
29	$197,814	$6,800
30	$237,376	$7,000

Let's look at another example to really hammer home the point. You must choose between the following two income alternatives.

ALTERNATIVE A

To receive income of $100,000 per year for 30 years.

ALTERNATIVE B

To receive only $1 in the first year, but that amount will double in each subsequent year. So, for clarity, you'll receive $1 in the first year, $2 in the second year, $4 in the third year, and so on.

Which option would you choose?

Figure 11 illustrates both alternatives side-by-side. If you opted for *Alternative A*, you would have ended up receiving $3,000,000 in total earnings over the 30-year period and would probably be very happy with that result. However, if you opted for *Alternative B*, you would have received substantially more. Your income in Year 30 alone would have amounted to an astronomical $536,870,911, and you would have received total income of $1,073,741,823 over the entire 30-year term. True, it would have taken 18 years for the annual income from *Alternative B* to pull ahead of *Alternative A*, and 22 years for the cumulative earnings of *Alternative B* to exceed those of *Alternative A*, but when *Alternative B* eventually pulled ahead, it quickly accelerated far beyond the reach of *Alternative A*.

FIGURE 11: ALTERNATIVE A ($100,000 PER YEAR) VERSUS ALTERNATIVE B ($1, DOUBLING EVERY YEAR)

End of Year	Alt A: Income	Alt A: Total Income	Alt B: Income	Alt B: Total Income
1	$100k	$100k	$1	$1
2	$100k	$200k	$2	$3
3	$100k	$300k	$4	$7
4	$100k	$400k	$8	$15
5	$100k	$500k	$16	$31
6	$100k	$600k	$32	$63
7	$100k	$700k	$64	$127
8	$100k	$800k	$128	$255
9	$100k	$900k	$256	$511
10	$100k	$1.0m	$512	$1,023
11	$100k	$1.1m	$1,024	$2,047
12	$100k	$1.2m	$2,048	$4,095
13	$100k	$1.3m	$4,096	$8,191
14	$100k	$1.4m	$8,192	$16,383
15	$100k	$1.5m	$16,384	$32,767
16	$100k	$1.6m	$32,768	$65,535
17	$100k	$1.7m	$65,536	$131,071
18	$100k	$1.8m	$131,072	$262,143
19	$100k	$1.9m	$262,144	$524,287
20	$100k	$2.0m	$524,288	$1,048,575
21	$100k	$2.1m	$1,048,576	$2,097,151
22	$100k	$2.2m	$2,097,152	$4,194,303
23	$100k	$2.3m	$4,194,304	$8,388,607
24	$100k	$2.4m	$8,388,608	$16,777,215
25	$100k	$2.5m	$16,777,216	$33,554,431
26	$100k	$2.6m	$33,554,432	$67,108,863
27	$100k	$2.7m	$67,108,864	$134,217,727
28	$100k	$2.8m	$134,217,728	$268,435,455
29	$100k	$2.9m	$268,435,456	$536,870,911
30	$100k	$3.0m	$536,870,912	$1,073,741,823

You can understand why Einstein described this mechanism as the most powerful force in the universe.

When you recall from the opening section of this chapter that Buffett compounded the market value of his company, Berkshire Hathaway, at 20.3% per annum for 55 years, you will immediately make a simple but binding connection between his fortune and the mechanism of compounding. Compounding is truly at the heart of his investment approach. His biography is even called *The Snowball*, a metaphor he uses to explain how even a small snowball can grow to an immense size as it rolls down a hill, gathering more and more snow as it does so.

Compounding is the key to Buffett's success and wealth. It is an essential concept to understand and an excellent investment mechanism to master and deploy within your investment portfolio. Later we will look at compounding in more detail, particularly how to compound your returns by owning great businesses and revealing the factors that can dilute your ability to compound.

COMPOUND ANNUAL GROWTH RATE (CAGR)

The Compound Annual Growth Rate, or CAGR, is the average annual growth of an investment over a specified period of time. We will use CAGR extensively throughout this book, so it is very important to take a moment to absorb the explanation that follows.

Using Berkshire Hathaway as an example, by mid-October 1964, Buffet had paid an average of $12.375 per share for his holding. At the end of 2019, after 55 years and 10 weeks of growth, the share price had risen to $339,590. So, what was Buffett's CAGR?

Beginning Value: $12.375 per share
Final Value: $339,590 per share
Investment Timeframe: 55 years 10 weeks, or 55.2 years

Compound Annual Growth Rate (CAGR)

$$= ((\text{Final Value} / \text{Beginning Value})^{(1/\text{Timeframe})} - 1) \times 100$$

$$= ((\$339,590 / \$12.375)^{(1/55.2)} - 1) \times 100$$

$$= ((27,441.6162)^{(0.01812)} - 1) \times 100$$

$$= (1.203 - 1) \times 100$$

$$= 0.203 \times 100$$

$$\text{CAGR} = 20.3\%$$

Note: The ^ symbol used in the equation means "to the power of".

This matches the 20.3% Compound Annual Growth calculated by Buffett in his 2019 Berkshire Hathaway Annual Report, summarised in Figure 7 above. It means that, on average, he earned a return of 20.3% every single year between October 1964 and 31st December 2019.

It is possible to use either per-share values in the CAGR calculation, or the value of an investment overall. To illustrate this, let's assume we purchased two shares of Berkshire when Buffett did. What would the CAGR be on our investment at the end of 2019?

Value of two share investment at start: $24.75
Value of two share investment at end of 2019: $ 679,180
Investment Timeframe: 55 years 10 weeks, or 55.2 years

Compound Annual Growth Rate (CAGR)

$$= ((\text{Final Value} / \text{Beginning Value})^{(1/\text{Timeframe})} - 1) \times 100$$

$$= (($679{,}180 / $24.75)^{(1/55.2)} - 1) \times 100$$

$$= ((27{,}441.6162)^{(0.01812)} - 1) \times 100$$

$$= (1.203 - 1) \times 100$$

$$= 0.203 \times 100$$

$$\text{CAGR} = 20.3\%$$

To help you calculate the formula for CAGR more efficiently, head to *theinvestorssolution.com* website and download the free *'Goal Planner & Stock Screen'* spreadsheet. The CAGR formula is set up and ready for you to use in the *'CAGR'* tab. Alternatively, create your own spreadsheet and enter the following inputs into the cells indicated, then change the format of cell A4 to a percentage:

Beginning Value	CELL A1	$12.375
Final Value	CELL A2	$339,590
Investment Timeframe	CELL A3	55.2
CAGR	CELL A4	=((A2/A1)^(1/A3)-1)

INVESTMENT MECHANISM 4: CAPITAL ALLOCATION

Capital allocation is the process of deciding how to deploy the firm's resources to generate the best possible return for shareholders. Two identical companies with different approaches to allocating capital will yield two very different long-term outcomes for shareholders. Buffett wants to see CEO's allocate capital in a rational, effective way.

In simple terms, a business has five methods of deploying capital:

1. INVESTING MONEY BACK INTO THE EXISTING BUSINESS

We know that Buffett looks for outstanding companies with above-average returns on equity, but he also wants those companies to reinvest their high returns back into their businesses, compounding those returns over time in order to generate even higher returns in the future.

2. PAYING OUT DIVIDENDS

By paying out dividends, a company is taking some of the earnings it has generated and is returning it to shareholders. This may be tax-inefficient for the shareholders and, more importantly, by paying cash out as a dividend it means that it can't be reinvested in the business to generate future growth. At Berkshire Hathaway, Buffett pays no dividend at all and believes that he serves his shareholders better by reinvesting their money back into the business to earn 20.3% per annum.

3. REPURCHASING ITS OWN SHARES

By repurchasing its own shares, a business reduces the number of shares in circulation, thereby driving the price of the remaining shares higher. However, like the purchase of any share, no business is worth an infinite price, so Buffett prefers share repurchases to be made only when Mr. Market undervalues those shares.

4. BUYING OTHER BUSINESSES

Buffett himself is in the business of buying businesses. But again, purchases must be made at valuations that make sense and don't reduce returns for shareholders.

5. PAYING OFF DEBT

Buffett isn't in favour of debt, using it only sparingly himself. He would prefer companies to err on the side of caution, maintaining modest levels of debt or paying them down over time, rather than over-leveraging their balance sheets.

Overall, Buffett would most like to see businesses reinvest their returns back into the existing businesses and at high rates of return. He'd like to see modest levels of dividends paid out, or no dividends at all. And for the cherry on top, he'd like to see a business repurchasing its own shares at favourable prices.

3.4
CHAPTER RECAP

Since Buffett talks so openly about his approach, and with such frequency, I believe that his words no longer cut through media noise. Or perhaps it is the case that, once we have heard something a number of times, we start to tune out the underlying message. However, if we take a moment to centre ourselves and to really listen to what he is telling us, the approach that has brought him immense success and wealth is so simple and elegant. We can distil it into the following four principles and mechanisms:

INVESTMENT PRINCIPLE 1:
SIMPLE IS BETTER
Look for simple businesses that you understand, good returns on equity and a consistent track record

Buffett's investment criteria have remained unchanged for decades and contain only a handful of criteria. The approach is so simple that he does not use a computer or calculator, and he can give an answer on a prospective investment within five minutes. He only invests in companies that he understands; those he can reasonably conclude will still be doing well 10-20 years from now.

INVESTMENT PRINCIPLE 2:
ANYONE CAN DO IT
All you need is a little time, a little money and the commitment to take action

Buffett talks about his approach openly in interviews, in the media, at his annual shareholder meetings and in his letter to Berkshire shareholders. He spends most of his time in a small, quiet office, reading. He maintains that you don't need a high IQ to achieve great investment returns, and the stocks he buys are big, household names that everybody is familiar with.

INVESTMENT PRINCIPLE 3:
OWN PART OF A BUSINESS NOT A STOCK
Don't speculate on fleeting price fluctuations, think of your investments like purchases of productive assets, which compound their returns over time

Buffett doesn't think of Apple as a stock, he thinks of it as his third largest business. He believes that we'd be better off if we said, "*I bought a business today*," not, "*I bought a stock today*," because that gives a crucially different perspective on our investment. By thinking of an investment as though we are buying a productive asset, we remove the tendency to follow fleeting price fluctuations and avoid the trap of being influenced by short-term news headlines.

INVESTMENT PRINCIPLE 4:
HOLD FOR A LONG TIME
Before buying a stock, ask yourself whether you'd be perfectly happy to hold your investment if the market shut down for ten years

Make your money based on inactivity. We can achieve

fantastic returns over long timeframes, even when starting small. The longer we hold, the bigger the payoff, and Buffett uses the power of compounding to let his investments grow and grow. He will only sell if a business he has purchased fundamentally changes and the expected returns are no longer likely to materialise.

INVESTMENT MECHANISM 1: RETURN ON EQUITY

Return on Equity is the fuel for our compound growth engine; seek out companies with high ROEs

If a business does well, the stock price eventually follows. In our search for investments we will seek companies with above-average returns on equity. The higher the return a company earns on equity, the more earnings it is generating and the greater its value over time. Buffett would rather have a $10 million business making 15% than a $100 million business making 4%. Look for high-quality companies with above-average ROEs and you have found the fuel for your compound growth engine.

INVESTMENT MECHANISM 2: PRICE

Buy at a price that enables you to realise above-average returns

Price is what you pay but value is what you get. We cannot simply look for companies that generate above-average returns on equity - no stock is worth an infinite price. Instead we will identify high-quality businesses that generate above-average ROEs and wait for Mr. Market to offer them to us at compelling prices.

INVESTMENT MECHANISM 3: COMPOUND GROWTH

Accelerate your returns by utilising the most powerful tool in an investor's arsenal - compound growth

Compounding is the key to Buffett's wealth and success. It sits at the very heart of his approach. Earning consistent, above-average returns on a capital base that is ever increasing accelerates your path to wealth and financial freedom like nothing else.

INVESTMENT MECHANISM 4:
CAPITAL ALLOCATION
Seek out companies that retain the majority of their earnings and reinvest them for future growth

Watch management's approach to capital allocation. To maximise the compound growth potential of a company we want as much money as possible to be reinvested and redeployed within that business. That means that the business should pay out only a modest proportion of earnings as dividends, should only make acquisitions that increase shareholder value, and should repurchase its own shares only when Mr. Market undervalues them.

Despite Buffett's success, of the trillions of dollars of investments managed on Wall Street, the amount of money following Buffett's approach is insignificant. As Munger observed at the 2007 Berkshire Hathaway Annual Meeting, *"Our system ought to be more copied than it is."*[53] This is likely due to Wall Street's inclination to chase short-term profits and results over larger, long-term growth.

Much has been written about Buffett over the years, with hundreds of books offering unique interpretations of his approach. Some books contain complex calculations of intrinsic value and of owner earnings. Some assess companies using comprehensive 'value' investment techniques. Some, which, in my view, hold a more accurate interpretation of his approach, combine 'value' investing with 'growth' investing. Some introduce techniques to forecast a company's prospects into the future and then discount the resulting cash flows back to present value. Some assess the talent and effectiveness of management while others dedicate chapters to assessing the competitive advantages of the companies he buys. Many books go on to conclude that only by being Warren Buffett can you obtain Buffett-like results. They reference his extensive knowledge and particular nuances of his deals, implying that his investments are 'unique' and cannot be replicated.

I have a different perspective. While all of these books are well-written, interesting and I have certainly learned something from each of them, I believe that a lot of the details contained within their pages can simply be stripped away, leaving a core set of principles and mechanisms which describe Buffett's approach on a more universal basis. After all, if each of his deals were uniquely different, he wouldn't keep insisting that "*Anyone can do it*" and "*Simple is better.*" I believe anyone can work out that Coca-Cola or Apple are great companies. I believe that anyone can work out a suitable price to pay for their shares. And I certainly believe anybody can hold them for a long time – that's the really easy bit.

The more I listen to Buffett and the more I hear him say the same things over and over again, the more clarity I have obtained. This book is my attempt to communicate that clarity. I believe it focuses on Buffett's timeless, universal, principles rather than unnecessary technical jargon. With a few key concepts, and a few simple calculations, which I call "*The Investor's Solution*", investors can garner significant upside with only minimal effort. After reading this book, every time you hear Buffett speak, or read his words, you will be able to mentally tick off the things he is saying against each of these principles. *The Investor's Solution* will just make sense.

CHAPTER 4:
FINANCIAL STATEMENTS AT A GLANCE

CHAPTER SUMMARY
4.1 FINANCIAL YEAR
4.2 FINANCIAL STATEMENTS
4.3 THE KEY COMPONENTS
    4.3.1 THE INCOME STATEMENT
    4.3.2 THE BALANCE SHEET
4.4 WHERE TO FIND THEM

Before we dive into *The Investor's Solution* in more detail, it is important to develop a high-level understanding of the financial statements that companies prepare and report.

4.1
FINANCIAL YEAR

To begin with, recognise that every company has a 'financial year' for which its results are recorded. Most companies select 31st December as their year-end, although you will find some companies with alternative year-ends.

4.2
FINANCIAL STATEMENTS

Throughout the year, a company must record all of its transactions. On a periodic basis they then collate and summarise these transactions into financial statements. Financial statements are reported to investors on a periodic basis, usually quarterly. However, it is the end-of-year annual report that is the most detailed and useful as it contains explanations of results plus other contextual information, such as progress towards strategic goals and dividend policies.

Different countries call the financial statements slightly different things, but their content is broadly the same. In the U.S. for example, companies must file their annual results in a report called Form 10-K. This provides a comprehensive overview of the company's business and financial condition and includes audited financial statements. On a quarterly basis they must file Form 10-Q, which includes unaudited financial statements and provides a view of the company's financial position during the year. In the U.K. companies are more likely to submit their accounts on a half-yearly basis. The year-end results are usually called the 'Annual Report' and the half-yearly update is referred to as the 'Interim Results'.

4.3
THE KEY COMPONENTS OF FINANCIAL STATEMENTS

Within the financial statements there are two key statements we are most interested in.

4.3.1 THE INCOME STATEMENT

The Income Statement shows a company's sales, expenses and any taxes incurred during a specific period. It may also be called the 'Statement of Operations,' the 'Statement of Comprehensive Income,' or the 'Profit & Loss Account'. Most of the companies we will examine are comprised of several smaller entities, wrapped up within a parent company. Where this is the case, the rolled-up accounts will be labelled as 'Consolidated' or 'Group' accounts. These are the accounts we will use in our analysis. Where no such consolidation of companies is required, we will simply examine accounts labelled 'Company'.

Figure 12 shows the Income Statement for Facebook for the year ended 31st December 2019. I have provided a short description of each component, and, for ease of reference, I have noted the key elements you will need to recall later in the book.

FIGURE 12: FACEBOOK, INC. CONSOLIDATED STATEMENTS OF INCOME YEAR ENDED 31 DECEMBER 2019

	$m	Explanation	Used in Book?
Revenue	70,697	Sales generated by selling a product or service	Yes
Costs and Expenses	(46,711)	Cost of raw materials, employees, marketing etc.	
Income from Operations	23,986	= Sales - Costs	
Interest and Other Income	826	Interest and investment income etc.	
Income before Tax	24,812	Income earned before tax	
Provision for Income Taxes	(6,327)	Tax due on income	
Net Income	18,485	Income earned after tax	Yes

4.3.2 THE BALANCE SHEET

The Balance Sheet shows the assets a company has and the liabilities it owes at a particular point in time. You may sometimes see it called the 'Statement of Financial Position'. As for the Income Statement, it may be labelled as 'Consolidated' or 'Group' if it contains a rolled-up view of performance.

Figure 13 shows the Balance Sheet for Facebook as at 31st December 2019. I have again provided a short description of each component and noted the key elements you will need to recall later in the book.

FIGURE 13: FACEBOOK, INC. CONSOLIDATED BALANCE SHEET AS AT 31 DECEMBER 2019

		$m	Explanation	Used in Book?
ASSETS	**Current Assets**	66,225	Cash, marketable securities, accounts receivable etc.	
	Property and Equipment	35,323	Land, buildings, machines, computers, equipment etc.	
	Operating Lease	9,460	Value of leased assets such as land, offices, equipment etc.	
	Intangible Assets	894	Intellectual property, patents, trademarks etc.	
	Goodwill	18,715	Excess paid to acquire other companies over fair value	
	Other Assets	2,759	Any assets not categorised above	
	TOTAL ASSETS	**133,376**		Yes
LIABILITIES	**Current Liabilities**	(15,053)	Any accounts payable, interest or expenses owed	
	Operating Leases	(9,524)	Liabilities arising from obtaining right-of-use assets such as leases, land etc.	
	Other Liabilities	(7,745)	Any liabilities not categorised above	
	TOTAL LIABILITIES	(32,322)		Yes
	STOCKHOLDERS EQUITY	(101,054)		Yes
	TOTAL LIABILITIES & STOCKHOLDERS EQUITY	**(133,376)**	=Total Liabilities + Stockholders Equity	Yes

I realise that we have found ourselves, once again, encountering financial jargon - different names used interchangeably for the same thing. Don't let it hold you back. You will get a good sense of the layout of financial statements very quickly and will learn to recognise differences in names and formats. In no time, you will be flicking through the pages of an annual report, a 10-K Form or 10-Q Form, and will easily find the Income Statement and Balance Sheet. Additionally, many financial websites, like *Yahoo Finance*, make life easier for you by collating all of these results in a sensible format and use consistent, straightforward language to describe each component.

4.4
WHERE TO FIND FINANCIAL STATEMENTS

You can find company accounts easily by looking at the 'Investors' or 'Investor Relations' section of corporate websites. On the Apple website, for example, I can head down to the footer, located at the bottom of each web page. Here, under the 'About Apple' section I find a link to 'Investors'. Once there, I can scroll down to the section 'Annual Reports on Form 10-K' or 'Quarterly Earnings Reports' for the 10-Q's.

The good news is that most financial websites quote this information freely. For example, if I am looking for the financial statements of Facebook, I can go to *Yahoo Finance*, type 'Facebook' into their search bar to locate that stock. Once the Facebook stock information is up on the screen, I can select the 'Statistics' sub-heading and see a wide range of information relating to Facebook. If I select the 'Financials' sub-heading I can see the financial statements set out for me and can switch between 'Income statement' and 'Balance sheet'. So as to not limit this to one reference, another source you could try is *Marketwatch.com*. Type 'Facebook' into their search bar. Once Facebook's stock information is up on the screen, select the 'Financials' sub-heading to reveal the 'Income Statement' and 'Balance Sheet'.

CHAPTER 5:
THE INVESTOR'S SHORT-TERM RETURN

CHAPTER SUMMARY
5.1 RETURN ON EQUITY (ROE)
5.2 PRICE: THE PRICE/BOOK RATIO
5.3 THE INVESTOR'S SHORT-TERM RETURN
5.4 CHAPTER RECAP

5.1
RETURN ON EQUITY (ROE)

In Chapter 3 we walked through the calculation of Return on Equity. In that example, a company started the year with Equity of $600 and generated a Return of $42 for the year, giving a Return on Equity of 7.0%:

Return on Equity (ROE) = (Return / Equity) x 100

Return on Equity (ROE) = ($42 / $600) x 100

Return on Equity (ROE) = 0.07 x 100

Return on Equity (ROE) = 7.0%

This calculation was simplified slightly in order to convey the concept of ROE as effectively as possible. Extending the concept further, it is important to note that, within the financial markets, ROEs aren't calculated based solely on the Equity at the start of the year; instead, they are calculated using the *average* of the start- and end-of-year values. This is because companies don't generate all of their sales on the last day of the year; they generate sales gradually as the year progresses. Each time a sale is made, the Equity of the company increases slightly, so using the start-of-year Equity, while approximately right, will tend to overstate the ROE. The financial industry uses average Equity as the denominator in the ROE equation in order to take this into account.

Let's perform this calculation using Facebook's results for the years ended 31 December 2018 and 2019, summarised in Figures 14 and 15.

Scanning the bottom rows of Facebook's Balance Sheet, we see that it ended 2018 with Equity of $84,127m. By default, this means it started 2019 with this same amount. It ended 2019 with Equity of $101,054m. The average for 2019 is therefore:

Starting Equity: $84,127m

Ending Equity: $101,054m

Average Equity = ($84,127 + $101,054) / 2

Average Equity = $92,591m

FIGURE 14: FACEBOOK, INC. CONSOLIDATED BALANCE SHEET AS AT 31 DECEMBER 2018 AND 2019

		2019 $m	2018 $m	Also called
ASSETS	Current Assets	66,225	50,480	
	Property and Equipment	35,323	24,683	
	Operating Lease	9,460	-	
	Intangible Assets	894	1,294	
	Goodwill	18.715	18,301	
	Other Assets	2,759	2,576	
	TOTAL ASSETS	133,376	97,334	
LIABILITIES	Current Liabilities	(15,053)	(7,017)	
	Operating Leases	(9,524)	-	
	Other Liabilities	(7,745)	(6,190)	
	TOTAL LIABILITIES	(32,322)	(13,207)	
	STOCKHOLDERS EQUITY	(101,054)	(84,127)	Shareholders Equity, Book Value
	TOTAL LIABILITIES & STOCKHOLDERS EQUITY	(133,376)	(97,334)	

FIGURE 15: FACEBOOK, INC. CONSOLIDATED STATEMENTS OF INCOME YEAR ENDED 31 DECEMBER 2019

	$m	Also called
Revenue	70,697	Sales
Costs and Expenses	(46,711)	
Income from Operations	23,986	Operating Income
Interest and Other Income	826	
Income before Tax	**24,812**	
Provision for Income Taxes	(6,327)	
Net Income	**18,485**	Earnings, Return

Turning our attention to the Income Statement, we see the Net Income for 2019 was $18,485m. The ROE for Facebook for 2019 was therefore:

$$ROE = Return / Average Equity$$

$$ROE = \$18,485 / \$92,591 \times 100$$

$$ROE = 20.0\%$$

Thus, in 2019, Facebook generated a return in line with Buffett's long-term track record of 20% per annum.

If we had used the simple version of the calculation, taking only the 2019 starting Equity, the result would have been:

$$ROE = Return / Starting Equity$$

$$ROE = \$18,485 / \$84,127 \times 100$$

$$ROE = 22.0\%$$

This simple calculation is fine as a quick gauge, so long as we recognise that it may overstate actual results.

LOCATING ROE

You can determine the ROE of a company yourself, as we have just done for Facebook, by locating their accounts and performing the calculation above. As noted earlier, accounts can be found in the 'Investors' or 'Investor Relations' section of corporate websites. We can also find the source Equity and Return figures for the ROE calculation on financial websites such as *Yahoo Finance* or *Marketwatch.com*.

But the quickest way to determine a company's ROE is to look directly for a pre-calculated ROE ratio on financial websites. Go to *Marketwatch.com*, type 'Facebook' into their search bar at the top of the page. Once Facebook stock data is up on screen, select the 'Profile' sub-heading in order to see a wide variety of information relating to the company. Scroll down to find the Return on Equity ratio listed.

Try another example. Head to *Yahoo Finance* and, once again, type 'Facebook' into their search bar. Once on screen, select the 'Statistics' sub-heading in order to see a wide variety of information relating to the company. Scroll down to find the 'Return on equity' value.

5.2
PRICE: THE PRICE/BOOK RATIO

Buffett's mentor, Ben Graham, taught him that "*Price is what you pay; value is what you get,*"[50] and it is true that the price we pay has an important impact on our ability to generate above-average returns. To illustrate this point, and several follow-on points revealed later in this chapter, let's examine a simple case study based on a straightforward company.

To keep things easy to follow in written format, any ROE calculations in this section will be based on the Return/Starting Equity, rather than Return/Average Equity.

CASE STUDY - SCENARIO A

At the start of the year we had $1,000 to invest. Mr. Market offered us the chance to buy an entire company, Company A, for that price. We made the investment, purchasing both of the company's two outstanding shares at a price of $500 each. At the point we made the investment, Company A had $1,000 of cash in the bank and no liabilities. During the year it made sales and generated a Return of $200.

FIGURE 16: CASE STUDY SCENARIO A

Company A	Scenario A
Price per share	$500
Number of shares outstanding	2
Total purchase cost	$1,000
Assets (cash)	$1,000
Liabilities	-
Shareholders' Equity (Assets – Liabilities)	$1,000
Earnings for the year	$200

CALCULATING THE ROE

Since Company A was able to generate earnings of $200 for the year, the ROE is:

ROE = Earnings / Shareholders' Equity

ROE = $200 / $1,000

ROE = 20%

CALCULATING OUR INVESTOR'S RETURN

We can also work out the return that we ourselves received as an investor. It is easy to calculate and can be done at a company level or on a per-share basis.

Investor's Return = Earnings / Cost of Investment

Investor's Return = $200 / $1,000

Investor's Return = 20%

Or alternatively…

Investor's Return = Earnings per share / Price per share

Investor's Return = $100 / $500

Investor's Return = 20%

GETTING A GAUGE OF VALUE: THE PRICE TO BOOK (P/B) RATIO

We know the *price* we paid was $500 per share, or $1,000 to acquire the entire company. However, we don't yet have a gauge of *value*. For that we will turn to the Price/Book ratio, or P/B ratio for short. Remember that Wall Street tries to confuse us, so whereas they could have kept things consistent and called it the 'Price/Shareholders' Equity' you will see it written everywhere in mainstream media as 'Price/Book'.

Price/Book can be calculated in two ways, either by dividing the total value of the company (called its 'Market Capitalisation' or 'Market Value') by the total Book Value of the business…

P/B = Market Value of company / Book Value of company

P/B = $1,000 / $1,000

P/B = 1.0

…or by using the per-share values:

P/B = Price per share / Book Value per share

P/B = $500 / $500

P/B = 1.0

The answer is the same in either case.

Examining our transaction through the lens of the P/B ratio, it seems like we got a fair deal from Mr. Market. We paid $1,000 to acquire a company with cash of $1,000. The resulting Price/Book ratio was 1.0. A P/B ratio higher than 1.0 would have implied that we paid more for the company than it was worth, while a ratio below 1.0 would have implied that we paid less for the company than it was worth.

The fact that we paid a fair price, leading to a P/B ratio of 1.0, is why the Investor's Return we calculated above of 20% matches the ROE of the company overall, also 20%.

What if we had paid more for the company than $1,000, or $500 per share? And what if we paid less? What impact does the price we pay have on the P/B ratio and our Investor's Return?

CASE STUDY - IMPACT OF PRICE CHANGES – SCENARIOS B and C

As we know, sometimes Mr. Market has mood swings and offers us prices that are either above or below fair value. Let's see what happens to the ratios as we change the price paid.

In Scenario A the business had two shares outstanding and we paid $500 per share to acquire them. In Figure 17, we introduce two new scenarios. Scenario B assumes we pay $750 per share and Scenario C assumes we pay only $400 per share.

FIGURE 17: CASE STUDY SCENARIOS A, B AND C

Company A	Scenario A	Scenario B	Scenario C
Price per share	$500	$750	$400
Number of shares outstanding	2	2	2
Total purchase cost	$1,000	$1,500	$800
Assets	$1,000	$1,000	$1,000
Liabilities	-	-	-
Shareholders' Equity	$1,000	$1,000	$1,000
Earnings for the year	$200	$200	$200
Outputs			
ROE	20%	20%	20%
P/B	1.0	1.5	0.8
Investor's Short-Term Return	20.0%	13.3%	25.0%

Notice within the table that the price paid is the only input that changes; all of the other inputs remain the same. That particular stock doesn't care that we bought it. The price we paid has zero influence on the number of shares outstanding, the assets, the liabilities, or the earnings. The nature of the business and all of those performance elements remain completely unchanged. However, the price we paid **does** have a significant impact on the **outputs**.

IMPACT OF PRICE CHANGE ON MARKET VALUE

By changing the amount we were willing to pay Mr. Market we change the market value of the business. Increasing our bid from $500 to $750 per share increased the perceived value of the company from $1,000 to $1,500. Reducing the amount we were willing to pay from $500 to $400 per share reduced the perceived market value of the company from $1,000 to $800. Here, one of Buffett's key investment principles comes to mind: Buy a business not a stock. By bidding more for the shares we chased up the price and the company's market valuation, even though the underlying economics of the business had not changed. Taken to extremes, this is how bubbles can form and subsequently pop.

IMPACT OF PRICE CHANGE ON ROE

The price we pay as investors has no impact on the ROE.

IMPACT OF PRICE CHANGE ON THE P/B RATIO

In Scenario A our P/B ratio was 1.0. In Scenario B we paid $1,500 ($750 per share for 2 shares) for a company with a Book Value of $1,000 so our P/B ratio increases to 1.5 ($1,500/$1,000). In Scenario C we paid $800 ($400 per share for 2 shares) for a company with a Book Value of $1,000, so our P/B ratio drops to 0.8.

IMPACT OF PRICE CHANGE ON INVESTOR'S RETURN

In Scenario A we paid a fair price with a Price/Book ratio of 1.0, so our Investor's Return was the same as the ROE of the company overall, 20% ($200/$1,000). In Scenario B, however, even though the company generated the same $200 of earnings and ROE of 20%, we only earned an Investor's Return of 13.3% ($200/$1,500). This is because we used more cash to buy the same $200 of earnings. The extra $500 we paid to acquire the two shares diminished our Investor's Return. Conversely, in Scenario C, by underpaying for our shares and investing only $800 to purchase $200 of earning power, we were able to generate a fantastic Investor's Return of 25.0% ($200/$800).

So, focusing on ROE alone is not enough to determine the level of return we will generate by investing in a business. The price we pay is also key in the determination of our return. The P/B ratio provides a quick gauge of the *value* we are getting for our money. Like ROE, P/B ratios are published extensively on financial websites and are easy to find.

5.3
THE INVESTOR'S SHORT-TERM RETURN

At this point we reveal the first component of *The Investor's Solution*, "***The Investor's Short-Term Return***." This is the theoretical rate of return that we ourselves can expect to receive as investors over the short-term. I tend to think of this as the Year 1 return.

The Investor's Short-Term Return can be calculated simply and quickly as follows, using readily available ROE and P/B ratio as inputs:

Investor's Short-Term Return = ROE / P/B Ratio x 100

For our three scenarios, *The Investor's Short-Term Returns* are therefore:

Scenario A: 20% / 1.0 x 100 = 20.0%

Scenario B: 20% / 1.5 x 100 = 13.3%

Scenario C: 20% / 0.8 x 100 = 25.0%

These match back to the Investor's Returns calculated in the bottom row of Figure 17. It is a much quicker way of calculating them.

5.4
THE INVESTOR'S SHORT-TERM RETURN RECAP

From this point onwards we are no longer going to be distracted by the arbitrary measure that is today's stock price. From now on, we are focused on price relative to value.

Earlier we learned to seek out companies generating consistently high ROEs. But focusing on ROE alone is not enough. The price we pay has a big impact on our returns. Now we have expanded our approach to incorporate the Price/Book ratio. Combining ROE and P/B, *The Investor's Short-Term Return* provides us with a quick and practical assessment of our theoretical first-year return, a single measure that balances both *return* and *value*.

Investor's Short-Term Return = ROE / P/B Ratio x 100

I say 'theoretical' return because the earnings a company generates aren't guaranteed. Even if we did own an entire business, its earnings could still be impacted factors outside of our control, such as customer orders, increased costs, changes to the tax rate, to name just a few of the many variables that can impact our return.

Furthermore, if we haven't bought an entire business but have instead purchased shares in a publicly listed company, then fluctuations of the share price will also impact our return. For example, the business may boast an *Investor's Short-Term Return* of 20% on paper, but if the share price also rose 7% in the first year, then our overall return would theoretically be closer to 27% (the 20% earnings generated and held in the company, plus the 7% increase in the price of our shares).

With *The Investor's Solution*, we are not trying to be

perfect. We are adopting a robust, yet quick and practical way to assess investments, enabling us to select those that will offer us the best return over time. Since we are investing for the long-term, the accuracy of the first year return isn't vitally important. The real value of *The Investor's Short-Term Return* is its utility in enabling us to compare multiple investment opportunities and stock screen ideas quickly, and side-by-side.

CHAPTER 6:
THE INVESTOR'S LONG-TERM RETURN

CHAPTER SUMMARY
6.1 COMPOUND GROWTH
6.2 CAPITAL ALLOCATION & COMPOUND GROWTH
6.3 THE INVESTOR'S RETURN CURVE
6.4 THE INVESTOR'S LONG-TERM RETURN
6.5 CHAPTER RECAP

6.1
COMPOUND GROWTH

Chapter 3 introduced the concept of compound growth and the calculation of the compound annual growth rate (CAGR). We know that it is one of the most powerful forces in the investment universe and that Buffett utilised compounding to achieve a phenomenal CAGR of 20.3% between 1964 and 2019, becoming one of the richest men in the world in the process. So, how can we emulate his performance?

A series of short lessons follow, designed to increase our understanding of compound growth and to demonstrate key investment concepts.

To provide context as we move between lessons, we will use the same compound growth base case we saw in Chapter 3, labelled as *Option 1* in Figure 10. I have replicated this base case for you below in Figure 18. In that base case we invested $1,000 for 30 years, earning 20% interest per annum. We elected to reinvest our interest income throughout. At the end of 30-year period our investment had grown from $1,000 to a very substantial $237,376.

FIGURE 18: COMPOUND GROWTH BASE CASE – BANK ACCOUNT BALANCE COMPOUNDED AT 20% PER ANNUM FOR 30 YEARS

End of Year...	Reinvest Interest Earned
Start	$1,000
1	$1,200
2	$1,440
3	$1,728
4	$2,074
5	$2,488
6	$2,986
7	$3,583
8	$4,300
9	$5,160
10	$6,192
11	$7,430
12	$8,916
13	$10,699
14	$12,839
15	$15,407
16	$18,488

17	$22,186
18	$26,623
19	$31,948
20	$38,338
21	$46,005
22	$55,206
23	$66,247
24	$79,497
25	$95,396
26	$114,475
27	$137,371
28	$164,845
29	$197,814
30	$237,376

LESSON 1: START COMPOUNDING AS EARLY AS POSSIBLE

Let's see how our Base Case is impacted when we delay investment. Instead of investing $1,000 in Year 1, we delay making that investment for 10 years.

FIGURE 19: BASE CASE VERSUS INVESTOR 1.0

End of Year...	Base Case	Investor 1.0: 10 Year Delay
Start	$1,000	
1	$1,200	
2	$1,440	
3	$1,728	
4	$2,074	
5	$2,488	
6	$2,986	
7	$3,583	
8	$4,300	
9	$5,160	

10	$6,192	$1,000
11	$7,430	$1,200
12	$8,916	$1,440
13	$10,699	$1,728
14	$12,839	$2,074
15	$15,407	$2,488
16	$18,488	$2,986
17	$22,186	$3,583
18	$26,623	$4,300
19	$31,948	$5,160
20	$38,338	$6,192
21	$46,005	$7,430
22	$55,206	$8,916
23	$66,247	$10,699
24	$79,497	$12,839
25	$95,396	$15,407
26	$114,475	$18,488
27	$137,371	$22,186
28	$164,845	$26,623
29	$197,814	$31,948
30	$237,376	$38,338

At the end of the 30-year term *Investor 1.0*'s investment has only been compounding for 20 years, 10 years fewer than the Base Case. The original $1,000 has grown to $38,338, significantly less than our base value of $237,376. If we were relying on this investment to retire, that 10-year delay made a significant difference to our retirement income and quality of life.

Wherever possible, start compounding as early as possible!

LESSON 2: START COMPOUNDING AS EARLY AS POSSIBLE, EVEN IF IT IS WITH A SMALL AMOUNT

We've just seen that the number of years over which we are able to compound is a key driver of growth. To further demonstrate this fact, we'll compare *Investor 1.0* to *Investor 2.0*, who has $162 to invest but can invest for the full 30-year term.

FIGURE 20: INVESTOR 1.0 VERSUS INVESTOR 2.0

End of Year...	Investor 1.0: 10 Year Delay	Investor 2.0: $162 Invested for 30 Years
Start		$162
1		$194
2		$233
3		$279
4		$335
5		$402
6		$482
7		$579
8		$694
9		$833
10	$1,000	$1,000
11	$1,200	$1,200
12	$1,440	$1,440
13	$1,728	$1,728
14	$2,074	$2,074
15	$2,488	$2,488
16	$2,986	$2,986
17	$3,583	$3,583
18	$4,300	$4,300
19	$5,160	$5,160
20	$6,192	$6,192
21	$7,430	$7,430
22	$8,916	$8,916
23	$10,699	$10,699

24	$12,839	$12,839
25	$15,407	$15,407
26	$18,488	$18,488
27	$22,186	$22,186
28	$26,623	$26,623
29	$31,948	$31,948
30	$38,338	$38,338

In this case, despite investing a smaller amount, *Investor 2.0* still ends up with the same $38,338 as *Investor 1.0*, who invested $1,000 in Year 10.

Starting early really helps growth, even when starting with a small amount.

LESSON 3: IF YOU COULDN'T START EARLY, MAKE UP LOST GROUND BY INVESTING A BIGGER LUMP SUM LATER ON

Many of us don't have spare money available to invest early on in life. And many only start to think about saving and investing when we settle down and start planning for the future.

It is still possible to achieve a large investment pot even if we are starting later. But to do so, we will need to invest a larger lump sum in order to make up for lost time. If we were to invest nothing for 10 years, but then made a lump sum investment of $6,192, our investment pot would grow to match the Base Case value of $237,376 by Year 30.

FIGURE 21: BASE CASE VERSUS INVESTOR 3.0

End of Year...	Base Case	Investor 3.0: Year 10 Lump Sum
Start	$1,000	
1	$1,200	
2	$1,440	
3	$1,728	
4	$2,074	
5	$2,488	
6	$2,986	
7	$3,583	
8	$4,300	
9	$5,160	
10	$6,192	$6,192
11	$7,430	$7,430
12	$8,916	$8,916
13	$10,699	$10,699
14	$12,839	$12,839
15	$15,407	$15,407
16	$18,488	$18,488
17	$22,186	$22,186
18	$26,623	$26,623
19	$31,948	$31,948
20	$38,338	$38,338
21	$46,005	$46,005
22	$55,206	$55,206
23	$66,247	$66,247
24	$79,497	$79,497
25	$95,396	$95,396
26	$114,475	$114,475
27	$137,371	$137,371
28	$164,845	$164,845
29	$197,814	$197,814
30	$237,376	$237,376

So, where we are unable to invest early, we can make up for lost time by making a larger lump sum investment at a later date.

LESSON 4: START EARLY, EVEN WHEN MAKING FREQUENT INVESTMENTS

Investor 4.0 makes a contribution of $1,000 per year for four years, then no more contributions for the rest of the 30-year term. The total invested is therefore $4,000. Each of those payments earns the usual return of 20% per annum.

Investor 5.0 makes no investment for the first 4 years. However, starting in year 5, *Investor 5.0* makes contributions of $1,000 per year and continues to do so for the rest of the 30-year term. Total contributions are therefore $26,000. *Investor 5.0* also earns a return of 20% per annum.

FIGURE 22: INVESTOR 4.0 (CONTRIBUTIONS OF $1,000 FOR 4 YEARS) VERSUS INVESTOR 5.0 (CONTRIBUTIONS OF $1,000 FROM YEARS 5 TO 30)

End of Year...	Investor 4.0: Contributions	Investor 4.0: Year-end Value	Investor 5.0: Contributions	Investor 5.0: Year-end Value
Start				
1	$1,000	$1,200		
2	$1,000	$2,640		
3	$1,000	$4,368		
4	$1,000	$6,442		
5		$7,730	$1,000	$1,200
6		$9,276	$1,000	$2,640
7		$11,131	$1,000	$4,368
8		$13,357	$1,000	$6,442
9		$16,029	$1,000	$8,930
10		$19,235	$1,000	$11,916
11		$23,081	$1,000	$15,499

12		$27,698	$1,000	$19,799
13		$33,237	$1,000	$24,959
14		$39,885	$1,000	$31,150
15		$47,862	$1,000	$38,581
16		$57,434	$1,000	$47,497
17		$68,921	$1,000	$58,196
18		$82,705	$1,000	$71,035
19		$99,246	$1,000	$86,442
20		$119,095	$1,000	$104,931
21		$142,914	$1,000	$127,117
22		$171,497	$1,000	$153,740
23		$205,796	$1,000	$185,688
24		$246,955	$1,000	$224,026
25		$296,347	$1,000	$270,031
26		$355,616	$1,000	$325,237
27		$426,739	$1,000	$391,484
28		$512,087	$1,000	$470,981
29		$614,504	$1,000	$566,377
30		$737,405	$1,000	$680,853
Total Contributions	$4,000		$26,000	
Investment Pot at End		$737,405		$680,853
Investment Pot Less Contributions		$733,405		$654,853
'Investor 4.0' Excess Over 'Investor 5.0'		$78,552		

Despite contributing only $4,000 over the duration of the example, being $22,000 less than the contributions made by *Investor 5.0*, *Investor 4.0* still ends up with more money. If we subtract the contributions, they each made from their ending investment pots, *Investor 4.0* has $78,552 (or 12%) more than *Investor 5.0*. This excess is 19-times the value of *Investor 4.0*'s original $4,000 contribution.

The key difference between the two is that *Investor 4.0* secured four extra years of compounding. Those four early years were worth a significant amount. So, even when making frequent investments, the importance of starting early cannot be over-emphasised.

LESSON 5: INVEST IN A TAX EFFICIENT WAY - TAXES REDUCE YOUR RETURN

This is one key reason not to trade in and out of positions. Closing one position so as to move capital to another position, particularly if you crystallise a gain in the process, can incur a lot of taxes.

To illustrate the negative impact of taxes, let's once again use our Base Case as context. *Investor 6.0* starts with an investment of $1,000, which compounds at 20% per annum. *Investor 6.0* sells that investment once per annum, at the end of each year, and must immediately pay a 10% tax charge. The net proceeds of the sale are then reinvested on the first day of the following year. This pattern is repeated for the full 30-year term.

FIGURE 23: INVESTOR 6.0 AND THE IMPACT OF TAXES

Year	Start of Year Value	20% Return (Pre-Tax)	10% Tax on Gain	Gain After Tax	End of Year Value
1	$1,000	$200	($20)	$180	$1,180
2	$1,180	$236	($24)	$212	$1,392
3	$1,392	$278	($28)	$251	$1,643
4	$1,643	$329	($33)	$296	$1,939
5	$1,939	$388	($39)	$349	$2,288
6	$2,288	$458	($46)	$412	$2,700
7	$2,700	$540	($54)	$486	$3,185
8	$3,185	$637	($64)	$573	$3,759
9	$3,759	$752	($75)	$677	$4,435

10	$4,435	$887	($89)	$798	$5,234
11	$5,234	$1,047	($105)	$942	$6,176
12	$6,176	$1,235	($124)	$1,112	$7,288
13	$7,288	$1,458	($146)	$1,312	$8,599
14	$8,599	$1,720	($172)	$1,548	$10,147
15	$10,147	$2,029	($203)	$1,827	$11,974
16	$11,974	$2,395	($239)	$2,155	$14,129
17	$14,129	$2,826	($283)	$2,543	$16,672
18	$16,672	$3,334	($333)	$3,001	$19,673
19	$19,673	$3,935	($393)	$3,541	$23,214
20	$23,214	$4,643	($464)	$4,179	$27,393
21	$27,393	$5,479	($548)	$4,931	$32,324
22	$32,324	$6,465	($646)	$5,818	$38,142
23	$38,142	$7,628	($763)	$6,866	$45,008
24	$45,008	$9,002	($900)	$8,101	$53,109
25	$53,109	$10,622	($1,062)	$9,560	$62,669
26	$62,669	$12,534	($1,253)	$11,280	$73,949
27	$73,949	$14,790	($1,479)	$13,311	$87,260
28	$87,260	$17,452	($1,745)	$15,707	$102,967
29	$102,967	$20,593	($2,059)	$18,534	$121,501
30	$121,501	$24,300	($2,430)	$21,870	$143,371
Total Tax Paid			($15,819)		

Despite the very modest tax rate of 10%, each time cash was taken out of the investment pot to pay the tax bill, the amount of capital available to reinvest was reduced. The total tax bill for the 30-year term amounted to $15,819, but the damage done was much deeper. At the end of the 30-year period *Investor 6.0* only ended up with a pot worth $143,271k, some $94,005 less than the Base Case pot of $237,376.

If you can invest through tax efficient vehicles, so that you don't have to pay tax on gains, this headache goes away. If you must still pay tax, try to limit the number of times you have to crystallise gains in order to minimise tax payments and maximise the capital available for growth. Buffett's principle of "Holding for a long time" helps in this respect.

LESSON 6: AVOID UNNECESSARY TRANSACTION COSTS, THEY REDUCE YOUR RETURN

Holding for the long-term not only helps to minimise tax, it also helps avoid unnecessary transaction costs.

Investor 7.0 starts with an investment of $1,000, which compounds at 20% per annum. *Investor 7.0* sells that investment once per annum, at the end of each year, and must pay $25 in trading transaction costs to do so. The net proceeds of the sale are then reinvested on the first day of the following year, free of charge. This pattern is repeated for the full 30-year term. For simplicity, we will ignore tax implications in this example.

FIGURE 24: INVESTOR 7.0 AND THE IMPACT OF TRANSACTION COSTS

Year	Start of Year Value	20% Return (Pre-Tax)	Transaction Cost of $25	Gain After Costs	End of Year Value
1	$1,000	$200	($25)	$175	$1,175
2	$1,175	$235	($25)	$210	$1,385
3	$1,385	$277	($25)	$252	$1,637
4	$1,637	$327	($25)	$302	$1,939
5	$1,939	$388	($25)	$363	$2,302
6	$2,302	$460	($25)	$435	$2,738
7	$2,738	$548	($25)	$523	$3,260
8	$3,260	$652	($25)	$627	$3,887
9	$3,887	$777	($25)	$752	$4,640
10	$4,640	$928	($25)	$903	$5,543
11	$5,543	$1,109	($25)	$1,084	$6,626
12	$6,626	$1,325	($25)	$1,300	$7,927
13	$7,927	$1,585	($25)	$1,560	$9,487

14	$9,487	$1,897	($25)	$1,872	$11,359
15	$11,359	$2,272	($25)	$2,247	$13,606
16	$13,606	$2,721	($25)	$2,696	$16,302
17	$16,302	$3,260	($25)	$3,235	$19,538
18	$19,538	$3,908	($25)	$3,883	$23,420
19	$23,420	$4,684	($25)	$4,659	$28,079
20	$28,079	$5,616	($25)	$5,591	$33,670
21	$33,670	$6,734	($25)	$6,709	$40,379
22	$40,379	$8,076	($25)	$8,051	$48,430
23	$48,430	$9,686	($25)	$9,661	$58,091
24	$58,091	$11,618	($25)	$11,593	$69,685
25	$69,685	$13,937	($25)	$13,912	$83,597
26	$83,597	$16,719	($25)	$16,694	$100,291
27	$100,291	$20,058	($25)	$20,033	$120,324
28	$120,324	$24,065	($25)	$24,040	$144,364
29	$144,364	$28,873	($25)	$28,848	$173,212
30	$173,212	$34,642	($25)	$34,617	$207,829
Total Tax Paid			($750)		

Despite the modest size of the $25 annual transaction costs, each transaction reduced the amount of capital available for reinvestment. Over the full 30-year term, transaction costs totaled only $750, but the Year 30 investment pot ended up at $207,829, some $29,547 smaller than in the Base Case pot of $237,376. Removing $750 of cash from the pot over 30 years had an impact on the investment pot almost 40x greater than the transaction costs themselves.

COMPOUNDING WITHIN A BUSINESS

So far, we've looked at examples of compounding within a straightforward bank or brokerage account, in which we invest a lump sum, say $1,000, and let it compound at 20%

per year for 30 years. But our ultimate aim is to invest in businesses, so how does compounding work within a company? The good news is that it's not much more complicated than the examples you've already seen.

Once again, for simplicity in written format, we'll base the ROE calculations on the Equity at the start of each year, rather than the average Equity over the year.

A BUSINESS CONTAINING ONLY ASSETS

In the Base Case we invested $1,000 cash in a bank account, and let it grow at 20% per annum. We can create an analogous example for a business by making the assumption that a company has $1,000 in cash, with no other assets or liabilities - just a simple balance of $1,000 cash, ready to deploy in its operations, to generate sales and to make a profit.

Equity = (Assets - Liabilities) = ($1,000 - $0) = $1,000

In its first year the business generates Sales of $500. It incurs expenses of $214 in doing so and pays a 30% tax charge on its profits.

FIGURE 25: INCOME STATEMENT FOR THE YEAR ENDED 2019

Sales generated	$500
Cost of raw materials and expenses	($214)
Net income before taxes	**$286**
Tax charge at 30%	($86)
Net income after taxes (or 'Earnings' or 'Return')	**$200**

Return on Equity (ROE) = (Return / Equity) x 100

Return on Equity (ROE) = ($200 / $1,000) x 100

Return on Equity (ROE) = 0.2 x 100

Return on Equity (ROE) = 20.0%

So, we started the year with cash of $1,000, which was the Equity of the business. We used that money to generate sales and make a profit after taxes of $200, which equates to a Return on Equity (ROE) of 20%. At the end of the year the business has $1,200 of cash, which equates to $1,200 of Equity.

The concept of compounding is the same within a company as it is for a bank account, so if the business can repeat this pattern for 30 years the company will end up with Equity of $237,376, exactly the same as the pot we had in our bank account.

A BUSINESS CONTAINING BOTH ASSETS AND LIABILITIES

We just saw a very clean example in which the business started with cash in the bank and had no liabilities. Now let's add a loan into the mix.

This business has $3,000 in cash and adds a further $2,000 of cash by taking out a bank loan.

Equity = (Assets - Liabilities) = ($5,000 - $2,000) = $3,000

The company has 3 shares outstanding, each valued at $1,000, making the total market value of the company $3,000.

In its first year the business generates Sales of $2,500. It incurs expenses of $1,643 in doing so, including an interest charge on the loan. It pays a 30% tax charge on its Net Income.

FIGURE 26: INCOME STATEMENT FOR THE YEAR ENDED 2019

Sales generated	$2,500
Cost of raw materials and expenses	($1,300)
Interest Expense	($343)
Net income before taxes	**$857**
Tax charge at 30%	($257)
Net income after taxes (or 'Earnings' or 'Return')	**$600**

Return on Equity (ROE) = (Return / Equity) x 100

Return on Equity (ROE) = ($600 / $3,000) x 100

Return on Equity (ROE) = 0.2 x 100

Return on Equity (ROE) = 20.0%

In this example, we started with the year with total cash available of $5,000 ($3,000 cash plus $2,000 from the loan), and a loan liability of $2,000, resulting in Equity of $3,000. We used that money to generate sales and make a profit after taxes of $600, which equates to a Return on Equity (ROE) of 20%. At the end of the year the business's Equity has therefore grown to $3,600, being $5,600 in total cash minus the $2,000 bank loan.

If we considered investing in this company at the start of the year, we would only have been able to purchase one of the three shares outstanding with our budget of $1,000. This represents ownership of one third of the business, so Equity of $3,000/3 = $1,000. At the end of the year our investment would have grown to $3,600/3 = $1,200, an increase of 20%. Once again, if this business were able to keep generating those returns for 30 years, our $1,000 investment would grow to $237,376.

6.2
CAPITAL ALLOCATION &
COMPOUND GROWTH

When a company generates earnings, it has the option of keeping that money within the business and reinvesting it to generate additional earnings. It could also pay out some of the earnings to its shareholders in the form of dividends.

A BUSINESS CONTAINING BOTH ASSETS AND LIABILITIES, AND ALSO PAYING A DIVIDEND

Using the same company that we did in the preceding example, let's see what happens to its compound returns when it opts to pay a dividend.

The business has $3,000 in cash and adds a further $2,000 of cash by taking out a bank loan.

Equity = (Assets - Liabilities) = ($5,000 - $2,000) = $3,000

The company has 3 shares outstanding, each valued at $1,000, making the total market value of the company $3,000.

In its first year the business generates Sales of $2,500. It incurs expenses of $1,643 in doing so, including an interest charge on the loan. It pays a 30% tax charge on its Net Income and its policy is to pay out 10% of after-tax Net Income to shareholders as dividends at the end of every year.

FIGURE 27: INCOME STATEMENT FOR THE YEAR ENDED 2019

Sales generated	$2,500
Cost of raw materials and expenses	($1,300)
Interest Expense	($343)
Net income before taxes	**$857**
Tax charge at 30%	($257)
Net income after taxes (or 'Earnings' or 'Return')	**$600**
Dividend paid to shareholders (10% of Earnings paid out)	($60)
Earnings retained in the business (90% retained)	**$540**

Return on Equity (ROE) = (Return / Equity) x 100

Return on Equity (ROE) = ($600 / $3,000) x 100

Return on Equity (ROE) = 0.2 x 100

Return on Equity (ROE) = 20.0%

In this example the businesses started in an identical financial position, it earned the same Net Income After Taxes, and it generated the same ROE. However, contrary to the previous example, the company paid out $60 of Earnings as a dividend to shareholders. Since $60 was paid out, only $540 was 'retained' in the business. This is called 'Retained Earnings'.

The business therefore ended the year with Equity of $3,540 ($5,540 in total cash minus the $2,000 bank loan), $60 less than the previous example. Paying a dividend reduced the amount of equity available for reinvestment and compound growth. For this reason, a company that pays dividends will generally underperform a non-dividend paying company over the long-term.

Investors may have benefited from the receipt of $60 of dividends ($20 per share), but unless those shareholders are adept enough to invest the dividend income themselves and generate an equivalent 20% return, they would have been better served by having the company retain the cash and reinvest it for them.

We can see the results of both scenarios side-by-side in Figure 28. Over 30 years, the company that pays dividends ends up with Equity of $430,112, having paid out $47,457 in dividends to shareholders. The total of those amounts is $477,569. This is significantly below the value of the company which paid no dividends and which has amassed Equity of $712,129 over that same period.

FIGURE 28: ALL EARNINGS RETAINED VERSUS 90% EARNINGS RETAINED

Equity at Year...	Non-Dividend-Paying Business (All Earnings are Retained and Reinvested)	Dividend-Paying Business (90% of Earnings are Retained and Reinvested)
Start	$3,000	$3,000
1	$3,600	$3,540
2	$4,320	$4,177
3	$5,184	$4,929
4	$6,221	$5,816
5	$7,645	$6,863
6	$8,958	$8,099
7	$10,750	$9,556
8	$12,899	$11,277
9	$15,479	$13,306
10	$18,575	$15,702
11	$22,290	$18,528
12	$26,748	$21,863

13	$32,098	$25,798
14	$38,518	$30,422
15	$46,221	$35,921
16	$55,465	$42,387
17	$66,558	$50,017
18	$79,870	$59,020
19	$95,884	$69,643
20	$115,013	$82,179
21	$138,015	$96,971
22	$165,618	$114,426
23	$198,742	$135,023
24	$238,491	$159,327
25	$286,189	$188,006
26	$343,426	$221,847
27	$412,112	$261,779
28	$494,534	$308,900
29	$593,441	$364,502
30	$712,129	$430,112
Total Dividends	**$0**	**$47,457**
Total Value at Year 30	**$712,129**	**$477,569**
Excess over Dividend-Paying Business	**$234,560**	

Thus, much like the examples in which we paid taxes or transaction costs, paying out dividends reduces the amount of equity available for reinvestment and reduces a company's ability to maximise compound growth.

"We don't get rich on our dividends that we receive…we get rich on fact that the retained earnings are used to build new earning power."[54]

Warren Buffett – Interview with Becky Quick, CNBC

EARNINGS RETENTION RATE

As a general rule, therefore, we want to see a high growth company retain its earnings and reinvest them into the business. By default, that means that we'd like it to pay only a small portion of earnings out as dividends, or no dividend at all. To determine the impact dividend payments have on our long-term return we use a measure called the 'Earnings Retention Rate'. There are three main methods for calculating it:

METHOD 1: USING EARNINGS AND RETAINED EARNINGS

Earnings Retention Rate

= (Earnings Retained / Earnings) x 100

= ($540 / $600) x 100

= 90%

METHOD 2: USING THE PAYOUT RATIO

Sometimes we will not have access to an Earnings Retention Rate metric, or we may not want to dig the Earnings and Earnings Retained values out of a company's accounts. Many financial websites provide an alternative, ready-made measure, the 'Payout Ratio'. The Payout Ratio is the proportion of earnings that are paid out as dividends. To obtain the Earnings Retention Rate, determine the Payout Ratio and then subtract it from 100%.

Payout Ratio = Dividends / Earnings

Payout Ratio = $60 / $600

Payout Ratio = 10%

Earnings Retention Rate = 100% - Payout Ratio

Earnings Retention Rate = 90%

This can be calculated on an overall company basis, or per-share basis.

METHOD 3: USING PER-SHARE EARNINGS AND DIVIDEND INFORMATION

This method is a little more accessible since Earnings Per Share (EPS) and Dividend Per Share (DPS) are widely available in the financial media.

EPS is the Earnings of the business divided by the number of shares outstanding.

Earnings Per Share = Earnings / Number of Shares

Earnings Per Share = $600 / 3

Earnings Per Share = $200

There are a few different types of EPS, depending on whether the company had any unusual events during the year, and whether the company has issued stock options to its employees, which dilutes the earnings each private shareholder receives. I use the EPS measure called '*Diluted Normalised Earnings per Share*' which takes into account the effects of all shares outstanding and non-recurring, unusual or one-off or extraordinary items. It may also be called *'Diluted Earnings per Share'* where no unusual, one-off or extraordinary items occurred.

Dividend Per Share is abbreviated to 'DPS'.

Dividend Per Share = Dividends / Number of Shares

Dividend Per Share = $60 / 3

Dividend Per Share = $20

To calculate the Earnings Retention Rate from per-share data, perform the following calculation:

Earnings Retention Rate = ((EPS - DPS) / EPS) x 100

Earnings Retention Rate = (($200 - $20) / $200) x 100

Earnings Retention Rate = ($180 / $200) x 100

Earnings Retention Rate = 90%

When examining businesses, it is important to be aware of the fact that as soon as the Earnings Retention Rate falls below 50%, over half of that company's earnings are being paid out and the ability to generate above-average compound growth is reduced dramatically.

6.3
THE INVESTOR'S RETURN CURVE

The second element of *The Investor's Solution*, which I will now introduce, is called "***The Investor's Return Curve***".

To explain this, let's bring together everything we've gone through so far – ROE, P/B Ratio, Compound Growth and the Earnings Retention Rate – in a new example.

Company A has 100 shares outstanding, priced at $160 each. We buy the entire company at this price, for a total investment of $16,000 (100 x $160).

The company has $5,000 in cash and owes $1,000 as a loan, resulting in Shareholders' Equity (Book Value) of $4,000 ($5,000-$1,000).

The Price/Book Ratio we paid for the shares is therefore $16,000/$4,000 = 4.0. Clearly this is above the benchmark ratio of 1.0, suggesting we have overpaid for the company. In effect, we have paid $4,000 for the Shareholders' Equity and an excess of $12,000 for the chance to earn above-average future returns. Later we will discover whether this overpayment is warranted by the company's long-term return prospects.

In its first year the company generated earnings of $1,600, resulting in a very strong ROE of 40% ($1,600/$4,000). *The Investor's Short-Term Return* was therefore ROE / P/B = 40%/4.0 = 10%. This is a great first-year return.

A moderate $400 of dividends were paid out of the $1,600 earnings, leaving $1,200 retained within the business. This increased the Shareholders' Equity at the end of Year 1 to $5,200 ($4,000+$1,200). This is also the *starting* Shareholders' Equity for Year 2.

FIGURE 29: COMPANY A: YEAR 1

Dark border = data input cell		YEAR 1	EXPLANATION
a. Price per share	Input	$160	
b. Number of Shares Outstanding	Input	100	
c. Market Value	= (a x b)	$16,000	= Price per share x Shares Outstanding
d. Assets: Cash	Input	$5,000	
e. Liabilities: Loan	Input	($1,000)	
f. Shareholders' Equity (Book Value) at start of year	= (d - e)	$4,000	= Year 1 Cash - Year 1 Loan
g. Price/Book Ratio	= (c / f)	4.0	= Market Value / Shareholders' Equity
h. Earnings	Input	$1,600	
i. Return on Equity (ROE)	= (h / f)	40%	= Earnings / Shareholders' Equity
j. Investor's Short-Term Return	= ROE / P/B	10%	= ROE / P/B
k. Earnings paid out as dividends	Input	$400	
l. Earnings retained increasing Shareholders' Equity	= (h - k)	$1,200	= Earnings - Dividends
m.Shareholders' Equity (Book Value) at end of year	= (f + l)	$5,200	= Year 1 Shareholders' Equity at start + Earnings Retained
n. Earnings per Share (EPS)	= (h / b)	$16.00	= Year 1 Earnings / Year 1 Shares Outstanding
o. Dividends per share (DPS)	= (k / b)	$4.00	= Year 1 Dividends / Year 1 Shares Outstanding
p. Earnings Retention Rate	= (EPS-DPS)/EPS	75%	= (EPS-DPS) / EPS

The Earnings Retention Rate is 75%. This could be calculated using either of our three methods:

METHOD 1:

Earnings Retention Rate

= (Earnings Retained / Earnings) x 100

Earnings Retention Rate = ($1,200 / $1,600) x 100

Earnings Retention Rate = 75%

METHOD 2:

Payout Ratio = Dividends / Earnings

Payout Ratio = $400 / $1,600

Payout Ratio = 25%

Earnings Retention Rate = 100% - Payout Ratio

Earnings Retention Rate = 75%

METHOD 3:

Earnings Retention Rate = ((EPS - DPS) / EPS) x 100

Earnings Retention Rate = (($16 - $4) / $16) x 100

Earnings Retention Rate = 75%

Let's assume in the second year that business conditions remain stable. The company therefore earns the same ROE of 40% and the Earnings Retention Rate also remains unchanged at 75%.

We can see that the $1,200 of Retained Earnings from the first year increased our starting cash balance to $6,200. Since the loan remained unchanged at $1,000 we can confirm that the starting Shareholders' Equity increased to $5,200 ($6,200-$1,000), which is, by default, identical to the ending equity from the prior year.

The stable ROE of 40%, when multiplied by the enlarged Shareholders' Equity, generated second year Earnings of $2,080 (40% x $5,200). With a stable Earnings Retention Rate of 75% we can deduce that 25% of Earnings were paid out as dividends (25% x $2,080 = $520). $1,560 (75% x $2,080) of Earnings were retained and added to Shareholders' Equity. The Year 2 ending Shareholders' Equity rose to $6,760 ($5,200+$1,560).

FIGURE 30: COMPANY A: YEAR 2

		YEAR 1	YEAR 2	EXPLANATION
Dark border = data input cell				
a. Price per share	Input	**$160**		
b. Number of Shares Outstanding	Input	**100**	100	No change (assuming not bought/sold shares)
c. Market Value	= (a x b)	$16,000		
d. Assets: Cash	Input	$5,000	$6,200	= Year 1 Cash + Year 1 Retained Earnings
e. Liabilities: Loan	Input	($1,000)	($1,000)	No change
f. Shareholders' Equity (Book Value) at start of year	= (d - e)	$4,000	$5,200	= Year 2 Cash - Year 2 Loan
g. Price/Book Ratio	= (c / f)	4.0		
h. Earnings	Input	**$1,600**	$2,080	= Yr.1 ROE x Yr.2 Shareholders' Equity at start of year
i. Return on Equity (ROE)	= (h / f)	40%		
j. Investor's Short-Term Return	= ROE / P/B	10%		
k. Earnings paid out as dividends	Input	**$400**	$520	= Year 2 Earnings - Year 2 Earnings Retained
l. Earnings retained increasing Shareholders' Equity	= (h - k)	$1,200	$1,560	= Year 2 Earnings x Year 1 Earnings Ret Rate
m. Shareholders' Equity (Book Value) at end of year	= (f + l)	$5,200	$6,760	= Yr.2 Shareholders' Equity at start + Earnings Retained
n. Earnings per Share (EPS)	= (h / b)	$16.00	$20.80	= Year 2 Earnings / Year 2 Shares Outstanding
o. Dividends per share (DPS)	= (k / b)	$4.00	$5.20	= Year 2 Dividends / Year 2 Shares Outstanding
p. Earnings Retention Rate	= (EPS-DPS)/EPS	75%		

In the third year we will again assume that the ROE and the Earnings Retention Rate remain stable.

The $1,560 of Earnings retained in the second year increased our starting cash balance to $7,760. Yet again, the loan remained unchanged at $1,000 so the starting Shareholders' Equity increased to $6,760 ($7,760-$1,000), which is, by default, identical to the ending equity from the prior year.

The ROE of 40%, when multiplied by the starting Shareholders' Equity, generated Earnings of $2,704 (40% x $6,760). Since the same 75% of earnings were retained, we added $2,028 (75% x $2,704) to Shareholders' Equity at year-end. Shareholders' Equity now stands at $8,788 ($6,760+$2,028). The remaining 25% of earnings, or $676 (25% x $2,704), were paid out as dividends.

FIGURE 31: COMPANY A: YEAR 3

	Formula	YEAR 1	YEAR 2	YEAR 3	EXPLANATION
Dark border = data input cell					
a. Price per share	Input	**$160**			
b. Number of Shares Outstanding	Input	100	100	100	No change (assuming not bought/sold)
c. Market Value	= (a x b)	$16,000			
d. Assets: Cash	Input	**$5,000**	$6,200	$7,760	= Year 2 Cash + Year 2 Retained Earnings
e. Liabilities: Loan	Input	**($1,000)**	($1,000)	($1,000)	No change
f. Shareholders' Equity (Book Value) at start of year	= (d - e)	$4,000	$5,200	$6,760	= Year 3 Cash - Year 3 Loan
g. Price/Book Ratio	= (c / f)	4.0			
h. Earnings	Input	**$1,600**	$2,080	$2,704	= Year 1 ROE x Year 3 Shareholders' Equity at start of year
i. Return on Equity (ROE)	= (h / f)	40%			
j. Investor's Short-Term Return	= ROE / P/B	10%			
k. Earnings paid out as dividends	Input	**$400**	$520	$676	= Yr. 3 Earnings - Yr. 3 Earnings Retained
l. Earnings retained increasing Shareholders' Equity	= (h - k)	$1,200	$1,560	$2,028	= Yr. 3 Earnings x Yr. 1 Earnings Ret Rate
m. Shareholders' Equity (Book Value) at end of year	= (f + l)	$5,200	$6,760	$8,788	= Yr.3 Shareholders' Equity at start + Earnings Retained
n. Earnings per Share (EPS)	= (h / b)	$16.00	$20.80	$27.04	= Yr.3 Earnings / Yr.3 Shares Outstanding
o. Dividends per share (DPS)	= (k / b)	$4.00	$5.20	$6.76	= Yr.3 Dividends / Yr.3 Shares Outstanding
p. Earnings Retention Rate	= (EPS-DPS)/EPS	75%			

VISUALISING YOUR RETURNS

In Figure 32, I have created a visual illustration of the initial $16,000 investment and the first year returns it generated. As described earlier, the investment can be considered as two components, the $4,000 we spent to acquire the Shareholders' Equity portion of the business, and a $12,000 excess over Shareholders' Equity. If Shareholders' Equity represents 1.0 of our P/B ratio of 4.0, then the excess portion is the additional 3.0 that we paid.

YEAR 1

Our Year 1 Earnings are generated from the 40% return on the company's $4,000 of Equity. $1,600 of Earnings are generated in total, of which $400 is paid out as a Dividend and $1,200 is retained, growing Shareholders' Equity to $5,200.

Overall, the $1,600 of Earnings, divided by our initial $16,000 investment, gives us a return for Year 1 of 10.0%. This is expected and matches Investor's Short-Term Return calculated in Figure 29.

FIGURE 32: VISUALISATION OF INITIAL INVESTMENT AND YEAR 1 RETURN

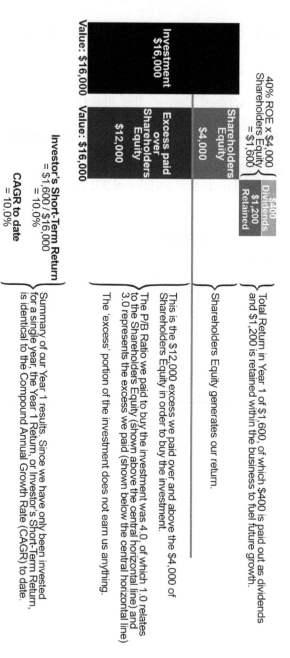

INITIAL INVESTMENT   YEAR 1

Investment
$16,000

Shareholders
Equity
$4,000

Excess paid
over
Shareholders
Equity
$12,000

40% ROE x $4,000
Shareholders Equity
= $1,600

$400
Dividends
$1,200
Retained

Value: $16,000   Value: $16,000

Total Return in Year 1 of $1,600, of which $400 is paid out as dividends and $1,200 is retained within the business to fuel future growth.

Shareholders Equity generates our return.

This is the $12,000 excess we paid over and above the $4,000 of Shareholders Equity in order to buy the investment.

The P/B Ratio we paid to buy the investment was 4.0, of which 1.0 relates to the Shareholders Equity (shown above the central horizontal line) and 3.0 represents the excess we paid (shown below the central horizontal line)

The 'excess' portion of the investment does not earn us anything.

Investor's Short-Term Return
= $1,600 / $16,000
= 10.0%

CAGR to date
= 10.0%

Summary of our Year 1 results. Since we have only been invested for a single year, the Year 1 Return, or Investor's Short-Term Return, is identical to the Compound Annual Growth Rate (CAGR) to date.

134

YEAR 2

Our Year 2 Earnings are generated from a 40% ROE on the now enlarged equity. We generate $2,080 of Earnings, of which $520 is paid out as a Dividend and $1,560 is retained, growing Shareholders' Equity to $6,760 by the end of the year. Overall, the $2,080 of Earnings, divided by our initial $16,000 investment, gives us a return for Year 2 of 13.0%. Since we earned 10.0% in Year 1 and 13.0% in Year 2, our Compound Annual Growth Rate (CAGR) has risen to 10.9%.

YEAR 3

Our Year 3 Earnings are generated from a 40% ROE on the further enlarged equity. We generate $2,704 of Earnings, of which $676 is paid out as a Dividend and $2,028 is retained, growing Shareholders' Equity to $8,788 by year-end. Overall, the $2,704 of Earnings, divided by our initial $16,000 investment, gives us a return for Year 3 of 16.9%. Since we earned 10.0% in Year 1, 13.0% in Year 2, and 16.9% in Year 3, our CAGR since the start has grown to 11.8%.

FIGURE 33: VISUALISATION OF YEAR 1 & 2 RETURNS

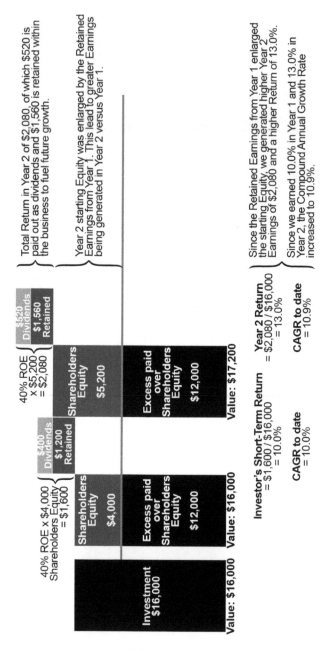

136

FIGURE 34: VISUALISATION OF YEAR 1-3 RETURNS

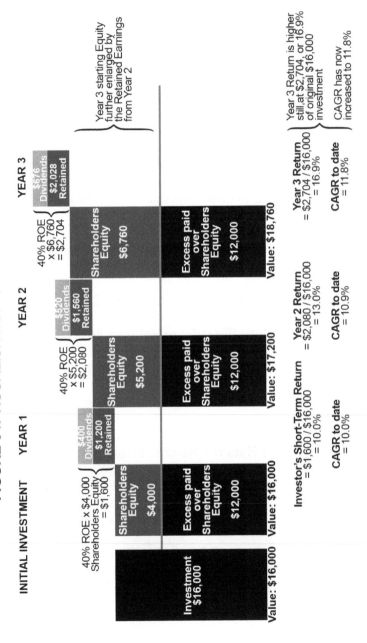

WHY IS THE CAGR INCREASING?

When we made the initial $16,000 investment, our return for the first year was 10.0%. Since the company retained earnings and grew its Equity, it was able to generate even larger returns in the second year. This led to an increase in our Year 2 return, which increased to 13.0%. The same process continued into the third year, increasing our return yet again, to 16.9%.

Our Compound Annual Growth Rate (CAGR), which was explained in Chapter 3, is the average annual growth of an investment over a specified period of time. So, as the returns increase in each individual year, our CAGR, which is the average, increases too.

YEAR 1: Our return is for the first year, *The Investor's Short-Term Return*:

Investor's Short-Term Return = ROE / P/B x 100

Investor's Short-Term Return = 40% / 4.0

Investor's Short-Term Return = 10.0%

Or, calculated from our initial $16,000 investment and the Year 1 return:

Year 1 Return = Return / Investment x 100

Year 1 Return = $1,600 / $16,000 x 100

Year 1 Return = 10.0%

YEAR 2: Using the CAGR calculation we learned in Chapter 3, we can deduce what the CAGR for a two-year period is:

Beginning Value: $16,000

Final Value: $19,680 ($16,000 investment + Year 1 Return of $1,600 + Year 2 Return of $2,080)
Investment Timeframe: 2 years

CAGR

$$= ((\text{Final Value} / \text{Beginning Value})^{(1/\text{Timeframe})} - 1) \times 100$$

$$= ((\$19{,}680 / \$16{,}000)^{(1/2)} - 1) \times 100$$

$$= ((1.23)^{(0.5)} - 1) \times 100$$

$$= (1.109 - 1) \times 100$$

$$= 0.109 \times 100$$

$$= 10.9\%$$

YEAR 3: The CAGR calculation for the entire three-year period is:

Beginning Value: $16,000
Final Value: $22,384 ($16,000 investment + Year 1 Return of $1,600 + Year 2 Return of $2,080 + Year 3 Return of $2,704)
Investment Timeframe: 3 years

CAGR

$$= ((\text{Final Value} / \text{Beginning Value})^{(1/\text{Timeframe})} - 1) \times 100$$

$$\text{CAGR} = ((\$22{,}384 / \$16{,}000)^{(1/3)} - 1) \times 100$$

$$\text{CAGR} = ((1.399)^{(0.333)} - 1) \times 100$$

$$CAGR = (1.118 - 1) \times 100$$

$$CAGR = 0.118 \times 100$$

$$CAGR = 11.8\%$$

The fact is, the longer we hold the investment, the higher our CAGR will become. The easiest way to think about this is:

For every year that passes we earn our first-year return, *The Investor's Short-Term Return*, on our initial investment. In this example, this means we will theoretically earn 10% on our $16,000 investment for every year we hold it. *On top* of that, we earn the full ROE rate, in this case 40%, on any earnings that are generated and retained by the business from the date of our purchase onwards. So, the more earnings that are generated and retained, the more equity we have earning us a rate of 40%. This pulls our first-year return of 10% upwards over time.

FIGURE 35: RETURN FROM INITIAL INVESTMENT VERSUS RETAINED EARNINGS

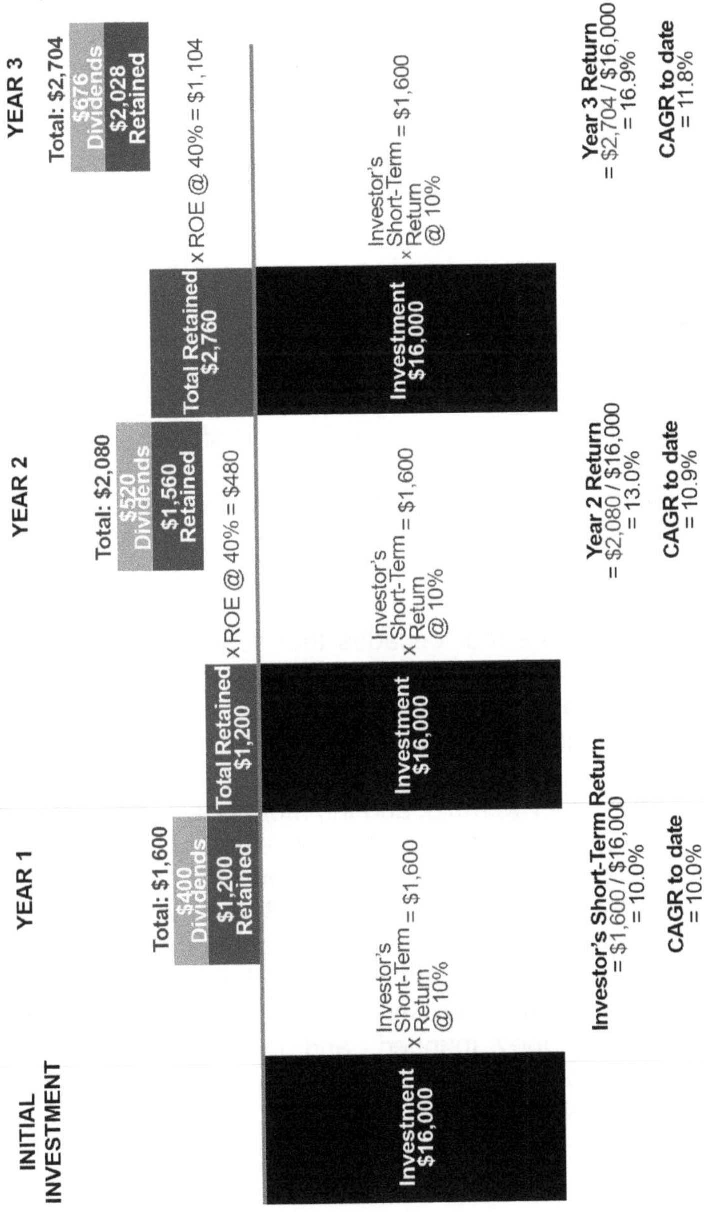

INITIAL INVESTMENT

YEAR 1

YEAR 2

YEAR 3

Total: $1,600
$400 Dividends
$1,200 Retained

Total: $2,080
$520 Dividends
$1,560 Retained

Total: $2,704
$676 Dividends
$2,028 Retained

Total Retained $1,200 × ROE @ 40% = $480

Total Retained $2,760 × ROE @ 40% = $1,104

Investment $16,000

Investment $16,000

Investment $16,000

Investment $16,000

Investor's × Short-Term = $1,600 Return @ 10%

Investor's × Short-Term = $1,600 Return @ 10%

Investor's × Short-Term = $1,600 Return @ 10%

Investor's Short-Term Return
= $1,600 / $16,000
= 10.0%

CAGR to date
= 10.0%

Year 2 Return
= $2,080 / $16,000
= 13.0%

CAGR to date
= 10.9%

Year 3 Return
= $2,704 / $16,000
= 16.9%

CAGR to date
= 11.8%

141

In his May 1977 Fortune article, *How Inflation Swindles the Equity Investor*, Buffett discusses this very notion, explaining that companies can retain earnings and reinvest them at the full ROE rate of return. He uses the example of a company with a ROE of 12%, "*...on their retained earnings, investors could earn [the full] 12%...The right to reinvest automatically a portion of the equity coupon at 12% was of enormous value.*"[55]

Flashing forward forty-two years we find that Buffett's Berkshire Hathaway 2019 Annual Report contains a section titled '*The Power of Retained Earnings*'. In it, he discusses a 1924 book written by Edgar Lawrence Smith called '*Common Stocks as Long Term Investments*'. Smith noted that wherever companies retain a part of their profits and put them back into the business, an element of compound interest operates in favour of the investor. Buffett goes on to explain that he and Charlie Munger have always utilised retained earnings advantageously and that they are of major importance to the growth of Berkshire.[56]

Despite the four decades that separate his words, the different economic environments he encountered along the way, the wars, the booms, the busts, and the creation of new financial instruments, Buffett didn't change his message or approach.

The longer we hold, and the more retained earnings that build up relative to our initial investment, the higher our annual return becomes. This is how Buffett has been able to earn a 20.3% annual return for Berkshire Hathaway.

In that same vein, Buffett's neighbors at the top of the world's richest list, Jeff Bezos and Bill Gates, amassed tremendous fortunes by holding large positions in the companies they founded, and by reinvesting company earnings to fund ever-greater profits and growth at Amazon and Microsoft, respectively.

IS THERE A CAP ON THE CAGR ACHIEVABLE?

If we were to extend our example forward, by Year 10 our CAGR would reach 18.1% and by Year 100 it would reach 28.6%. In the early years the CAGR grows rapidly as the proportion of earnings retained and generating 40% grows rapidly relative to our initial investment. However, as time goes by, more and more retained earnings have been added to the company's equity and this eventually outweighs the size of our initial investment. In effect, it becomes increasingly difficult to lift the CAGR as time goes by.

The result is a curve, which rises to begin with but flattens over time, reaching a plateau after around 50 years. I call this pattern "*The Investor's Return Curve*". This curve enables us to determine the theoretical return we can achieve at any point in time, given the three inputs of ROE, P/B and Earnings Retention Rate.

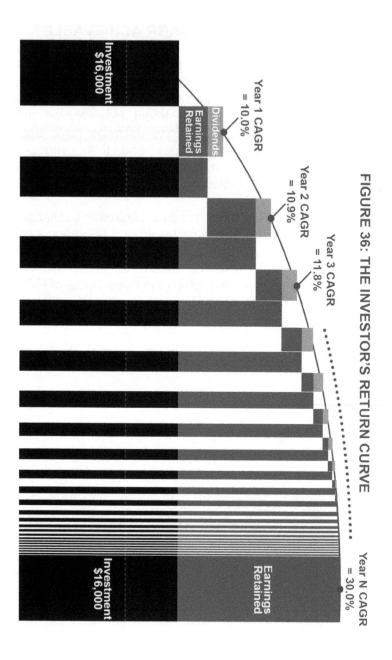

FIGURE 36: THE INVESTOR'S RETURN CURVE

Now here's a mini test for you. So far, you've been introduced to a small number of key metrics. If we have a ROE of 40%, a P/B of 4.0, and an Earnings Retention Rate of 75%, which two of those metrics could you combine to give you the expected long-term CAGR? For context, in our example the CAGR had reached 28.6% by Year 100.

6.4
THE INVESTOR'S LONG-TERM RETURN

It's time to reveal the third and final component of *The Investor's Solution*, "***The Investor's Long-Term Return***." This is the theoretical CAGR that we can expect to achieve as an investor over the long-term.

In order to determine the theoretical *Investor's Long-Term Return*, multiply the ROE by the Earnings Retention Rate.

Investor's Long-Term Return

= ROE x Earnings Retention Rate

= 40% x 75%

= 30%

After 100 years we are up to 28.6%, but if we held the investment long enough the CAGR would get closer and closer to 30.0%.

6.5
THE INVESTOR'S LONG-TERM RETURN RECAP

In this chapter we learned different ways to maximise compound growth.

Lesson 1
Invest early to secure as many years of compound growth as possible

Lesson 2
Invest early even if you only have a small amount to invest

Lesson 3
If you can't invest early, make up for lost time by investing a lump sum

Lesson 4
Invest early, even when making frequent investments/Invest often in order to maximise the amount of money put to work

Lesson 5
Invest in tax efficient ways since taxes reduce your return

Lesson 6
Minimise transaction costs since they reduce your return

We learned that compound growth occurs within a business in much the same way as it does in a bank account:

- Use ROE to gauge the size of a company's compound growth potential

We learned the impact Capital Allocation has on compound growth:

- Look for companies with a high Earnings Retention Rate; companies that pay excessive Dividends reduce the amount of Equity available for reinvestment

We learned three methods for calculating the Earnings Retention Rate:

Method 1: Using Earnings and Retained Earnings
Method 2: Using the Payout Ratio
Method 3: Using per-share Earnings and Dividend information

We learned how Retained Earnings build up in a company, increasing the amount of equity present within the business. As more and more earnings are retained, our CAGR increases, since any Earnings that are reinvested earn us the full ROE rate of return. This has the effect of increasing our CAGR for every year we hold the investment, up to a maximum of ROE x Earnings Retention Rate, which is *The Investor's Long-Term Return*.

Investor's Long-Term Return

= ROE x Earnings Retention Rate

The curve that connects the *Investor's Short-* and *Long-Term Returns* is called '*The Investor's Return Curve*'. This curve enables us to determine the theoretical CAGR we will achieve at any point in time, making it an incredibly useful tool for planning ahead.

RICHARD WORNER

CHAPTER 7:
THE INVESTOR'S SOLUTION

CHAPTER SUMMARY
7.1 THE INVESTOR'S SOLUTION
7.2 ADVANTAGES OF THE INVESTOR'S SOLUTION
7.3 THE ASPIRATIONAL INVESTOR'S RETURN CURVE
7.4 OPTIMISING THE INVESTOR'S SOLUTION
7.5 CHAPTER RECAP

7.1
THE INVESTOR'S SOLUTION

So, there is a simple calculation we can perform to determine the theoretical *Investor's Short-Term Return*, an equally quick and simple calculation to determine the theoretical *Investor's Long-Term Return*, and an *Investor's Return Curve* that connects the two. The curve shows us the theoretical return at any point in time, given the three simple inputs of ROE, P/B and Earnings Retention Rate.

THE INVESTOR'S SHORT-TERM RETURN

= ROE / P/B

The ROE gives us an indication of the magnitude of returns a business is able to generate. And by incorporating the Book Value of a business into our assessment of Price, the P/B ratio gives us a gauge of the value we are getting, rather than just the price we are paying.

THE INVESTOR'S LONG-TERM RETURN

= ROE x EARNINGS RETENTION RATE

As above, ROE gives us an indication of the magnitude of returns a business can generate. The Earnings Retention Rate gives us an indication of the proportion of those returns that will be retained in the business. Together, these metrics provide investors with a gauge of the portion of ROE they will capture as investors over the long-term.

THE INVESTOR'S RETURN CURVE

The Investor's Return Curve connects the short and long-term returns. It tells us the theoretical CAGR return we can expect to receive at any point in time.

THE INVESTOR'S SOLUTION

Most investors start out with two targets in mind: a target CAGR and a target time horizon. The thing they'd really like to know is, "*What investments will get me there?*" Using knowledge gained from this book, together with the action plan set out later on and the tools I have made available for free on *theinvestorssolution.com*, you can:

- Input your target time horizon
- Determine your overall investment goal

- Determine the CAGR required to achieve your goal
- Screen for stock opportunities
- Identify the stocks that meet your own particular investment criteria
- Assess and tailor your overall portfolio to ensure it meets your goals

Want to know the theoretical CAGR you will have earned 20 years from now for a stock you are screening? No problem, *The Investor's Solution* tells you. Want to know how a portfolio of several stock investments will have theoretically performed at the point you expect to retire? No problem, *The Investor's Solution* tells you that too.

7.2
ADVANTAGES OF THE INVESTOR'S SOLUTION

SIMPLE INPUTS

Only three metrics are used to generate *The Investor's Solution*: ROE, P/B and Earnings Retention Rate. They are easy to understand and easy to find or calculate.

STRAIGHTFORWARD LOGIC

The logic used is transparent and common sense. You can create substantial wealth by identifying and investing in companies that generate high returns. The higher the ROE, the higher your return is likely to be. By purchasing those high-returning businesses at prices that represent good value, you can secure above-average rates of return. By varying the ROE, P/B and Earnings Retention Rate, you can select stocks with particular return curve characteristics and tailor a portfolio of stocks to achieve your own particular goals.

EASY VISUALISATION

The *Investor's Short-Term Return* and *Investor's Long-Term Return* are not arbitrary points in isolation. They are connected by *The Investor's Return Curve*, which enables you to see the theoretical CAGR at any point in the investment's lifetime.

If you head to *theinvestorssolution.com* you can download a free '*Goal Planner & Stock Screen*' tool that enables you to enter the ROE, P/B and Earnings Retention Rate for a given stock and see the resulting curve.

ENABLES YOU TO DETERMINE THE CAGR THAT MEETS YOUR GOALS

If you have a *Target CAGR* in mind, then you can use *The Investor's Solution* to screen for stocks that are able to deliver that particular return.

ENABLES YOU TO PICK A TIME HORIZON THAT MEETS YOUR GOALS

If you have a particular time horizon in mind, say you want to retire in 25 years, *The Investor's Solution* enables you to screen for investments that will generate a suitable return over that particular period of time.

PROVIDES THE CONTEXT NEEDED TO COMPARE DIFFERENT INVESTMENT OPPORTUNITIES

Another advantage of *The Investor's Solution* is that it provides context against which you can compare multiple investment opportunities. You can also use it to compare other investment types, like cash in the bank, bonds or ETFs.

IT IS A COMPLETE SOLUTION THAT INCORPORATES EACH OF BUFFETT'S INVESTMENT PRINCIPLES AND MECHANISMS

The Investor's Solution combines all elements of Buffett's core approach:

INVESTMENT PRINCIPLES
- It is simple
- Anyone can do it
- We consider the performance of a business, not merely fluctuating stock prices
- Investments are held for the long-term

INVESTMENT MECHANISMS
- It is centred around Return on Equity
- It takes into account the *value* of your investment, not just the *price* paid
- It utilises the power of compounding to generate wealth
- It incorporates capital allocation by seeking out companies that retain the majority of their earnings and reinvest them in order to fuel future growth

7.3
THE ASPIRATIONAL INVESTOR'S RETURN CURVE

I am very much an advocate of investing for the long-term, however, not all of us have that option available to us. Each investor will have their own aspirations regarding the returns they would like to generate and the timeframe over which they would like to generate them. While it is impractical to illustrate an infinite array of possibilities, I can create some context. In a moment I will define a benchmark return curve around which you can tailor the ROE, P/B and Earnings Retention Rate to create return curves that match our own unique time and return requirements.

A simple, high-level principle governs this curve and all variations thereof: Build buffers in to both your short- and long-term return aspirations!

We don't want to introduce any unnecessary risk to either our short-term or long-term returns. We want buffers in place to insulate us from the risk that the companies we invest in will underperform and miss our expectations.

THE ASPIRATIONAL INVESTOR'S SHORT-TERM RETURN IS 10%

If the short-term return is too low, it implies that the stock is already selling at a high price because we'd have to pay a high P/B ratio to acquire it. A high price may indicate that future price appreciation has already been built into the current share price, leading to a sluggish price growth over the short- to medium-term, or perhaps a higher chance of an imminent stock correction. To insulate ourselves from this risk we must look for companies that provide us with an acceptable short-term return. For reasons that will become clear later, we are going to set our aspirational short-term return at 10%. If we make an investment and we subsequently turn out to be wrong, this aspirational return provides us with some downside protection because we haven't overpaid for that investment.

THE ASPIRATIONAL INVESTOR'S LONG-TERM RETURN IS 30%

If our aspiration over the long-term was to achieve Buffett-like CAGR's of 20% per annum, we can't simply seek out companies that deliver 20% and hope for the best. We would need to identify companies that provide an expected long-term return comfortably in excess of our CAGR goal.

In order to do so we must allow for slippage in both the ROE and the Earnings Retention Rate. If either of these metrics moves against us, our long-term returns, and thus our *Target CAGR*, will come under threat. If we desire Buffett-like returns of 20%, we should seek out investment candidates which, given current performance, will theoretically provide a long-term return of 30% or more.

Later in the book we will cover minimum short and long-term returns in more detail, setting out stocks screening rules which will not only help us to achieve our desired returns, but will also insulate us from downside risk. For the moment, fix in your mind that the *Aspirational Investor's Long-Term Return* is 30%.

As an example, a company possessing the following fundamentals meets both our short- and long-term criteria:

ROE: 40%
P/B Ratio: 4.0
Earnings Retention Rate: 75%

INVESTOR'S SHORT-TERM RETURN
= ROE / P/B ratio
= 40% / 4.0
= 10%

INVESTOR'S LONG-TERM RETURN
= ROE x Earnings Retention Rate
= 40% x 75%
= 30%

ASPIRATIONAL INVESTOR'S RETURN CURVE

If this company were to maintain its ROE and Earnings Retention Rate, our *Aspirational Investor's Return Curve* would start at 10% in the first year and grow to produce a CAGR of 30% over the long-term. The theoretical CAGR we would earn at different points in time are shown in Figure 37 below. *The Aspirational Investor's Return Curve* provides a Buffett-like CAGR of 20% from Year 13 onwards and after 30 years it provides us with a 5.3%-point buffer. This would allow for the overall CAGR to fall 20%, from 25.3% to 20% percent, without jeopardising our Buffett-like results.

FIGURE 37: THEORETICAL CAGR'S AT DIFFERENT POINTS ON THE ASPIRATIONAL INVESTOR'S RETURN CURVE

Year	CAGR
Year 1: Investor's Short-Term Return	10.0%
Year 10	18.1%
Year 13	20.1%
Year 15	21.1%
Year 20	23.1%
Year 30	25.3%
Investor's Long-Term Return	30.0%

We'll see this *Aspirational Investor's Return Curve* a lot throughout the remainder of the book, and we'll discover how it is closely linked to Buffett's present-day investment criteria. For convenience going forward, we will use the following abbreviation to describe the aspirational curve: 10%~30%

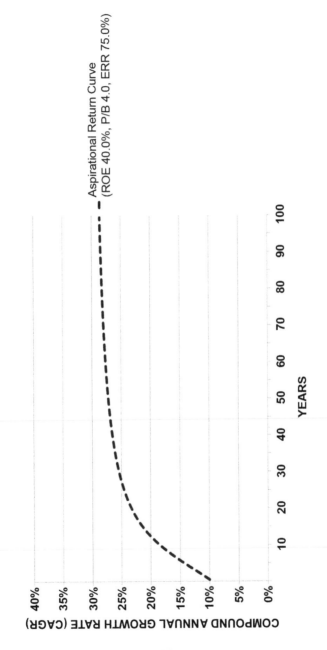

FIGURE 38: THE ASPIRATIONAL INVESTORS RETURN CURVE OVER 100 YEARS

Aspirational Return Curve
(ROE 40.0%, P/B 4.0, ERR 75.0%)

7.4
OPTIMISING THE INVESTOR'S SOLUTION

We can optimise *The Investor's Solution* to meet our specific requirements, adjusting the three input metrics to achieve very particular short- and long-term returns. Visualise this balancing act like a seesaw, with the left-hand side representing the *Investor's Short-Term Return* and the right-hand side representing the *Investor's Long-Term Return*.

ROE

The primary lever, affecting the short-term returns, long-term returns, and the return curve that connects them, is the ROE. Increasing the ROE elevates the short- and long-term returns and raises the entire return curve in the process. This is why the identification of companies with above-average ROEs is at the heart of this approach.

P/B

The primary lever impacting the short-term return on the left-hand side of the seesaw is the P/B ratio. Lowering the P/B ratio has the effect of raising the short-term return. This is because we effectively bought the stock at a lower price. Increasing the P/B ratio has the effect of lowering the short-term return. Overall, we want to find companies with low P/B ratios.

Earnings Retention Rate

The primary lever impacting the long-term return on the right-hand side of the seesaw is the Earnings Retention Rate. A high retention rate means more earnings remain in the business to fuel future growth. We want our companies to retain as much of their earnings as possible, fuelling the compound growth machine that will make us wealthy.

The reason we use a seesaw as the analogy is that it is unlikely that we'll be able to find a company that provides all of these conditions at once. We might find a company with a great ROE and a low P/B, but it might retain only a low proportion of its earnings. Alternatively, we might find a company with a great ROE, and which retains all of its earnings, but it is expensive and thus has a high P/B ratio.

The whole process is a balancing act. In the sections ahead you'll learn everything you need to know to identify suitable stocks and to create a portfolio tailored to our own particular requirements.

CHANGING ROE

We have learned that the primary lever affecting the short-term returns, long-term returns, and the overall *Investor's Return Curve* that connects them, is the ROE. Increasing the ROE increases both short and long-term returns and elevates the return curve. We'll demonstrate this by comparing our *Aspirational Investor's Return Curve* to the curve of a company with a higher ROE, at 50%, and a company with a lower ROE, at 30%, while keeping the P/B ratio and Earnings Retention Rate unchanged.

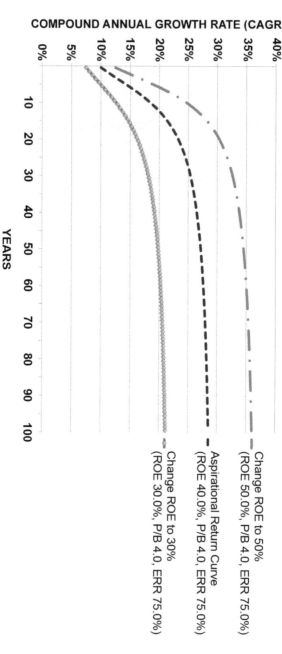

FIGURE 39: THE IMPACT OF RAISING AND LOWERING THE ROE

FIGURE 40: THE IMPACT OF RAISING AND LOWERING THE ROE

Company	Aspirational	Higher ROE	Lower ROE
ROE	40%	50%	30%
P/B	4.0	4.0	4.0
Earnings Retention Rate	75%	75%	75%
Investor's Short-Term Return	10.0%	12.5%	7.5%
Investor's Long-Term Return	30.0%	37.5%	22.5%

The company with the higher ROE raised the entire return curve, increasing the short-term return from our aspirational 10% up to 12.5%, and increasing the long-term return from our aspirational 30% up to 37.5%.

The company with the lower ROE lowered the entire return curve, decreasing the short-term return from our aspirational 10% down to 7.5%, and decreasing the long-term return from our aspirational 30% down to 22.5%.

CHANGING P/B

We learned that the lever most impacting the short-term return on the left-hand side of the seesaw is the P/B ratio. Lowering the P/B ratio has the effect of raising the short-term return and vice versa. We'll demonstrate this by comparing our *Aspirational Investor's Return Curve* to a company with a higher P/B ratio of 8.0, and a company with a lower P/B ratio of 2.0, while keeping the ROE and Earnings Retention Rate unchanged.

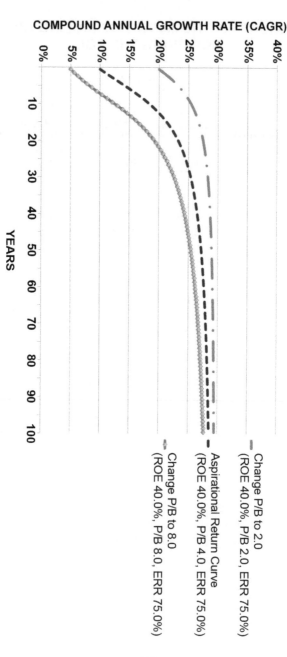

FIGURE 41: THE IMPACT OF RAISING AND LOWERING THE P/B RATIO

FIGURE 42: THE IMPACT OF RAISING AND LOWERING THE P/B RATIO

Company	Aspirational	Higher ROE	Lower ROE
ROE	40%	40%	40%
P/B	4.0	8.0	2.0
Earnings Retention Rate	75%	75%	75%
Investor's Short-Term Return	10.0%	5.0%	20.0%
Investor's Long-Term Return	30.0%	30.0%	30.0%

For the company with the higher P/B ratio, we can make two observations. Firstly, the left-hand side of the curve has dropped sharply, falling from an aspirational short-term return of 10% down to 5%. Secondly, the right-hand side of the curve, representing the long-term return *has* changed, but only by a small amount. To clarify this further, the end point on this particular chart has lowered slightly. This is because the chart only takes us up to Year 100. If we were to continue the chart beyond one hundred years, all lines would eventually converge at 30%, as determined by the *Investor's Long-Term Return* calculation. Since we, as investors, are necessarily more interested in returns over the first 0-40 years or so, we should be aware that changing the P/B ratio does change our long-term return, and the shorter your time horizon the more impact it will have.

For the company with the lower P/B ratio, the left-hand side of the curve has been raised sharply, increasing from an aspirational short-term return of 10% up to 20%. The right-hand side of the curve, representing the long-term return has also changed by a small amount.

The above demonstrates that the P/B ratio primarily acts to change the short-term return, although it has a knock-on impact on the medium- to long-term return.

The P/B ratio is also the most volatile of our three key measures since the price of a stock can fluctuate wildly in the financial markets. Luckily, this affords us the opportunity to buy great companies from Mr. Market at low prices, almost guaranteeing that we achieve above-average returns over the long-term.

CHANGING EARNINGS RETENTION RATE

We have learned that the lever most impacting the long-term return is the Earnings Retention Rate. We'll demonstrate this by comparing our *Aspirational Investor's Return Curve* to a company with a higher Earnings Retention Rate of 90%, and a company with a lower Earnings Retention Rate of 10%, while keeping the ROE and P/B ratio unchanged.

For the company with the higher Earnings Retention rate, we can make three observations. First, the far left-hand side of the curve is completely unchanged with the short-term return remaining at exactly 10%. Second, over the 0-40-year timeframe, the left-hand side of the curve has been elevated by the change in Earnings Retention Rate. Third, the long-term return curve on the right-hand side of the chart has risen from the aspirational 30% up to 36%, reflecting the higher portion of earnings reinvested in the business and used to generate growth.

For the company with the lower Earnings Retention Rate, we see a very different result from any of the other curves examined so far. This company pays out almost all of its earnings as dividends, retaining only 10% within the business. Its compound growth engine is therefore smaller. Much, much smaller. The short-term return remains unchanged at exactly 10%, but over the 0-40-year timeframe the curve has been lowered significantly. By the time we get to the long-term end of the curve the expected return has dropped to only 4%. In other words, the longer we hold this investment, the *lower* our CAGR becomes.

FIGURE 43: THE IMPACT OF RAISING AND LOWERING THE EARNINGS RETENTION RATE

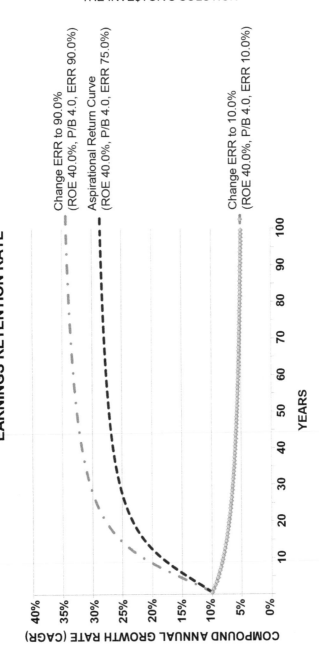

Change ERR to 90.0%
(ROE 40.0%, P/B 4.0, ERR 90.0%)

Aspirational Return Curve
(ROE 40.0%, P/B 4.0, ERR 75.0%)

Change ERR to 10.0%
(ROE 40.0%, P/B 4.0, ERR 10.0%)

YEARS

COMPOUND ANNUAL GROWTH RATE (CAGR)

FIGURE 44: THE IMPACT OF RAISING AND LOWERING THE EARNINGS RETENTION RATE

Company	Aspirational	Higher ROE	Lower ROE
ROE	40%	40%	40%
P/B	4.0	4.0	4.0
Earnings Retention Rate	**75%**	**90%**	**10%**
Investor's Short-Term Return	10.0%	10.0%	10.0%
Investor's Long-Term Return	30.0%	36.0%	4.0%

It is true that we would receive a lot of cash as dividends from this company over time, but we may incur a tax charge on those dividends and would be required to take a more active role in reinvesting them to achieve our desired level of compound growth. It would be much harder to achieve a Buffett-like CAGR of 20% in these circumstances.

The above demonstrates that the Earnings Retention Rate principally acts to change the long-term return, although it has a knock-on impact on returns from Year 2 onwards. We want companies with high Earnings Retention Rates and we definitely don't want companies with low retention rates.

Most companies maintain stable dividend policies and they are usually transparent about those policies, publishing them in their annual reports. A company will often state something along the lines of *"our intention to consistently pay out 25% of earnings as dividends."* We can't influence this policy ourselves, so it is best to look for companies with stable dividend policies favouring earnings retention right from the start.

7.5
THE INVESTOR'S SOLUTION RECAP

There is a simple calculation we can perform to determine the theoretical *Investor's Short-Term Return*, an equally quick and simple calculation to determine the theoretical *Investor's Long-Term Return*, and an *Investor's Return Curve* that connects the two. The curve shows us the theoretical return at any point in time, given the three simple inputs of ROE, P/B and Earnings Retention Rate.

INVESTOR'S SHORT-TERM RETURN = ROE / P/B

The ROE gives us an indication of the returns a business can generate.

By incorporating the Book Value of a business into our assessment of Price, the P/B ratio gives us a gauge of the *value* we are getting, rather than just the price we are paying.

INVESTOR'S LONG-TERM RETURN = ROE x EARNINGS RETENTION RATE

As above, ROE gives us an indication of the returns a business can generate.

The Earnings Retention Rate gives us an indication of the proportion of those returns that we can capture over the long-term.

THE ASPIRATIONAL INVESTOR'S RETURN CURVE

We must build buffers into our short- and long-term return aspirations to insulate us from the risk that the companies we invest in will underperform, missing our expectations.

- The Aspirational Investor's Short-Term Return is 10%
- The Aspirational Investor's Long-Term Return is 30%

OPTIMISING THE INVESTOR'S SOLUTION

We can optimise *The Investor's Solution* to meet our specific requirements, adjusting the three input metrics to achieve very particular short- and long-term returns.

ROE

The key to high short- and long-term returns is a high ROE. The higher the ROE, the higher our return is likely to be.

P/B

The P/B ratio primarily acts to change the short-term return, although it has a knock-on impact on the medium- to long-term return. We want to buy companies with low P/B ratios. It is the most volatile of our three input measures since the price of a stock can fluctuate wildly in the financial markets. Luckily, this affords us the opportunity to buy great companies from Mr. Market at low prices.

Earnings Retention Rate

The Earnings Retention Rate principally acts to change the long-term return, although it has a knock-on impact on returns from Year 2 onwards. We want companies with high Earnings Retention Rates and we definitely don't want companies with low retention rates.

GOAL PLANNER & STOCK SCREEN TOOL

To help you better understand the impact of different inputs on the short- and long-term returns and on the curve which connects them, head to *theinvestorssolution.com* for the free '*Goal Planner & Stock Screen*' tool. Use it to compare the return curves for different stocks and to determine the overall return curve for your portfolio.

CHAPTER 8: INVESTOR RETURN PROFILES

CHAPTER SUMMARY
8.1 EXAMPLE RETURN PROFILES
INVESTOR A: 30+ YEAR HORIZON; 25% TARGET CAGR
INVESTOR B: 20 YEAR HORIZON; 20% TARGET CAGR
INVESTOR C: 15 YEAR HORIZON; 15% TARGET CAGR
INVESTOR D: 10 YEAR HORIZON; 10% TARGET CAGR

8.1
EXAMPLE RETURN PROFILES

There are an infinite number of ways that ROE, P/B and Earnings Retention Rate can be combined, and an infinite number of resulting return curves. It is impossible to create an exhaustive list of examples to match every unique investment timeframe and target return. However, it is possible to illustrate a *range* of outcomes, categorised according to broad investor types. We will enlist the help of the four investor profiles introduced in Chapter 2, illustrating the stock characteristics that enable them to achieve their particular goals. We will include the *Aspirational Investor's Return Curve* in each profile, using it as a yardstick to highlight differences between them.

INVESTOR A:
NEW TO INVESTING

"I am a beginner investor...I'd like to learn how to invest so that I can build some cash reserves and one day be wealthy."

INVESTMENT HORIZON: 30+ years
TARGET CAGR: 25% by Year 30

KEY OUTCOMES:
- An effective approach that ensures my wealth will grow
- Financial freedom and flexibility
- To travel often and experience the world
- To create an independent income stream
- To retire early

WHAT WOULD BE USEFUL IS:
- A trusted guide to learn from
- To know what stocks to buy
- To know why I am buying so that I can understand more clearly and learn faster
- An effective, step-by-step process that anyone can follow
- An approach that doesn't require too much money
- A way of using market crashes to my advantage, making them work for me

Figure 45 shows five stocks, all of which achieve a

theoretical 30-year CAGR in excess of the 25% per annum *Target CAGR*; 25.3% to be exact, which is the return delivered by the *Aspirational Investor's Return Curve* in that year. By flexing the ROE, P/B ratio and Earnings Retention Rate, the other four stocks were engineered to deliver exactly the same CAGR at that point in time.

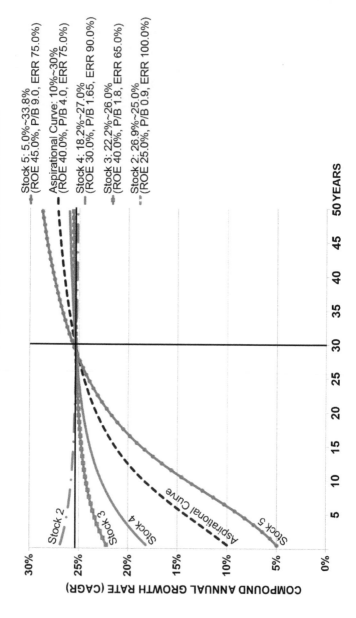

FIGURE 45: INVESTOR A: STOCK SCENARIOS CHART

FIGURE 46: INVESTOR A: STOCK SCENARIOS TABLE

	Aspiration	Stock 2	Stock 3	Stock 4	Stock 5
ROE	40%	25%	40%	30%	45%
P/B	4.00	0.93	1.80	1.65	9.00
Earnings Retention Rate	75%	75%	65%	90%	75%
Investors Short-Term Return	**10.0%**	**26.9%**	**22.2%**	**18.2%**	**5.0%**
Investors Long-Term Return	**30.0%**	**25.0%**	**26.0%**	**27.0%**	**33.8%**
CAGR after 30y	25.3%	25.3%	25.3%	25.3%	25.3%
CAGR after 20y	23.1%	25.4%	25.0%	24.5%	21.7%
CAGR after 15y	21.1%	25.6%	24.7%	23.8%	18.3%
CAGR after 10y	18.1%	25.8%	24.2%	22.6%	13.6%

STOCK 1 – THE ASPIRATIONAL RETURN
ROE: 40.0%
P/B: 4.00
Earnings Retention Rate: 75%
Investor's Return Curve: 10.0%~30.0%

As you already know, this return curve has an excellent short-term return of 10.0% and an outstanding long-term return of 30.0%. The ROE of the company generating this curve is 40%. This is sufficiently above our *Target CAGR* of 25% that it allows for some slippage in the ROE over time, and also allows for some reduction in the level of earnings retained. We have assumed a P/B ratio of 4.0, which is perfectly reasonable for a company with these economics.

Around this aspirational curve you will see the return curves of Stocks 2-5, all of which intersect at exactly 25.3% in Year 30. An infinite number of alternate curves exist within this area, but there are upper and lower limits that we need to be aware of - beyond these limits it is unlikely that *Investor A* can achieve the *Target CAGR* by sensible means. Stock 2 represents the upper limit, and Stock 5 represents the lower limit.

STOCK 2 – THE UPPER LIMIT
ROE: 25.0%
P/B: 0.93
Earnings Retention Rate: 100%
Investor's Return Curve: 26.9%~25.0%

This curve is possibly the simplest and most intuitive of the five stocks – find a company with a ROE matching or exceeding your *Target CAGR*, buy it for 1 x Book Value or less, and, assuming it retains 100% of its earnings, just hold it for thirty years.

In this example we have assumed that *Investor A* purchases a company with a ROE of 25%, and an Earnings

Retention Rate of 100%. *Investor A* manages to purchase the stock at 0.93 P/B, and because the price paid is less than Book Value, the return curve actually starts above 25% (at 26.9%, or ROE / P/B = 25.0%/0.93). However, the return curve then falls gradually over time towards our expected long-term return of 25.0% (ROE x Earnings Retention Rate = 25.0% x 100%).

The likelihood that a company will be able to maintain such stability in its results, so as to perfectly maintain the 25.0% ROE and 100% Earnings Retention Rate for 30 years, is negligible. On occasions we may be able to find a company with a ROE of 25.0% that retains all of its earnings, and we can endeavour to purchase it at a P/B ratio of 1.0 or below, but, if at any point the ROE falls even slightly, or the Earnings Retention Rate decreases, it becomes impossible to meet our *Target CAGR*.

Stock 2 is therefore denoted as the 'upper limit' because there is a high probability that we will *not* be able to achieve our target return over a 30-year period. It is an inherently riskier strategy than that offered by the *Aspirational Investor's Return Curve* represented by Stock 1.

To mitigate the risk of missing our *Target CAGR*, we could opt for a company with a ROE higher than our Target CAGR, at say 30%. In this case, assuming we can buy it at a P/B of 1.0, our return curve would start at an improved 30.0% (30.0%/1.0), providing us with some insulation should the company fail to perform to our expectations. In this scenario, there is a higher probability that we will achieve your 30-year *Target CAGR* of 25%, even if the ROE were to fall modestly or the company was to start paying a small dividend. However, I am not a fan of return curves that slope downward. Why make an investment in a company that will generate *lower* returns the longer we hold it? Instead, opt for stocks demonstrating upward-sloping return curves that provide us with the opportunity for our earnings and CAGR to grow in the future.

Even with a shorter-term goal, say a 10-15 year investment time horizon, we should still opt for companies that have upward-sloping curves. There is always the possibility that we will want to stay invested for longer than originally intended. An upward-sloping curve provides us with the greatest likelihood of growth and the most flexibility. Stock 2 forms the upper limit of what we should be willing to accept.

STOCK 3
ROE: 40.0%
P/B: 1.80
Earnings Retention Rate: 65%
Investor's Return Curve: 22.2%~26.0%

In this case, the company has the same ROE of 40.0% as Stock 1, but pays out more earnings as dividends, reducing the Earnings Retention Rate to 65%. Under these circumstances, *Investor A* must purchase the company at a P/B of 1.8 in order to achieve the 25.0% *Target CAGR* by Year 30. These factors result in a very high start return of 22.2% (40.0% / 1.8), but the curve does not rise very fast as a large portion of the company's earnings are not retained or reinvested to generate future growth. The ultimate long-term return works out as 26.0% (40.0% x 65%), enough to achieve the *Target CAGR*, but leaving little room for a misstep.

STOCK 4
ROE: 30.0%
P/B: 1.65
Earnings Retention Rate: 90%
Investor's Return Curve: 18.2%~27.0%

The ROE of Stock 4 is lower, at 30.0%, but the Earnings Retention Rate has increased to 90%. Despite the lower

ROE than that generated by Stock 3, this company can achieve a great return because it retains and reinvests more of its earnings. To achieve the *Target CAGR* after 30 years, *Investor A* must purchase this company at 1.65x Book Value or below. The result is an excellent starting return of 18.2% (30.0% / 1.65), rising gradually towards 27.0% (30.0% x 90%) over time.

STOCK 5 – THE LOWER LIMIT
ROE: 45.0%
P/B: 9.0
Earnings Retention Rate: 75%
Investor's Return Curve: 5.0%~33.8%

At the lower limit, Stock 5 generates a strong ROE of 45% and retains a sizeable 75% of its earnings. *Investor A* was required to pay Mr. Market a hefty price for the high earnings-generating power of this company, paying 9.0x Book Value. Despite the high price paid, *Investor A* still generates a reasonable starting return of 5.0% (45.0% / 9.0) and has the opportunity to grow the CAGR towards 33.8% (45.0% x 75%) longer-term.

A high-quality company such as this, which possesses strong earnings-generating power, is a desirable investment. In search of high returns, investors may drive the price of this stock upwards, pushing up the P/B ratio along with it. As a result, future earnings power may already be baked into current stock price, increasing the likelihood that the stock will pull back or correct in the short- to medium-term. This may jeopardise our returns, so we must put a sensible threshold in place to mitigate this risk. A minimum *Investor's Short-Term Return* of 5% is recommend, being half of the return delivered by the *Aspirational Investor's Return Curve*.

Stock 5 therefore represents the 'lower limit' of our five stock scenarios.

INVESTOR A: RECAP

Using the five stock scenarios from this section as a guide, we can start to think about some high-level rules we could use to screen for potential investment candidates.

ROE

The minimum ROE required to achieve an upward sloping, or at least flat, curve over your investment time horizon is dictated by your *Target CAGR*. ROE should always match or exceed the *Target CAGR*. ROE has no upper limit.

P/B

The P/B ratio has a huge impact on our short-term return. Of course, we'd always like to buy our investments as cheaply as possible, but the opportunity to buy great companies at low P/B ratios is extremely rare. We must usually pay more to acquire high earnings-generating power and must work out how much is acceptable to pay, without jeopardising our returns.

Since we know that the *Investor's Short-Term Return* is calculated as ROE / P/B, we can rearrange this equation in order to come up with some initial guidelines on the maximum P/B ratio to accept.

$$\text{Investor's Short-Term Return} = \text{ROE} / \text{P/B}$$

$$\text{P/B} = \text{ROE} / \text{Investor's Short-Term Return}$$

From the ROE rules we just created above, we know that there is no upper limit for ROE. We will use a very high ROE of 100% for indicative purposes. We also know that the minimum short-term return we will accept is 5.0%. Inserting these two variables into our equation we get the following result:

$$\text{P/B} = 100\% / 5.0 = 20.0$$

We will therefore screen for companies with P/B ratios of 20.0 or below.

EARNINGS RETENTION RATE

The lowest retention rate we saw across the five scenarios was 65%, exhibited by Stock 3. Since we want our long-term return to be at least the same as our *Target CAGR*, but preferably higher, we can balance ROE and Earnings Retention Rate to ensure we achieve our goals. To achieve the return and timeframe requirements of *Investor A*:

- A company with a ROE of 25% would need to retain all of its earnings to be in with a chance of meeting the *Target CAGR*
- A company with a ROE of 40% would require an Earnings Retention Rate of 62.5%
- A company with a ROE of 50% would require an Earnings Retention Rate of 50%, but a retention rate this low leads to a downward-sloping curve that isn't recommended

To avoid the formation of downward-sloping curves, and to narrow our search to companies with high growth potential, we will establish an Earnings Retention Rate of 60% as our lower limit.

INVESTOR'S SHORT-TERM RETURN

To minimise the risk of missing our target returns we defined the minimum short-term return to be 5.0%, being half of the *Aspirational Investor's Short-Term Return*.

INVESTOR'S LONG-TERM RETURN

We established the need to avoid downward sloping curves which result in lower returns the longer we hold them. The simplest criteria required to achieve an upward-sloping curve is simply that the *Investor's Long-Term Return* must equal or exceed the *Target CAGR*. However, we should also build a buffer into our returns, requiring that *the Investor's Long-Term Return* is at least 1.2x the *Target CAGR*. In the case of *Investor A*, this means that the minimum *Investor's Long-Term Return* is 1.2 x 25% = 30.0%.

SUMMARY: DRAFT STOCK SCREEN RULES
- ROE must match or exceed the *Target CAGR*.
- P/B ratio must be 20.0 or below.
- The Earnings Retention Rate must be 60% or above.
- *The Investor's Short-Term Return* must be 5.0% or above.
- *The Investor's Long-Term Return* must match or exceed 1.2x the *Target CAGR*.

APPLICATION OF OUR DRAFT STOCK SCREEN RULES FOR INVESTOR A
Applying these rules to *Investor A*'s list of five potential stock investments:

- All ROEs match or exceed the *Target CAGR* of 25%.
- All P/B ratios are below 20.0.
- The Earnings Retention Rate is 60% or above in all instances.
- *The Investor's Short-Term Return* is 5.0% or above in all instances.
- *The Investor's Long-Term Return* must match or exceed 1.2x *Target CAGR* (1.2 x 25% = 30.0%). This requirement is met in only two cases, for Stock 1 and Stock 5, which exhibit *Investor's Long-Term Returns* of 30.0% and 33.8% respectively.

If this process were part of our screen for investment opportunities we would eliminate Stocks 2, 3 and 4 and take Stocks 1 and 5 forward for further consideration.

INVESTOR B: FAMILY SECURITY AND PEACE OF MIND

"I am the parent of two young kids. I want a no-fuss way of investing for the long-term in a way that will generate meaningful returns for myself and my family."

INVESTMENT HORIZON: 20 years
TARGET CAGR: 20%

KEY OUTCOMES:
- To secure financial freedom for myself and my family
- To avoid unnecessary stress and achieve peace of mind
- An effective way of investing 10% of my income each month
- To know why I am buying so I have the courage to sit through price fluctuations
- A way to gauge whether I am likely to achieve my goals

WHAT WOULD BE USEFUL IS:
- Having the complex world of investing simplified for me
- Learning in digestible chunks and in plain language
- An approach that is easy to action
- An approach that doesn't take much time
- An approach that works for any income level

Figure 47 shows four new stock profiles (Stocks 6-9) against the original *Aspirational Investor's Return Curve*. All four new stocks achieve *Investor B's Target CAGR*, achieving 20% at the end of the 20-year timeframe. Once again, these curves were engineered to hit that CAGR of 20% by altering their ROEs, P/B ratios and Earnings Retention Rates.

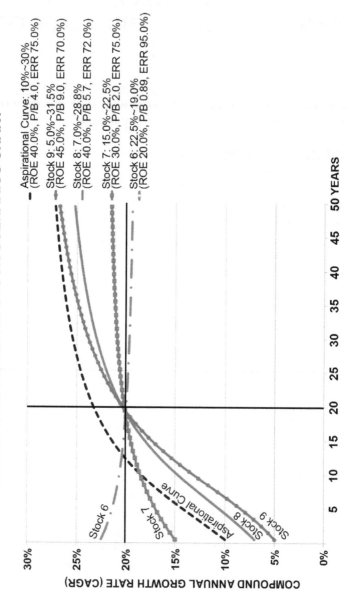

FIGURE 47: INVESTOR B: STOCK SCENARIOS CHART

FIGURE 48: INVESTOR B: STOCK SCENARIOS TABLE

	Aspiration	Stock 6	Stock 7	Stock 8	Stock 9
ROE	40%	20%	30%	40%	45%
P/B	4.00	0.89	2.00	5.70	9.00
Earnings Retention Rate	75%	95%	75%	72%	70%
Investors Short-Term Return	**10.0%**	**22.5%**	**15.0%**	**7.0%**	**5.0%**
Investors Long-Term Return	**30.0%**	**19.0%**	**22.5%**	**28.8%**	**31.5%**
CAGR after 30y	25.3%	19.7%	20.9%	22.9%	23.7%
CAGR after 20y	23.1%	20.0%	20.1%	20.0%	20.0%
CAGR after 15y	21.1%	20.2%	19.4%	17.8%	17.0%
CAGR after 10y	18.1%	20.7%	18.4%	14.3%	12.7%

As we transition from the requirements of *Investor A* to those of *Investor B*, a number of important elements change. First and foremost, the time horizon has reduced from 30 years to 20 years. Second, since we are now working with a shorter timeframe, it is prudent to lower the *Target CAGR*. Accordingly, the target has been reduced from 25% to 20% percent per annum. Third, the lower *Target CAGR* means we can lower our minimum ROE requirement to match that same level of 20%. This automatically lowers the 'upper limit' versus *Investor A*. The 'lower limit' changes very little.

SUMMARY: DRAFT STOCK SCREEN RULES

Revisiting the draft stock screen rules that we created for *Investor A*, we don't need to make any amendments - they all remain intact and unchanged. We did lower *Investor B*'s ROE requirement to 20% in order to match the new, lower, *Target CAGR*, but this change is allowed by the screen rules.

- ROE must match or exceed the *Target CAGR*.
- P/B ratio must be 20.0 or below.
- The Earnings Retention Rate must be 60% or above.
- *The Investor's Short-Term Return* must be 5.0% or above.
- *The Investor's Long-Term Return* must match or exceed 1.2x the *Target CAGR*.

APPLICATION OF OUR DRAFT STOCK SCREEN RULES FOR INVESTOR B

Applying these rules to *Investor B*'s list of five potential stock investments:

- All ROEs match or exceed the *Target CAGR* of 20%.
- All P/B ratios are below 20.0.
- The Earnings Retention Rate is 60% or above in all instances.

- *The Investor's Short-Term Return* is 5.0% or above in all instances.
- *The Investor's Long-Term Return* must match or exceed 1.2x *Target CAGR* (1.2 x 20% = 24.0%). This requirement is met in three cases, for Stocks 1, 8 and 9, which exhibit *Investor's Long-Term Returns* of 30.0%, 28.8% and 31.5% respectively.

If this process were part of our screen for investment opportunities, we would eliminate Stocks 6 and 7, and take Stocks 1, 8 and 9 forward for further consideration. If the stocks assessed for *Investor A* were also available to *Investor B*, all four additional stocks, Stocks 2-5, would pass *Investor B*'s screen rules and could also be taken forward for further consideration.

INVESTOR C:
SEEKING CERTAINTY OVER PENSION INCOME AND RETIREMENT TIMEFRAME

"I'd like more certainty so that I can plan ahead. I'd like to know how much I need to retire comfortably, and when retirement is likely to happen. I need an investment approach that will generate compelling capital growth over the medium-long term. I want my money to work for me."

INVESTMENT HORIZON: 15 years
TARGET CAGR: 15%

KEY OUTCOMES:
- To retire early and enjoy the freedom I've worked hard to achieve
- To have sufficient income in retirement that I can maintain our quality of life
- To sense check the expected value of my investments on retirement
- To know what to buy in order to bridge any shortfall
- To meet those financial goals without taking on too much risk

WHAT WOULD BE USEFUL IS:
- Knowing the most effective way of putting my money to work
- A way of projecting my returns into the future so I can course-correct my investments or add more savings over time if required
- A way of experimenting with different retirement dates to work out different retirement scenarios
- An approach that isn't overly complex and doesn't take too

much time

Figure 49 shows four new stock profiles (Stocks 10-13) against the original *Aspirational Investor's Return Curve*. All four new stocks achieve the *Target CAGR*, intersecting at 15% at the end of the 15-year timeframe. Once again, these curves were engineered to hit that CAGR of 15% by altering their ROEs, P/B ratios and Earnings Retention Rates.

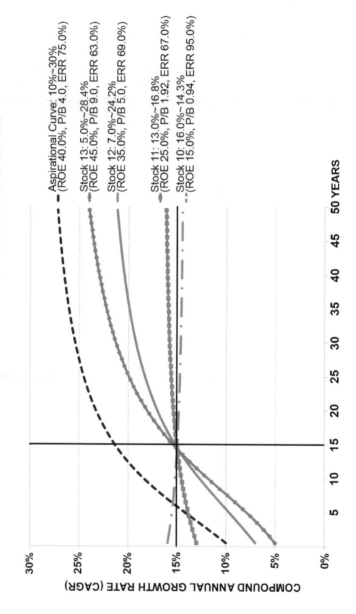

FIGURE 49: INVESTOR C: STOCK SCENARIOS CHART

FIGURE 50: INVESTOR C: STOCK SCENARIOS TABLE

	Aspiration	Stock 10	Stock 11	Stock 12	Stock 13
ROE	40%	15%	25%	35%	45%
P/B	4.00	0.94	1.92	5.00	9.00
Earnings Retention Rate	75%	95%	67%	69%	63%
Investors Short-Term Return	**10.0%**	**16.0%**	**13.0%**	**7.0%**	**5.0%**
Investors Long-Term Return	**30.0%**	**14.3%**	**16.8%**	**24.2%**	**28.4%**
CAGR after 30y	25.3%	14.7%	15.8%	19.1%	21.1%
CAGR after 20y	23.1%	14.9%	15.4%	16.9%	17.9%
CAGR after 15y	21.1%	15.0%	15.0%	15.0%	15.1%
CAGR after 10y	18.1%	15.2%	14.5%	12.4%	11.5%

Turning our attention towards *Investor C*, notice that the time horizon has once again reduced, from 20 years to 15 years. Since we are now working with a shorter timeframe, it is prudent to lower the *Target CAGR*. Accordingly, the target has been reduced from 20% to 15% percent per annum. The lower *Target CAGR* means we can lower our minimum ROE requirement to match that same level of 15%. This automatically lowers the 'upper limit' versus *Investor B*. The 'lower limit' has changed very little compared to that for *Investor B*.

SUMMARY: DRAFT STOCK SCREEN RULES

Revisiting the draft stock screen rules that we created for *Investor A* and subsequently re-examined for *Investor B*, all rules remain intact and unchanged. We did lower our ROE requirement to 15% in order to match the new, lower, *Target CAGR*, but this change is allowed by the screen rules.

- ROE must match or exceed the *Target CAGR*.
- P/B ratio must be 20.0 or below.
- The Earnings Retention Rate must be 60% or above.
- *The Investor's Short-Term Return* must be 5.0% or above.
- *The Investor's Long-Term Return* must match or exceed 1.2x the *Target CAGR*.

APPLICATION OF OUR DRAFT STOCK SCREEN RULES FOR INVESTOR C

Applying these rules to *Investor C*'s list of five potential stock investments:
- All ROEs match or exceed the *Target CAGR* of 15%.
- All P/B ratios are below 20.0.
- The Earnings Retention Rate is 60% or above in all instances.
- *The Investor's Short-Term Return* is 5.0% or above in all instances.
- *The Investor's Long-Term Return* must match or exceed

1.2x *Target CAGR* (1.2 x 15% = 18.0%). This requirement is met in three cases, for Stocks 1, 12 and 13, which exhibit *Investor's Long-Term Returns* of 30.0%, 24.2% and 28.4% respectively.

If this process were part of our screen for investment opportunities, we would eliminate Stocks 11 and 12, and take Stocks 1, 12 and 13 forward for further consideration. If the stocks assessed for *Investors A* and *B* were also available to *Investor C*, all eight additional stocks, Stocks 2-9, would pass *Investor C*'s screen rules and could also be taken forward for further consideration.

INVESTOR D:
LANDLORD SEEKING DIVERSIFICATION WITHOUT SACRIFICING RETURNS

"I am a landlord with an established property/real estate portfolio. The property portfolio is intended to act as my pension, but market volatility and uncertainty require that the concentration of risk be re-balanced into other asset types, diversifying the portfolio. By purchasing stocks and letting those returns compound over time, I hope to create returns in excess of those possible within the property portfolio while simultaneously reducing risk and leverage."

INVESTMENT HORIZON: 10 years
TARGET CAGR: 10%

KEY OUTCOMES:
- To maintain or enhance my independent source of income
- To diversify my holdings while maintaining or exceeding the long-term expected return
- To reduce the leverage inherent in a property portfolio
- To reduce exposure to a single investment sector (property/real estate)
- To take advantage of tax efficient vehicles

WHAT WOULD BE USEFUL IS:
- An investment approach that is transparent so that I can fully understand it
- To understand what returns will be generated and whether these are comparable to leveraged property investment
- Having stock market investing simplified for me
- New and effective ways of putting my money to work

Figure 51 shows three new stock profiles (Stocks 14-16) against the original *Aspirational Investor's Return Curve*. All three new stocks achieve the *Target CAGR*, intersecting at 10% at the end of the 10-year timeframe. Once again, these curves were engineered to hit that CAGR of 10% by altering their ROEs, P/B ratios and Earnings Retention Rates.

Examining our final investor profile, *Investor D*'s time horizon has once again reduced, from 15 years to 10 years. Since we are now working with a shorter timeframe, it is prudent to lower the *Target CAGR*. Accordingly, the target has been reduced from 15% to 10% percent per annum. The lower *Target CAGR* means we can lower our minimum ROE requirement to match that same level of 10%. This automatically lowers the 'upper limit' versus *Investor C*. The 'lower limit' has changed very little compared to that for *Investor C*.

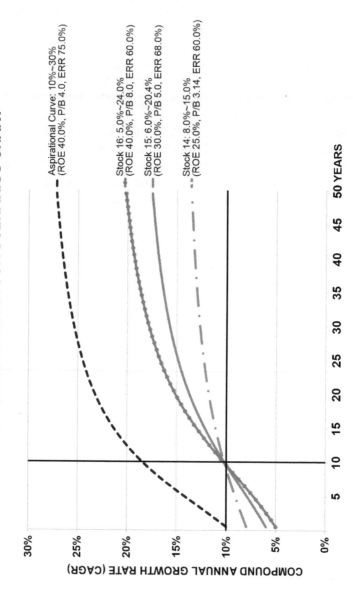

FIGURE 51: INVESTOR D: STOCK SCENARIOS CHART

FIGURE 52: INVESTOR D: STOCK SCENARIOS TABLE

	Aspiration	Stock 14	Stock 15	Stock 16
ROE	40%	25%	30%	40%
P/B	4.00	3.14	5.00	8.00
Earnings Retention Rate	75%	60%	68%	60%
Investors Short-Term Return	**10.0%**	**8.0%**	**6.0%**	**5.0%**
Investors Long-Term Return	**30.0%**	**15.0%**	**20.4%**	**24.0%**
CAGR after 30y	25.3%	12.6%	15.6%	17.7%
CAGR after 20y	23.1%	11.7%	13.6%	14.9%
CAGR after 15y	21.1%	11.0%	12.0%	12.7%
CAGR after 10y	18.1%	10.0%	10.0%	10.0%

SUMMARY: DRAFT STOCK SCREEN RULES

Revisiting the draft stock screen rules, we created for *Investor A* and subsequently re-examined for *Investors B* and *C*, all rules remain intact and unchanged. We did lower our ROE requirement to 10% in order to match the new, lower, *Target CAGR*, but this change is allowed by the screen rules.

- ROE must match or exceed the *Target CAGR*.
- P/B ratio must be 20.0 or below.
- The Earnings Retention Rate must be 60% or above.
- *The Investor's Short-Term Return* must be 5.0% or above.
- *The Investor's Long-Term Return* must match or exceed 1.2x the *Target CAGR*.

APPLICATION OF OUR DRAFT STOCK SCREEN RULES FOR INVESTOR D

Applying these rules to *Investor D*'s list of four potential stock investments:

- All ROEs match or exceed the *Target CAGR* of 15%.
- All P/B ratios are below 20.0.
- The Earnings Retention Rate is 60% or above in all instances.
- *The Investor's Short-Term Return* is 5.0% or above in all instances.
- *The Investor's Long-Term Return* must match or exceed 1.2x *Target CAGR* (1.2 x 10% = 12.0%). This requirement is met in all cases.

If this process were part of our screen for investment opportunities, we would take Stocks 1, 14, 15 and 16 forward for further consideration. If the stocks assessed for *Investors A*, *B* and *C* were also available to *Investor D*, all eleven additional stocks, Stocks 2-13, would pass *Investor*

D's screen rules and could also be taken forward for further consideration.

The eagle-eyed readers among you may have noticed that we did not observe a scenario of a flat 10% return curve for *Investor D*. We should always seek to maximise the opportunity for our returns to grow. With a short 10-year timeframe there will be a wide range of companies possessing the ability to generate a CAGR of 10% or more - so why pick ones with a flat (or downward-sloping) return curve? Opt for upward-sloping curves that provide us with upside potential and afford us the flexibility to stay invested for longer should we subsequently choose to do so.

CHAPTER 9: BUFFETT'S INVESTMENTS

CHAPTER SUMMARY

> *"That which goes up doesn't necessarily have to come down."*[57]
>
> Warren Buffett – The Tao of Warren Buffett

What do Buffett's investments look like when viewed through *The Investor's Solution* lens? In this chapter we examine some of the largest stock investments made by Buffett, together with the ROEs, P/B ratios, Earnings Retention Rates, *Investor's Short-Term Returns*, *Investor's Long-Term Returns* and *Investor's Return Curves* that characterise those investments.

Examining the most recent Berkshire Hathaway's Annual Report, for the year ended 31st December 2019, we can see the five biggest holdings based on market value were:[58]

- Apple ($73.7 billion)
- Bank of America ($33.4 billion)
- Coca-Cola ($22.1 billion)
- American Express ($18.8 billion)
- Wells Fargo ($18.6 billion)

In this Chapter we will examine Apple, Coca-Cola, Wells Fargo, a legacy $13.5 billion investment in IBM that Buffett has since sold, and a recent investment in Biogen. These examples provide a good mix of investments made at different stages of Buffett's career.

From the list of his five biggest current holdings above, we won't examine Bank of America or American Express. Buffett's Bank of America investment was made in 2011 following the atypical conditions of the 2007-2009 credit crisis and was more complex in nature. He purchased preferred stock that came with warrants allowing him to buy further shares, and the deal reflected bail out more than a typical long-term investment. His American Express purchase was made back in 1964, a time at which his investment approach was a little different from what it is today and was centred more on value investing. Strategic deals have also been excluded; those made for reasons other than pure investment gain. An example of this is the 1998 purchase of insurance company General Re that Buffett used to increase his insurance float and to rebalance his investment portfolio towards bonds ahead of the collapse of the Dot-com bubble.

9.1
COCA-COLA (1988)

Buffett started buying Coca-Cola towards the end of 1988. It quickly became his biggest investment. In the 1988 Shareholders Letter he stated, *"We expect to hold these securities for a long time. In fact, when we own portions of outstanding businesses with outstanding managements, our favorite holding period is forever."*[46] He considered Coca-Cola the world's most ubiquitous product, with sales overseas virtually exploding.

The last full year accounts available to him would have been those for the twelve months ended 31st December 1987.[59] We will therefore derive the ROE and Earnings Retention Rate from those accounts. Helpfully, the Coca-Cola accounts contain a ten-year summary that makes it easy to assess the consistency of its financial performance.

Examining that ten-year summary, the average ROE for the 5 years up to and including 1987 was 24.1%.

The Earnings Retention Rate increased over the five years, rising from 35.0% in 1983 to 53.9% in 1987. In other words, over time Coca-Cola was paying out fewer earnings as dividends, choosing instead to retain more within the business. For our calculations, we will take the most recent annual number available to him, the retention rate of 53.9% recorded for 1987.

Now turning to the P/B ratio, we can determine the average price Buffett paid for Coca-Cola by examining his 1989 Shareholders Letter[60] where he lists the number of shares owned and the cost of those shares. Here we are using the 1989 letter in preference to the 1987 letter because he built up his position over time, rather than making the entire purchase in one instant. Using the 1989 accounts gives us a better view of the full holding Buffett amassed between 1988 and 1989. By the end of 1989, he had acquired 23,350,000 shares in Coca-Cola at a cost of

$1,023.92m. He did not increase this holding in 1990 so we will take these numbers to fairly reflect his original investment. Dividing his cost by the number of shares acquired gives us an average cost per share of $43.85.

In terms of Book Value, we want to match this as closely as possible to the Book Value that Buffett was acquiring with his share purchases. The challenge with Book Value is that, since his purchases were spread out over a long period of time, the Book Value of the business will all not have remained constant. As a result, we will make a high-level assumption that the end of 1988 marks the mid-point of Buffett's acquisition phase, and therefore the Book Value at the end of 1988 acts as a reasonable proxy for use in our P/B calculations. At the end of 1988, Coca-Cola had a Book Value (Shareholders' Equity) of $3,345m and had 365m shares outstanding.[61] Thus, the Book Value per Share was $9.16 ($3,345m/365m), yielding a P/B ratio of 4.79 ($43.85/$9.16).

INVESTOR RETURNS

Investor's Short-Term Return
= ROE / P/B
= 24.1% / 4.79
= 5.0%

Investor's Long-Term Return
= ROE x Earnings Retention Rate
= 24.1% x 53.9%
= 13.0%

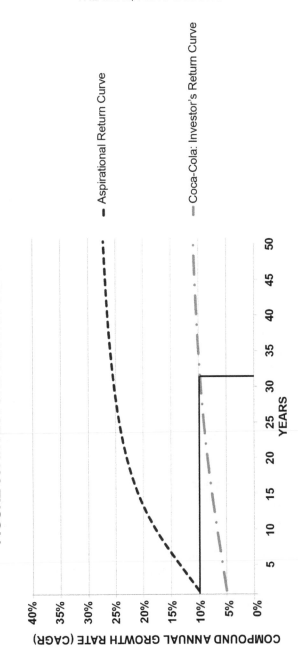

FIGURE 53: INVESTORS RETURN CURVE FOR COCA-COLA

Knowing the *Investor's Short-Term Return* and the *Investor's Long-term Return* we can deduce what we believe the CAGR should be at the end of 2019, 31 years after Buffett's purchase. Figure 53 reveals that the result is a CAGR of 9.7%. Let's see how this stacked up with the actual long-term performance of Coca-Cola.

INVESTMENT PERFORMANCE

Adjusting Buffett's purchase price of $43.85 for stock splits; the price of Coca-Cola increased from a split adjusted $2.74 to $55.25 at the end of 2019.[62] This was an increase of almost twenty-fold in stock price over 31 years. In addition, he received 31 years' worth of dividends from Coca-Cola, amounting to a total of $325 per share over that period[62] (also adjusted for stock splits). On an overall basis, combining the increase in share price with the dividend received, Buffett made $377.13 from his original $2.74 investment, which equates to a CAGR of 17.2% on Coca-Cola for 31 years.

This is higher than the 9.7% that we were expecting from the *Investor's Return Curve* and is even higher than the expected *Investor's Long-Term Return* of 13.0%. This difference arises from the fact that, following his purchase, the ROE of Coca-Cola rose significantly, driven by a rapid increase in overseas sales. From above, the five-year average ROE when Buffett bought was 24.1%. A year later, in 1988, it had risen to 34.7% and it continued to rise, reaching 52.0% in 1994.[63]

This would have had a significant impact on the *Investor's Return Curve*, elevating it. As an illustration, if we maintain the same P/B ratio and Earnings Retention Rate as in our original calculation, but use the average ROE for the five years from 1987 to 1991 instead (which was 36.8%), our Investor's Returns calculations provide the following improved result:

Investor's Short-Term Return
= ROE / P/B
= 36.8% / 4.79
= 7.7%

Investor's Long-Term Return
= ROE x Earnings Retention Rate
= 36.8% x 53.9%
= 19.8%

The new *Investor's Return Curve*, shown in Figure 55, suggests that by Year 31 we should have a CAGR of 16.2%. This is much closer to the actual performance Buffett realised of 17.2%. In any case, Coca-Cola outperformed his expectations and delivered tremendous value.

FIGURE 54: INVESTOR RETURNS SUMMARY FOR COCA-COLA

	Investor's Short-Term Return	CAGR After 31 Years	Investor's Long-Term Return
Expected	5.0%	9.7%	13.0%
Including ROE increases	7.7%	16.2%	19.8%
Actual CAGR		17.2%	

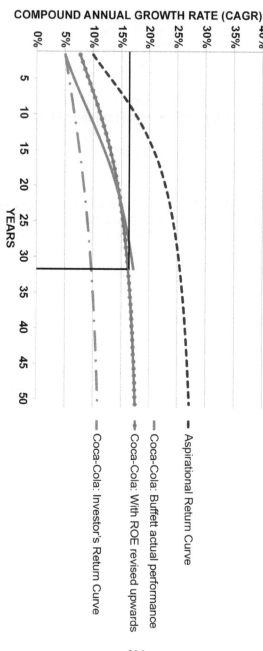

FIGURE 55: INVESTORS RETURN CURVE FOR COCA-COLA WITH ROE REVISED UPWARDS AND BUFFETTS ACTUAL PERFORMANCE

9.2
WELLS FARGO (1990)

Buffett started acquiring the shares of Wells Fargo in the latter half of 1990. The last full year accounts available to him would therefore have been the 12 months to 31st December 1989. We will derive the ROE and Earnings Retention Rate from these accounts.

Examining the accounts, the ROE for 1988 and 1989 were stable at 24.0% and 24.5% respectively,[64] providing an average ROE of 24.2%. Prior to 1988 the ROEs had been erratic, making the calculation of an average circumspect. While we would normally look for more consistency in results, we'll trust Buffett's judgment on the future prospects of Wells Fargo and stick to the average of the two most recent years.

The Earnings Retention Rate remained broadly stable in the previous five years, ranging from 70.1% to 73.4%,[65] with the exception of 1987. The 1989 accounts show a retention rate of 70.1% so we will use this most recent, and also most prudent, number for our calculations.

Turning to the P/B ratio, we can determine the price Buffett paid by examining his 1990 Shareholders Letter where he lists the number of shares owned and the cost of those shares. By the end of 1990, he had acquired 5,000,000 shares in Wells Fargo at a cost of $289.431m.[66] He did not increase this holding in 1991 so we will take these numbers to fairly reflect his original investment. Dividing the cost by the number of shares acquired we get an average cost per share of $57.89.

In terms of Book Value, we want to match this as closely as possible to the Book Value of Wells Fargo at the point Buffett was buying. As a result, we will make the high-level assumption that the end of 1990 marks the end of his acquisition phase, and therefore the Book Value at the end of 1990 acts as a reasonable proxy for use in our P/B calculations. At the end of 1990, Wells Fargo had a Book Value (Common Stockholders' Equity) of $3,360m and had 51.4m shares outstanding.[67] Thus; the Book Value per Share was $65.37 ($3,360m/51.4m). Consequently, the P/B ratio was 0.9 ($57.89/$65.37).

INVESTOR RETURNS

Investor's Short-Term Return
= ROE / P/B
= 24.2% / 0.9
= 26.9%

Investor's Long-Term Return
= ROE x Earnings Retention Rate
= 24.2% x 70.1%
= 17.0%

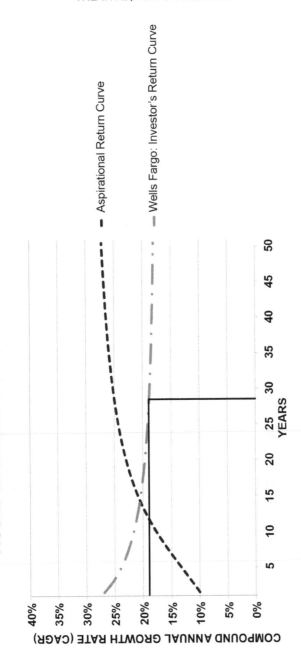

FIGURE 56: INVESTORS RETURN CURVE FOR WELLS FARGO

Knowing the *Investor's Short-Term Return* and the *Investor's Long-term Return* we can deduce what we believe the CAGR should be at the end of 2019, 29 years after Buffett's purchase. Figure 56 reveals that the result is a CAGR of 18.8%. Let's see how this stacked up with the actual long-term performance of Wells Fargo.

INVESTMENT PERFORMANCE

Adjusting Buffett's purchase price of $57.89 for stock splits, the price of Wells Fargo increased from a split adjusted $2.60 at the end of 1990 to $53.80 at the end of 2019.[68] This was an increase of over twenty-fold during the 29-year period. In addition, he received 29 years of dividends from Wells Fargo, amounting to a total of $181 per share (also adjusted for stock splits).[68] On an overall basis, combining the increase in share price with the dividends received, Buffett made $232 from his original $2.60 investment, which equates to a CAGR of 16.8% on Wells Fargo for 29 years.

The difference between this investment and Coca-Cola is that here he was tapping into a theoretically high return from the start. Wells Fargo's solid 24.2% Return on Equity would have generated a lot of earnings, but on top of this, Buffett managed to acquire the business at around 0.9 times Book Value. Coca-Cola, while having an almost identical ROE of 24.1% was more expensive, forcing him to pay almost 5 times Book Value, in part due to the power of the Coca-Cola brand name. Buffett had some comfort therefore; he was securing a high starting return that should only diminish slowly over time.

Since it is my own personal policy not to purchase stocks with downward-sloping curves, I would not have made this investment. However, considered in the context of Buffett's overall portfolio, I can understand why he would have found it advantageous to bring-forward some of his returns via Wells Fargo, while his other stock investments provided upward-sloping curves and the opportunity to grow.

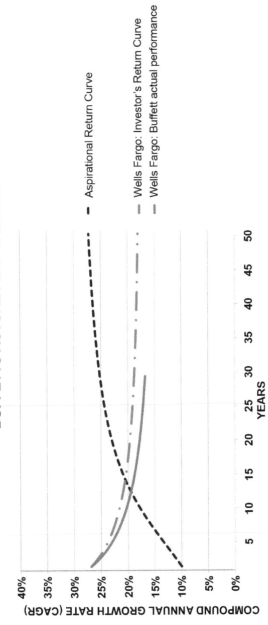

FIGURE 57: INVESTORS RETURN CURVE FOR WELLS FARGO AND BUFFETTS ACTUAL PERFORMANCE

FIGURE 58: INVESTOR RETURNS SUMMARY FOR WELLS FARGO

	Investor's Short-Term Return	CAGR After 29 Years	Investor's Long-Term Return
Expected	26.9%	18.8%	17.0%
Actual CAGR		16.8%	

9.3
IBM (2011)

IBM became one of Buffett's 'Big Four' Investments, with Berkshire building a position worth $13.5 billion at its peak.[69] Buffett was impressed with IBM, openly praising their financial management and flexibility in his 2011 Letter to Shareholders.[70] He started buying in the first half of 2011 so the last full year accounts available to him would have been the 12 months to 31st December 2010.

Examining the five-year summary in those accounts, the average ROE for the 5 years up to and including 2010 was 53.6%.[71]

The Earnings Retention Rate reduced slightly over the five-year period, falling from 82.0% in 2006 to 78.3% in 2010, but it always remained within that narrow band. For our calculations, we will take the most recent annual number available to Buffett, the retention rate of 78.3% in 2010, which is also very similar to the 2008 and 2009 numbers.[71]

Turning to the P/B ratio, we can determine the price Buffett paid by examining his 2011 Shareholders Letter where he lists the number of shares owned and the cost of those shares. By the end of 2011, he had acquired 63,905,931 shares in IBM at a cost of $10,856m.[72] While he did increase his holdings over the subsequent five years, this initial investment represented around 80% of his entire position so we will take these numbers to reasonably reflect his original investment. Dividing his cost by the number of shares acquired gives us an average cost per share of $169.87.

In terms of Book Value, we want to match this as closely as possible to the Book Value of IBM when Buffett was acquiring it. As a result, we will make a high-level assumption that the Book Value at the end of 2010 reasonably reflects the Book Value he was buying. At that time, IBM had a Book Value (Total IBM Stockholders' Equity) of $23,046m[73] and had 1,287.4m shares outstanding.[74] Thus; the Book Value per Share was $17.90 ($23,046m/1,287.4m), and the P/B ratio was 9.5 ($169.87/$17.90).

INVESTOR RETURNS

Investor's Short-Term Return
= ROE / P/B
= 53.6% / 9.5
= 5.6%

Investor's Long-Term Return
= ROE x Earnings Retention Rate
= 53.6% x 78.3%
= 42.0%

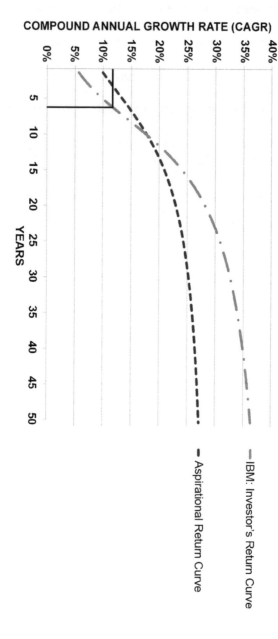

FIGURE 59: INVESTORS RETURN CURVE FOR IBM

Knowing the *Investor's Short-Term Return* and the *Investor's Long-term Return* we can deduce what we believe the CAGR should be at the end of 2019. However, for reasons we'll cover next, by the time this book was written, Buffett had already sold all of his IBM position. Thus, we will instead examine what the *Investor's Return Curve* tells us the CAGR would have been at the end of his roughly 6-year holding period to 2017. The result is a CAGR of 11.9%. Let's see how this stacked up with the actual performance of IBM over that short, 6-year period.

INVESTMENT PERFORMANCE

There were no stock splits for the period Buffett held the shares, so his purchase price remains at $169.87. Between his purchase in 2011 and the sale of the position, which was completed prior to the middle of 2017, the price of IBM actually fell slightly to around $152. However, he did receive 6 years of dividends from IBM, amounting to $32.00 per share.[75] On an overall basis, combining the decrease in share price with the dividend received, Buffett made $13.88 from his original $169.87 investment, which equates to a CAGR of 1.3% on IBM for 6 years.

Clearly this is below the expectation of 11.9% CAGR and explains why he sold. Speaking at the 2017 Shareholder Meeting Buffett said he'd been wrong and that he thought it would have done better in the six years since his purchase.[76]

If we had examined IBM's 2010 financial statements, along with its five-year track record prior to that, it would be easy to understand why Buffett believed he was investing in a high-quality company with great financials and management. IBM was highly profitable, had a solid return on equity and great cash generation. Management's capital allocation decisions were astute, their intentions were clear, and were detailed in the annual reports. The one chink in the armour was IBM's revenue, which didn't grow. If a business cannot grow its top line, it makes it very hard for earnings to grow. Back in his 2011 Letter to Shareholders Buffett noted that the success of his IBM investment would be principally determined by its future earnings.[77] Because sales did not grow, earnings did not grow, so the share price refused to rise.

Rising sales is one of the additional considerations we'll build into our investment screen later in the book. But, even if you do a lot of due diligence and the prospect of future sales growth looks certain, you never can tell. What's really interesting in this case is what Buffett did next. As he began selling his IBM position, he started accumulating a massive position in a one-time competitor of IBM, Apple.

FIGURE 60: INVESTOR RETURNS SUMMARY FOR IBM

	Investor's Short-Term Return	CAGR After 6 Years	Investor's Long-Term Return
Expected	5.6%	11.9%	42.0%
Actual CAGR		1.3%	

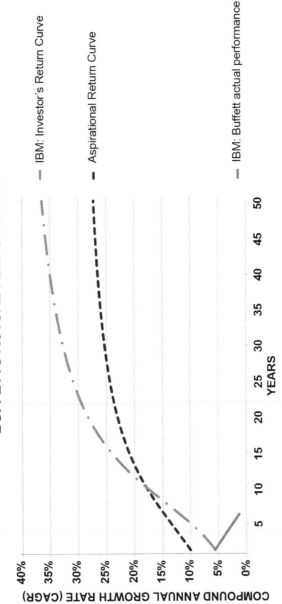

FIGURE 61: INVESTORS RETURN CURVE FOR IBM AND BUFFETTS ACTUAL PERFORMANCE

9.4
APPLE (2016)

Buffett started buying Apple during 2016. The holding wasn't big enough to show up in the Berkshire Hathaway 3rd Quarter results of that year but it did show up in the 2016 year-end accounts.[78] Buffett has continued to add to this holding over time, and per the 2019 Letter to Shareholders the investment had grown to a massive $73.7 billion, double the size of his next biggest holding.[79]

The last full year accounts available to Buffett would have been the 12 months to 26th September 2015. We will derive the ROE and Earnings Retention Rate from those accounts. The average ROE for the 5 years up to and including 2015 was 38.9%.[80]

The Earnings Retention Rate decreased from 100% in 2011, a year in which it paid no dividend, to 78.5% in 2015.[80] For our calculations, we will take the most recent annual number available to Buffett, the retention rate of 78.5% in 2015.

Turning to the P/B ratio, we can determine the price he paid by examining his 2016 Shareholders Letter where he lists the number of shares owned and the cost of those shares. By the end of 2016, Buffett had acquired 61,242,652 shares in Apple at a cost of $6,747m.[81] Dividing his cost by the number of shares acquired gives us an average cost per share of $110.17.

In terms of Book Value, we want to match this as closely as possible to the Book Value of Apple when Buffett was acquiring the bulk of his holding. As a result, we will make a high-level assumption that the accounts to the 12 months ended 24th September 2016 are the best reflection of Book Value acquired, and therefore acts as a reasonable proxy for use in our P/B calculations. At the end of September 2016, Apple had a Book Value (Shareholders' Equity) of $128,249m[82] and had 5,500.3m shares outstanding.[83] Thus

the Book Value per Share was $23.32
($128,249m/5,500.3m), and the P/B ratio was 4.7
($110.17/$23.32).

INVESTOR RETURNS

Investor's Short-Term Return
= ROE / P/B
= 38.9% / 4.7
= 8.3%

Investor's Long-Term Return
= ROE x Earnings Retention Rate
= 38.9% x 78.5%
= 30.5%

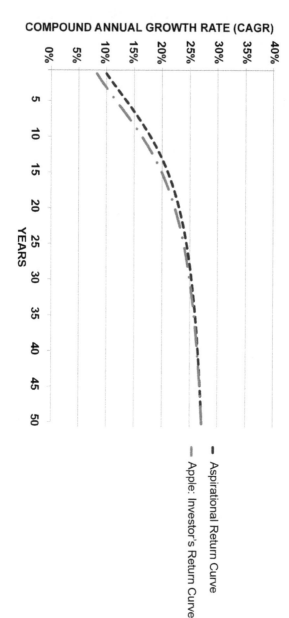

COMPOUND ANNUAL GROWTH RATE (CAGR)

FIGURE 62: INVESTORS RETURN CURVE FOR APPLE

- Aspirational Return Curve
- Apple: Investor's Return Curve

INVESTMENT PERFORMANCE AND INVESTOR'S RETURN CURVE

At present, it is too soon to fairly assess the success of Buffett's Apple acquisition. But where IBM failed to grow sales and earnings, Apple is making solid headway. Over the last five years, sales have increased by an average of 7% per annum and earnings per share have increased 13% per annum.[84] The share price has made solid progress too. In the decade prior to his purchase, Apple rose twelve-fold from the $9 level to the $110.17 Buffett paid. Since then, the Apple share price has risen further, reaching $290 by the end of 2019, representing an increase of 169% for Buffett over three years, or 38% per annum. But Buffett views Apple as a long-term investment, and he therefore plans to hold it so as to compound the growth.

Using the *Investor's Return Curve* for Apple, we can estimate that he will earn a 16.5% CAGR after 10 years, a 22.4% CAGR after 20 years and a 25.0% CAGR after 30 years. If Apple can continue to generate a ROE at this level, Buffett can just sit back and wait for the gains to rack up. And, much like the brand powerhouse that is Coca-Cola, it will be very difficult for any competitor to come along and knock Apple off its pedestal.

FIGURE 63: INVESTOR RETURNS SUMMARY FOR APPLE

	Investor's Short-Term Return	Expected CAGR	Investor's Long-Term Return
Expected	8.3%		30.5%
Expected CAGR after 10 years		16.5%	
Expected CAGR after 20 years		22.4%	
Expected CAGR after 30 years		25.0%	

9.5
APPLE FOR THE SMALL INVESTOR
(2016)

When conducting my research on Buffett's approach, and undertaking my analysis of his investments I consistently faced a key challenge - it was impossible to know exactly *when* he started buying. He does not openly discuss the timing of his purchases, and his quarterly and annual reports do not contain the level of detail needed to identify exact 'buy' decisions. It could be three or more months between him buying his first share in a company and that investment appearing in the quarterly or annual statements. And in any case, it will only show up in those statements if the investment is above a certain size at that point in time, or if Buffett decides to comment on it explicitly.

It was also impossible to discern the initial *price* at which he started buying. If he intends to put on a sizeable position, he cannot purchase his entire allocation all at once for fear of pushing up the price of the stock unduly. Instead he must purchase shares a little at a time. Inevitably, by the time Buffett has finished adding to a large position, particularly if that position does become public knowledge, the stock has probably risen since the point he made his first purchase. This means that, for analysis purposes, taking the number of shares and their corresponding cost from the quarterly or annual reports will likely provide a result that is higher than his initial purchase price. Here, the small investor has a big advantage over Buffett. The small investor can put on an entire position in the blink of an eye and not move the market.

I was intrigued as to the exact trigger point that causes Buffett to buy something. Considering all of the possible investments in the marketplace, and their constantly fluctuating prices, I wondered what threshold criteria might signal him to pick up the phone to his broker and say, "*start buying*".

We know that Buffett is happy making a decision on an investment in less than five minutes, which isn't enough time to conduct reams of complex analysis. And we discovered earlier that he has no computer or calculator in his office, further eliminating the likelihood that he creates intricate models to predict a company's future prospects.

We also know that he and Munger use filters[26,32] and checklists to assess investments.[85] I wondered whether there was a simple checklist of criteria Buffett might run through in his five-minute appraisal window, and whether we could replicate something similar to use for ourselves.

I decided to re-examine the Apple investment in more detail. We know from the annual accounts that he owned 61,242,652 shares at the 2016 year-end, with a total cost of $6.7 billion. That total position was not put on in one go; therefore, he must have started acquiring the position earlier in the year. Apple does not show up in the 2016 Third Quarter 10-Q report, but this is because its market value wasn't big enough to require disclosure. For that to happen the position would have already had to be bigger than American Express Company, a position with a market value of $9.7 billion. So, in all likelihood, he would have begun his purchases in the first half of the year. I looked back to the low in the share price, which occurred in May of that year, around the $92.70 level.

The Book Value of Apple at that point in time was $130,457m and there were 5,478m shares outstanding,[86] resulting in a Book Value per Share of $23.81 ($130,457/5,478). The P/B at that time would have therefore been 3.9 ($92.70/$23.81).

INVESTOR RETURNS

Investor's Short-Term Return
= ROE / P/B
= 38.9% / 3.9
= 10.0%

Investor's Long-Term Return
= ROE x Earnings Retention Rate
= 38.9% x 78.5%
= 30.5%

These short- and long-term investment returns seemed like nice, round numbers, easy to remember and reflective of a great investment opportunity: An *Investor's Short-Term Return* of 10.0%, rising over time to an *Investor's Long-Term Return* above 30%. As a small investor, you could have picked up your entire Apple position at these outstanding economics. Hold that thought for a moment, as we examine Buffett's next investment, Biogen.

FIGURE 64: INVESTOR RETURNS SUMMARY: APPLE FOR THE SMALL INVESTOR

	Investor's Short-Term Return	Expected CAGR	Investor's Long-Term Return
Expected	10.0%		30.5%
Expected CAGR after 10 years		18.3%	
Expected CAGR after 20 years		23.5%	
Expected CAGR after 30 years		25.8%	

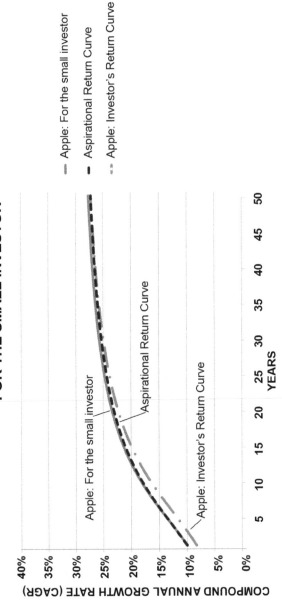

FIGURE 65: INVESTORS RETURN CURVE FOR APPLE AND FOR THE SMALL INVESTOR

9.6
BIOGEN (2019)

Buffett bought Biogen in 2019 after the price dropped abruptly from the $320 level down to around $220 in March of that year. The stock spent around six months undulating between $220 and $240, before rising back up to reach the $300 level by year end.

The last full year accounts available to him would have been the 12 months to 31st December 2018, so we will derive the ROE and Earnings Retention Rate from those accounts.[87]

The average ROE for the 5 years up to and including 2018 was 32.9%.

The Earnings Retention Rate was 100% throughout as Biogen pays no dividends and reinvests all of its earnings in order to grow the business.

Turning to the P/B ratio, here we normally determine the price Buffett paid by examining his Shareholders Letters. At the end of December 2019, Biogen was not a big enough position for that information to be disclosed, so we must form an estimate of our own. A few times between March and October 2019 the price of Biogen dropped to the $220 lows, but we'll assume a slightly more conservative purchase price of $225 per share over that time period.

In terms of Book Value, we want to match this as closely as possible to the Book Value at the time Buffett was acquiring. We will make a high-level assumption that the mid-year Book Value is the most appropriate, which we will find in the 10-Q report for the quarter ending 30th June 2019.[88] Here we can see that the Book Value (Shareholders' Equity) was $12,949m. We can also see that the number of shares outstanding was 190.4m,[89] resulting in a Book Value per Share of $68.00 ($12,949/190.4). The P/B ratio is therefore 3.3 ($225/$68.00).

INVESTOR RETURNS

Investor's Short-Term Return
= ROE / P/B
= 32.9% / 3.3
= 10.0%

Investor's Long-Term Return
= ROE x Earnings Retention Rate
= 32.9% x 100%
= 32.9%

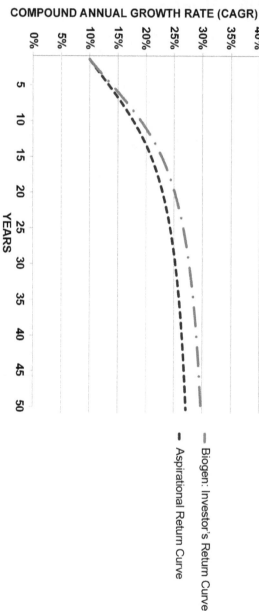

FIGURE 66: INVESTORS RETURN CURVE FOR BIOGEN

CREATION OF THE ASPIRATIONAL INVESTOR'S RETURN CURVE

It was at this point in my analysis that I was really struck by the similarity between the return possible for Apple, and that revealed for Biogen. Both exhibited an *Investor's Short-Term Return* of 10% and an *Investor's Long-term Return* above 30%.

In line with my objective of simplifying the complex, volatile world of investments for you, I adopted these thresholds as the foundation of the *Aspirational Investor's Return Curve*. This is also why I included the Aspirational Investor's Return Curve on each of the investor profile charts in the previous chapter, enabling you to compare Stocks 2-16 against a Buffett-like investment.

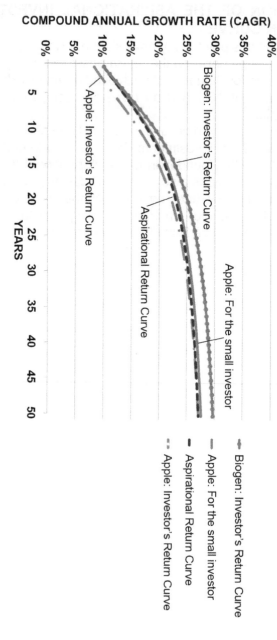

FIGURE 67: ASPIRATIONAL INVESTORS RETURN CURVE ALONGSIDE APPLE, APPLE FOR THE SMALL INVESTOR AND BIOGEN

COMPOUND ANNUAL GROWTH RATE (CAGR)

YEARS

Biogen: Investor's Return Curve

Apple: Investor's Return Curve

Aspirational Return Curve

Apple: For the small investor

↓ Biogen: Investor's Return Curve

Apple: For the small investor

Aspirational Return Curve

Apple: Investor's Return Curve

INVESTMENT PERFORMANCE AND INVESTOR'S RETURN CURVE

As was the case for Apple, it is too soon to fairly assess the success of the Biogen acquisition. Early signs are positive, however. Over the last decade Biogen's stock price has risen from $53.70 to $296, delivering a CAGR of 18.6%. And it currently has all of the financial attributes required to fuel that growth into the future, with five -year average sales growth over 8% per annum and earnings per share growth of 20% per annum.[102]

Using the *Investor's Return Curve*, we can estimate that Buffett will earn a 19.4% CAGR after 10 years, a 25.2% CAGR after 20 years and a 27.7% CAGR after 30 years.

FIGURE 68: INVESTOR RETURNS SUMMARY FOR BIOGEN

	Investor's Short-Term Return	Expected CAGR	Investor's Long-Term Return
Expected	10.0%		32.9%
Expected CAGR after 10 years		19.4%	
Expected CAGR after 20 years		25.2%	
Expected CAGR after 30 years		27.7%	

9.7
CHAPTER RECAP

We opened this chapter with the Buffett quote, "*That which goes up doesn't necessarily have to come down*," and we can see that borne out in the long-term CAGR's he has achieved with Coca-Cola (17.2%) and Wells Fargo (16.8%). IBM did not perform in the way he expected, principally driven by a lack of sales and earnings growth, so Buffett cut the position just above break-even (1.3% CAGR).

Nevertheless, from this we learned the importance of checking for sales and earnings growth and we will bake these criteria into our stock screens. While early signs are encouraging, it is too early to conclude on the performance of Apple and Biogen.

The concrete track record of Buffett's investments in Coca-Cola and Wells Fargo, offer us a way to reconcile his approach to the stellar 20.3% per annum results he has delivered for Berkshire shareholders. Coca-Cola and Wells Fargo didn't quite match 20.3%, but then he had no control of the Earnings Retention Rate of these companies. Over the years, Buffett has purchased more entire businesses than he has made major stock investments. With full ownership comes the ability to control capital allocation decisions, to retain a higher proportion of earnings and to drive future growth. Had he been in the position to reduce the proportion of earnings that Coca-Cola and Wells Fargo paid out as dividends, their performance would most likely have matched or exceeded his long-term CAGR of 20.3%.

Crucially, Buffett's investments offer solid proof that "*anyone can do it.*" Coca-Cola and Wells Fargo are big brand names of which we are all aware; they are easy to understand; and when held long-term they delivered excellent compound annual growth rates. Everybody knows Apple and understands what it does; it is currently the biggest company in the world, and Buffett's biggest investment.

Any investor on the lookout for great companies such as these can mirror Buffett's track record. Using *The Investor's Solution* and *The Investor's Return Curve*, you can gauge a stock's theoretical return at any point in time, and compare prospective investments side-by-side. If you can identify a company that you understand, one that possesses a consistent track record of generating above-average returns, and you have the opportunity to buy that company at a reasonable price, fill your boots.

CHAPTER 10:
OTHER INVESTMENT CONSIDERATIONS

We have set the bar high for our investments, aiming to achieve Buffett-like returns of 20% per annum. To increase our chances of achieving that return, we set our aspirational return even higher, at 30% or more. This helps insulate us should things not go according to plan. Remember, despite our best efforts, not every investment will work out the way we hope. Earlier, I elected to review Buffett's investment in IBM so as to demonstrate that very point - even the best get it wrong sometimes!

There are some additional considerations we must be aware of before we start identifying prospective investments. These will help us to make the most of opportunities that arise, while avoiding many of the pitfalls, like sales failing to rise, or being shaken out of a position by a market correction.

10.1
VARIABILITY OF RETURNS

A key objective of this book was to simplify the complex world of financial markets, providing the beginner investor with access to Buffett-like returns. In order to deliver that simplicity, it was necessary to strip away layer upon layer of complexity so as to arrive at a set of straightforward principles and investment mechanisms. The outflow of *The Investor's Solution* is a set of simple calculations that enable us to determine our theoretical short- and long-term returns using three simple metrics. However, the world remains a complex place, and these metrics are not static. All three variables will shift over time, leading to variations in the returns we achieve.

Stock prices are the most volatile of the variables. While I was writing this book, the world was hit by the COVID-19 pandemic, which sent financial markets around the world into a nosedive in the Spring of 2020. In addition to tumbling prices, companies slashed dividends, seeking to keep as much cash on hand as possible. The aftermath of the pandemic saw the biggest economic contraction in history.

At extreme times like this, investors can begin to question their approach, the merits of their investments and whether or not to sell their positions. The COVID-19 pandemic provided an excellent stress test of *The Investor's Solution*, which I am pleased to report, remained unchanged throughout. Decisions to hold were automatic as the businesses held were high quality, unaffected over the long-term by a temporarily market correction. Falling prices meant that great businesses were on sale at bargain prices, and my stock screen was filled with first class names.

A panic such as this clearly highlights the volatile and unpredictable nature of the financial markets. In real life, our short- and long-term returns will never perfectly match our calculations. The stock price performance and dividend income will not combine to mirror the *Investor's Return Curve* perfectly. There *will* be variability in our results; this is inevitable. In contrast, there will be absolutely *no* variability in our approach.

10.2
FACTORS INFLUENCING ROE

We select companies with high ROEs for three principle reasons. First, these generally represent high-quality companies that possess strong brand names. Second, they provide us with the opportunity to share in those high returns. Third, they provide us with downside protection should the initial ROE fall in subsequent years. If the ROE of a company falls from 40% to 30%, this may not have a significant impact on an investor's long-term Target CAGR set at 20%.

In reality, business, customer, economic and market fluctuations make it impossible for a company to maintain a perfectly stable ROE over the long-term. And, variability in the ROE doesn't mean that the ROE has to *fall*; as we saw for Buffett's investment in Coca-Cola, a company's ROE can also *improve* in subsequent years. But the simple fact of the matter is; the ROE can and will vary over time.

There are five principle factors that influence ROE. Two are what we might call *global* factors, in that they impact all companies in the market, and three are *company-specific* characteristics.

GLOBAL FACTORS

HIGHER TAX RATES REDUCE ROE

The massive government stimulus and spending which followed the 2007/08 Credit Crisis and the COVID-19 pandemic will, at some point, need to be repaid. It is highly likely that at least a portion of that repayment will come in the form of higher taxes. Since Return on Equity is the after-tax earnings of a company divided by its equity base, an increase in the tax rate has the direct impact of reducing after-tax earnings and thus ROE.

HIGHER INTEREST RATES REDUCE ROE

Companies can borrow money as a source of additional funding in order to amplify their returns. If you buy a home for $100,000 and the price rises 10% in the first year, you would generate a return of $10,000 / $100,000 = 10%. If you only use $10,000 of capital instead, borrowing the remaining $90,000, the 10% increase in the house price leads to a much higher return on that investment of $10,000 / $10,000 = 100%. By borrowing money to increase your capital base you can amplify your return.

We are currently experiencing unprecedented low levels of interest rates. Borrowing costs are at historically low levels as a result. Since interest rates tend to move in long cycles, spanning 30 years or so, the probability of interest rates rising in the future is much higher than the probability that they will move lower still. Higher interest rates increase the cost of borrowing, increasing interest expense, thus lowering earnings and ROE.

COMPANY-SPECIFIC FACTORS

LEVERAGE

Taking advantage of unprecedented low interest rates, most companies have taken on more debt in order to amplify their returns. Each dollar of equity is now leveraged much more heavily than it used to be. This had the effect of increasing ROEs in the past, but has the opposite implication for ROEs in the future. It would be imprudent for companies to take on even more debt at this point. Therefore, ROEs are unlikely to be boosted by additional leverage in the future. However, as borrowing costs rise, companies may choose to *reduce* leverage, removing the amplification effect from their returns, ultimately reducing their ROEs.

ASSET TURNOVER

A fall in the ratio between sales and the assets employed in a business would cause ROE to fall. Asset Turnover is the ratio of Sales divided by Total Assets. It measures how efficiently a business uses its assets to generate sales. The more assets required to generate a dollar of sales, the lower the ROE.

The three major categories of assets we have to think about are accounts receivable, inventories, and fixed assets such as plant and machinery.

Accounts receivable is the money owed to a company. It usually moves in proportion to sales: if you sell more, you are owed more by those you sell to; if you sell less, you are owed less. Since it is linked to sales in this way, both parts of the Sales/Total Assets formula will move together, and ROE will remain broadly unaffected by changes.

An increase in **inventories** relative to sales can reduce ROE. During the recent COVID-19 pandemic, some companies experienced a dramatic fall in sales, causing stock inventories to pile up in their warehouses. Any time an increase in inventories is not the result of a corresponding increase in sales, the efficiency of the company is reduced and the ROE falls. Conversely, the pandemic also disrupted supply chains across the world leading some companies to experience stock shortages, since deliveries could not be made to their warehouses. This will have temporarily improved their ROEs. However, these companies may now elect to hold more stock on hand in order to protect themselves against future supply shocks, leading to a subsequent reduction in ROE from pre-COVID-19 levels.

Finally, generating sales may require an investment in new assets such as new **plant and machinery**. Such investments can be costly to the business and may increase the value of assets on the balance sheet. Since sales are unlikely to increase lock step with investments in new plant and machinery, with sales coming through much later than the investment outlay, the Asset Turnover ratio will generally fall, and the ROE will be reduced.

Over the long-term, the impact of changes in these three categories will have a modest impact on ROE, either to the upside or to the downside.

INCREASED EXPENSES

Increased expenses reduce earnings and thus ROE. For every dollar of sales there are a lot of costs that must be taken into account. We've already noted that tax and interest rates are likely to increase, but the pressure on labour, raw materials and energy are unlikely to offer any respite. We are likely to see modest upward pressure on costs and thus lower earnings and ROEs in the future.

ROE SUMMARY

The likelihood is that ROEs will fall in the future. Between higher taxes, higher interest rates, lower leverage, higher inventories and upward cost pressures, corporate earnings will most likely decrease, lowering ROEs in the process. High-quality companies will fare better. The brand power they have built will act like a protective moat, helping them to maintain pricing power and protect margins. As long as we maintain our focus on identifying high-quality companies, we will continue to be able to generate above-average returns in the future, even if ROE does fall.

10.3
PRICE VOLATILITY AND P/B

The P/B ratio is the most volatile of our three key inputs since stock prices can fluctuate wildly in the financial markets. You can use this to your advantage, however. All markets move in cycles and opportunities will arise continuously, enabling you to boost your returns by purchasing great companies at excellent P/B ratios. By seizing such opportunities, you can almost guarantee the realisation of above-average returns over the long-term.

10.4
CAPITAL ALLOCATION POLICIES & EARNINGS RETENTION RATES

Earnings Retention Rate is the most stable of the three key inputs. The high-quality companies that we seek will tend to have stable dividend policies that span many years, if not decades. These policies are often based on paying out a fixed and therefore predictable portion of their earnings each year, offering some comfort that retention rates will remain consistent over time.

10.5
TIMING INVESTMENTS

Earlier, when we learned about compound growth, we discovered that the sooner we start investing the better, even if starting with a small amount. However, each of us will begin our investment journey at a different time, starting on different days, weeks, months and years. As a beginner, making your first investment can be one of the most stressful decisions you make. You might read this book, find that it makes perfect sense, develop a clear plan...and then lift your head from its pages to be bombarded by market noise. You'll constantly be shown conflicting information and will hear conflicting opinions. Market pundits will scramble over themselves to call market tops and market bottoms.

Ignore it all. The markets are so unpredictable; there is no "best" time to buy. Stick to the approach set out in this book...understand it and follow it. As you'll see shortly, if the market is overextended, very few, if any, stocks will show up in your screens. If the market has corrected, your screen will be full of fantastic investment opportunities. In either case, the approach set out in this book, and the contents of your stock screen (or lack thereof), will lead the way.

AVOIDING BUBBLES AND MAKING THE MOST OF CORRECTIONS

Over long periods of time, financial markets undulate up and down, driven by wider credit and economic cycles. Credit and economic cycles can also be overridden by human psychology. Due to the fallible nature of human perception, differences can arise between the price we are willing to pay for assets and the economic fundamentals that underpin them. In some circumstances, the faulty perception can be self-reinforcing, creating an asset bubble in which valuations enter far-from-equilibrium territory. During the Dot-com bubble investors chased the price of technology stocks up to unprecedented levels based on nothing more than the observation that technology stocks were prone to rise. Many of these companies never turned a profit, and the market collapsed below equilibrium when the dream proved illusory. We will not get swept up in such hysteria.

BUBBLES

Fortunately, *The Investor's Solution* helps us to avoid that trap. Since we use the P/B ratio to calculate the *Investor's Short-Term Return*, we have a gauge of price *and* value built into our approach. When stocks are in far-from-equilibrium bubble territory, no opportunities will show up in our stock screens. The short-term returns of bubble stocks will simply be too low to meet our minimum criteria of 5%.

CORRECTIONS

The opposite of a bubble is a correction/bust/collapse. Often, these are result of a preceding bubble bursting, but they are sometimes the result of other unforeseen circumstances, like the COVID-19 pandemic. During a correction, asset prices fall below equilibrium. Market corrections are a powerful weapon in an investor's arsenal. It is during these periods of turmoil that we can find compelling investment opportunities, adding high quality businesses to our portfolio at knockdown prices. Buying during a correction is a great way to boost our long-term return. Once again, *The Investor's Solution* helps in this respect. During a correction our stock screen will likely be filled with plenty of investment opportunities, possessing all of the investment characteristics we desire.

EMOTIONAL UNCERTAINTY DURING CORRECTIONS

Human emotions can foster bubbles and trigger corrections. They can also prevent us from capitalising on great opportunities at very the time it is most advantageous to do so.

When we are in bubble territory, stock prices are going up. Despite the fact that stocks are becoming more expensive to purchase, the upward trajectory and the hope of riches means we feel happy and content. Conversely, when we enter market corrections, prices are plunging, everything seems too risky, and investors are at their most nervous. Ironically, this is usually the best time to buy!

These feelings are very natural – they are what make us human – and we shouldn't seek to bury them. Instead, we must be aware of them when they arise, acknowledge their presence, but act rationally in accordance with our approach.

One of the big advantages of a rule-based approach such as *The Investor's Solution* is that it eliminates the impact of emotions on the decision-making process. This is partly the reason that Buffett and Munger use checklists. By using the stock screening rules set out in this book, together with the examination of the short- and long-term returns, we will know whether or not a stock is a suitable investment candidate. If the market is rising, there may be only a couple of investment candidates present at any one time. If the market has corrected, we'll likely have several high-quality stocks to choose from. The way we *feel* about investing won't have gone away, but it will have been put back in its box.

TIMING INVESTMENTS DURING BIG CORRECTIONS

Nobody can predict the future, so we're not going to pretend we can do so. However, as a market starts to correct and prices start to fall, two very reasonable questions arise; "*When should I buy?*" and "*Should I invest all of my cash in one go?"*

During a major correction the stock market will often continue to go down week after week, and month after month. Investment candidates will start popping up in our stock screens. Often, the market will continue to fall even after we have made a purchase or two, taking the price of our new investments down with it.

In such cases, those investments offer even better value at the new, lower price, than they did when we originally purchased them. Technically we should buy more! Nobody can predict how deep the correction will be and how long it will last, so at some point we need to jump in and buy, otherwise we will miss great opportunities. At the same time, we don't want to invest all of our capital too early in the correction, paying too much for the companies. This uncertainty adds a lot of emotional stress into the mix.

Whenever I find myself in this situation, I mitigate the negative emotions as follows:

a) SPLIT AND DIVIDE PURCHASES

There is no need to go 'all in' at a particular point in time. If you have $10,000 of cash on the sidelines, and have four investment candidates showing up in your screen, you could decide to *split* your purchases, putting $2,500 into one of the candidates, then waiting to see how the market performs before putting on a second $2,500 position in another candidate, and so on. Alternatively, you could *divide* your purchases, investing $1,000 in each of the four candidates. By observing how each performs relative to the others you could invest more in the stock demonstrating the best relative strength.

b) USE A TIME-BASED RULE TO DRIP FEED INVESTMENTS

You could also use a time-based rule, establishing that you won't invest more than a certain amount per week or per month. This protects you from investing too much too soon. At the start of a correction, such as that which followed the collapse of the Dot-com bubble, an investor had no idea whether it would last three weeks, three months, or three years. By electing to invest $1,000 of your $10,000 per month, you give the market time to show you whether there is more downside to come. If you are five months into a correction that still shows no sign of reversing, reduce the pace of investment, amending your rule to now invest $1,000 every *two* months.

BE PATIENT

If you are seeking to make an investment but are not in the midst of a market correction, you will generally find slim pickings. At any particular point in time there will likely be very few stocks that meet your criteria. Be patient. Do not chase returns by lowering your standards.

"In the securities business, you literally, every day, have thousands of the major American corporations offered to you, at a price that changes daily, and you don't have to make any decisions...nothing is forced upon you."[90]

Warren Buffett

Opportunities will always arise, and they will arise frequently. There may not be an entire market correction around the corner, but a particular high-quality stock could issue a performance update that is criticised by the media, knocking 10% off its share price and dropping it right into your stock screen. Despite the fleeting, inconsequential news, it is still a high-quality stock, and it will still generate a great return over the long-term.

On a regular basis, say once per month, screen the

market for potential opportunities. The presence of great quality companies that meet your screen criteria will confirm whether or not it is an opportune time to buy. The absence of any suitable companies suggests that the market is overinflated, and prices are too high. Keep an eye on the market, but let the opportunities come to you.

10.6
INDEX INVESTING

If you have a low amount of capital to invest up-front, or perhaps want to invest a small amount on a regular basis, then investing in stock indices such as the S&P500 is a great alternative to outright stock selection and purchase. Investing small amounts on a frequent basis has the added benefit of reducing the overall volatility of your portfolio since your purchases are spread over a long period of time. This 'small and often' approach is called 'dollar-cost averaging'.

Nowadays, large selections of Exchange Traded Funds (ETFs) exist, enabling you to buy exposure to a vast array of indices. ETFs contain collections of tens or hundreds of stocks or bonds in a single fund, and can also contain commodities, providing you with the opportunity to buy exposure to precious metals, oil, and so on. They are traded on the major stock markets and can be purchased through your regular brokerage account and through tax-efficient accounts. They are low cost, which is key if you're making small purchases on a regular basis.

As an example, Vanguard offers the Vanguard S&P 500 ETF (stock code VOO) that is listed on the New York Stock Exchange and invests in the stocks making up the S&P 500 Index, representing 500 of the largest U.S. companies. Its goal is to closely track the return of the S&P500 index and has an annual fee of only 0.3% per annum.

Investing in indices in this way is a great way to get

exposure to the broad stock market. While the aim of this book is to achieve above-average returns, there is absolutely no harm in simply mirroring the market. Over long periods of time this approach will also yield solid returns. You can actually use *The Investor's Solution* to compare ETF returns to those of individual stocks or to other ETFs, so long as their ROE, P/B and Earnings Retention Rate can be found or calculated. At the end of March 2020, near the bottom of the COVID-19 correction, I examined the return profile for VOO. From the Vanguard website I located the ROE, which was 19.3% at that time, and the P/B ratio, which was 3.1.[91]

$$\text{Investor's Short-Term Return} = \text{ROE} / \text{P/B}$$

$$\text{Investor's Short-Term Return} = 19.3\% / 3.1 = 6.2\%$$

To determine the Earnings Retention Rate, I first determined the Earnings per Share of VOO. Per the Vanguard website, the price of VOO at that point was $225 and the Price/Earnings ratio was 19.7.[92]

$$\text{Price} / \text{Earnings} = 19.7$$

$$\text{Earnings} = \text{Price} / 19.7$$

$$\text{Earnings} = \$225 / 19.7$$

$$\text{Earnings} = \$11.42$$

Vanguard also publishes the dividend yield, which was 1.58%, meaning that the dividends paid out are 1.58% x $225 = $3.55.[92]

$$\text{Earnings Retention Rate} = (\text{EPS} - \text{DPS}) / \text{EPS}$$

Earnings Retention Rate = ($11.42 - $3.55) / $11.42

Earnings Retention Rate = 69%

Thus…

Investor's Long-Term Return

= ROE x Earnings Retention Rate

= 19.3% x 69%

= 13.3%

These returns are actually very similar to Buffett's projected return for Coca-Cola, which we calculated to have a short-term return of 5.0% and a long-term return of 13.0% in the previous chapter. In fact, Buffett regularly endorses the use of index funds for the beginner investor, recommending that they buy low cost index funds on a regular basis in order to weather the ups and downs of the market.[93]

10.7
SUPPLEMENTARY SCREEN RULES

In addition to the three key *Investor's Solution* metrics of ROE, P/B and Earnings Retention Rate, we will incorporate a number of additional metrics into our stock screening process to ensure we only select high-quality, financially strong companies with consistent track records.

Finding investment opportunities will be easiest if you use some form of online stock screening tool that enables you to search the entire market for companies possessing your desired characteristics.

Head to *theinvestorssolution.com* for an up-to-date list of recommended tools and services. However, use of a screening tool is not essential. All criteria described below can be found easily without a screening tool, and any calculations, where required, are simple to perform yourself.

MARKET CAPITALISATION

The Market Capitalisation, or 'Market Cap' for short, is a measure of a company's size. We want the businesses we purchase to be established enterprises, which will generally mean more stability and a greater competitive advantage over newcomers. Market Capitalisation is calculated by multiplying the current share price by the current number of shares outstanding. For example, at the end of 2019, Apple had a share price of $293.65 and 4,443,236,000 shares outstanding.[94] Therefore its Market Cap is $293.65 x 4,443,236,000 = $1,304,756,250,000, or $1.3 Trillion. Apple is one of the largest companies in the market. We don't need our businesses to be as big as this, but we do require their current Market Cap to exceed $1 billion.

SALES GROWTH

Consistency of performance is one of the key ingredients Buffett looks for, and consistency in Sales growth is essential. Consistent Sales growth helps us avoid the pitfall Buffett faced with his investment in IBM. In addition to consistency, we want Sales to comfortably outperform inflation. Sales that are increasing at 2% per annum are simply keeping pace with inflation, not growing in real terms. We require average Sales growth over the last 5 years of 5% per annum or more. Most annual accounts will contain five- to ten-year summaries of key statistics and will detail the track record of Sales growth for you.

EARNINGS GROWTH

Consistency in Earnings growth is just as essential as

consistency in Sales growth. We demand a little more from our potential investments in this instance, requiring average Earnings growth over the last 5 years of 10% per annum or more. The easiest metric to focus on is Earnings per Share, or EPS. As was the case for Sales, most annual accounts will contain five- to ten-year summaries of key statistics and will detail the EPS growth track record.

NET PROFIT MARGIN (NET INCOME / SALES)

We also require our investments to exhibit strong profit margins. The Net Profit Margin is a measure of how much profit a company has left over after paying all of its expenses, including interest and taxes. It is either displayed as a metric in financial accounts, or can be calculated easily by dividing the Net Income by Sales.

Net Profit Margin provides an indication of company strength. A company with a small Net Profit Margin has little buffer against adverse market conditions that might quickly send the company into loss-making territory. We require a strong Net Profit Margin of 15% or above in every year for the last five years.

FINANCIAL LEVERAGE (TOTAL ASSETS / EQUITY)

A number of times, we have noted that Buffett prefers companies to generate good returns on equity while employing little or no debt. To screen for this characteristic we will use a metric called 'Financial Leverage', which is calculated as Total Assets divided by Equity. We are interested in the most recent number, or that for the last financial year where a more recent reading is not available. A relatively high number, indicating lots of Assets and very little Equity, may indicate the company has taken on substantial debt.

To provide some context, earlier we worked out from the 2016 Apple accounts that Buffett bought Apple when it had Shareholders' Equity (Book Value) of $128,249m. Total

Assets listed on the Balance Sheet at that time amounted to $321,686m.[95] Thus the Financial Leverage of Apple when Buffett bought was $321,686m/$128,249m = 2.5. You will sometimes see this presented as a percentage, in which case 2.5 x 100% = 250%. At the time of writing, when Apple has become Buffett's biggest position, the Financial Leverage has increased to 3.74 or 374%.[94] Biogen had Financial Leverage of 2.04 or 204%[96] when Buffett bought.

We will use 4.00 or 400% as the maximum Financial Leverage for our screen. This enables us to capture high quality companies like Apple and Biogen but eliminates businesses with higher debt burdens.

When examining the requirements of the four Investor Profiles in Chapter 2, you may recall that *Investor D*, the landlord seeking to diversify returns, already has a property portfolio that was built using debt and leverage. The landlord's equity constituted 20% of the entire portfolio, meaning that the leverage employed is 5.0 or 500% (Assets of 100 / Equity of 20). In this case, *Investor D* should opt for companies with lower Financial Leverage ratios than those recommended here, so as to reduce the impact of leverage on the portfolio overall.

CURRENT RATIO (CURRENT ASSETS / CURRENT LIABILITIES)

The Current Ratio is used to determine the ability of a company to meet its current liabilities. It is calculated as Total Current Assets divided by Total Current Liabilities. We are interested in the most recent Current Ratio, or that for the last financial year where a more recent reading is not available. A ratio below 1.0 indicates that the company has fewer current assets than current liabilities and thus might struggle to meet its obligations in the coming months. To protect against this, our screen requires that the Current Ratio be above 1.0.

Banks and insurance companies record short- and long-term assets and liabilities in a different way. A Current Ratio is therefore not available for those kinds of businesses and may be ignored as a screen requirement.

AN UPWARD SLOPING PRICE CHART OVER THE LAST 10 YEARS

We want to buy stocks that have a proven track record of translating returns on equity into added value for shareholders. The stocks we buy should therefore exhibit charts with relative linearity in their trend, rising upwards from left to right over a 10-year period, or longer. We don't want stocks with a share price that has gone nowhere for prolonged periods, or stocks which swing all over the place. Of course, we must allow for occasional consolidations and market corrections. Despite such falls, which are often market-wide, great companies will exhibit solid growth in their share prices over time.

ENSURE THAT YOU UNDERSTAND THE BUSINESS

Introduced in *Investment Principle 1: Simple is Better*, you must ensure that you understand the business you are buying. Buffett purchases only businesses that he understands and can reasonably conclude will still be doing well 10-20 years from now, businesses like Apple, Coca-Cola, Gillette, American Express, Visa, Wells Fargo and Kraft Heinz.

Taking what we have learned so far throughout this book, let's now pull all of the principles, mechanisms, metrics, calculations and rules together in one place, before taking definitive action and screening for investment opportunities.

CHAPTER 11:
BRINGING IT ALL TOGETHER

Before you start creating investment goals, screening for stocks, examining investment opportunities and assessing your theoretical return at an overall portfolio level, let's bring together everything you've learned so far so that it is fresh in your mind and ready to implement.

INVESTMENT PRINCIPLE 1:
SIMPLE IS BETTER
Look for simple businesses that you understand, good returns on equity and a consistent track record

The Investor's Solution uses only a few simple metrics that are easy to understand and easy to find or calculate. Those metrics are used to power two simple equations that determine your theoretical short- and long-term returns. Return on Equity is built into the core of both equations; it is the fuel for your compound growth engine. Invest in companies that you understand and can reasonably conclude will still be doing well 10-20 years from now.

INVESTMENT PRINCIPLE 2:
ANYONE CAN DO IT
All you need is a little time, a little money and the commitment to take action

The inputs for *The Investor's Solution* are widely available and cost-free. Once located, they can be used within the short- and long-term equations with little investment of time or effort. You do not need a high IQ to be able to understand the input metrics or the equation outputs. And you've learned that, using compounding, you can achieve great returns over long time periods even when starting with a small amount of money. There are really no barriers that prevent you from becoming financially free and wealthy.

INVESTMENT PRINCIPLE 3:
OWN PART OF A BUSINESS NOT A STOCK
Don't speculate on fleeting price fluctuations, think of your investments like purchases of productive assets, which compound their returns over time

"I bought a business today" gives a crucially different perspective on your investment versus, *"I bought a stock today."* By thinking of an investment as a productive asset, you remove the tendency to follow fleeting price fluctuations and avoid the trap of being influenced by short-term news headlines.

INVESTMENT PRINCIPLE 4:
HOLD FOR A LONG TIME
Before buying a stock, ask yourself whether you'd be perfectly happy to hold your investment if the market shut down for ten years

Make your money based on inactivity. You can achieve fantastic returns over long timeframes, even when starting small. The longer you hold, the bigger the payoff, and Buffett uses the power of compounding to let his investments grow and grow. He will only sell if a business he has purchased fundamentally changes and the expected returns are no longer likely to materialise.

INVESTMENT MECHANISM 1:
RETURN ON EQUITY
Return on Equity is the fuel for our compound growth engine, seek out companies with consistently high ROEs

If a business does well, the stock price eventually follows. The key to above-average short- and long-term returns is a high ROE. The higher the ROE, the higher your returns are likely to be.

As a minimum, the ROE must match or exceed your *Target CAGR*. To ensure our screen is not circumvented by fluctuations in the ROE, we added more rigour to this rule. First, we require that the average ROE over the last five years exceeds the *Target CAGR*. Next, to ensure that the ROE is not falling over time, we require that the ROE exceeds the *Target CAGR* in each of the three most recent years.

STOCK SCREEN RULE 1:
ROE must consistently match or exceed the Target CAGR

STOCK SCREEN RULE 1a:
Average ROE for last five years must exceed the
Target CAGR

STOCK SCREEN RULE 1b:
ROE must exceed the Target CAGR in each of the
three most recent years

INVESTMENT MECHANISM 2:
PRICE
Buy at a price that enables you to realise above-
average returns

Price is what you pay but value is what you get. You cannot simply look for companies that generate above-average returns on equity - no stock is worth an infinite price. Instead you must identify high-quality businesses that generate above-average ROEs and wait for Mr. Market to offer them to you at compelling prices.

STOCK SCREEN RULE 2:
The P/B ratio must be 20.0 or below

INVESTMENT MECHANISM 3:
COMPOUND GROWTH
Accelerate your returns by utilising the most powerful
tool in an investor's arsenal - compound growth

Compounding is the key to Buffett's wealth and success. It sits at the very heart of his approach. Earning consistent, above-average returns on a capital base that is ever increasing accelerates your path to wealth and freedom like nothing else.

INVESTMENT MECHANISM 4:
CAPITAL ALLOCATION
Seek out companies that retain the majority of their earnings and reinvest them for future growth

You want your companies to retain and reinvest as much of their earnings as possible, fuelling the compound growth machine that will make you wealthy. The higher the Earnings Retention Rate the higher the returns. Avoid companies that retain less than 60% of their earnings as this limits the possibility of future growth.

STOCK SCREEN RULE 3:
The Earnings Retention Rate must be consistently 60% or more, or the Payout Ratio consistently 40% or less

STOCK SCREEN RULE 4:
Current Market Capitalisation must exceed $1 billion

STOCK SCREEN RULE 5:
Five year average Sales growth of 5% or more per annum

STOCK SCREEN RULE 6:
Five year average Earnings per Share (EPS) growth of 10% or more per annum

STOCK SCREEN RULE 7:
Net Profit Margin (Net Income/Sales) consistently above 15% in each of the last 5 years

STOCK SCREEN RULE 8:
Financial Leverage (Assets/Equity) less than 4.00 or less than 400% (currently and/or last year)

STOCK SCREEN RULE 9:
Current Ratio (Current Assets/Current Liabilities) above 1.0 (currently and/or last year)

STOCK SCREEN RULE 10:
An upward-sloping share price chart over the last ten years

STOCK SCREEN RULE 11:
Acknowledge whether or not you understand the business

THE INVESTOR'S SHORT-TERM RETURN

Investor's Short-Term Return = ROE / P/B

If we were to examine the short-term return in isolation, we would want the ROE to be as high as possible and the P/B ratio to be as low as possible. However, we must balance the short-term return with the long-term return in order to meet our overall goal. For instance, we may well be willing to accept a low short-term return if that return grows rapidly and results in a very high return 10 to 30 years down the line. That being said, we would never want to accept a short-term return approaching zero, so there must be a minimum accepted limit. Very low starting returns increase the risk that we will never realise our long-term aspirations, so we established 5% as the minimum short-term return we would accept, being half of the short-term return of our aspirational curve.

STOCK SCREEN RULE 12:
The Investor's Short-Term Return must be 5.0% or above

THE INVESTOR'S RETURN CURVE

The Investor's Return Curve connects the short- and long-term returns. It enables us to determine the theoretical return achievable from a prospective investment at any point in time. Here we must ensure that the theoretical return expected at our *Target Timeframe* exceeds the *Target CAGR*. So as to build in a performance buffer, should things not end up going to plan, we must enhance this rule. We require that the theoretical return at the *Target Timeframe* exceeds 1.1 x the *Target CAGR*. So, if you were *Investor C* and had the ambition to achieve a return of 15% over 15 years, you must check that *The Investor's Return Curve* indicates a return of 16.5% (15.0% x 1.1) or more after 15 years. This check will be described in more detail in the next chapter.

STOCK SCREEN RULE 13:
The return must match or exceed 1.1x the Target CAGR at your Target Timeframe

THE INVESTOR'S LONG-TERM RETURN

Investor's Long-Term Return

= ROE x Earnings Retention Rate

If we were to examine the long-term return in isolation, we would want both the ROE and the Earnings Retention Rate to be as high as possible. In some cases, we may identify a company with a short-term return higher than the long-term return, resulting in a downward sloping curve. Generally, we should avoid downward sloping curves since this implies that our CAGR will fall with each passing year.

The criteria for ensuring an upward sloping curve is simply that the long-term return is the same as, or higher, than the *Target CAGR*. So as to build in a performance buffer, should things not end up going to plan, we require that the long-term return must exceed 1.2 x the *Target CAGR*.

STOCK SCREEN RULE 14:
The Investor's Long-Term Return must match or exceed 1.2x the Target CAGR

We've reached the point at which it is time to take action. In the next chapter we'll walk through everything we've learned step by step, and screen for investment opportunities.

CHAPTER 12:
TAKING ACTION

CHAPTER SUMMARY
12.1 DEFINE YOUR DREAM
12.2 DETERMINE YOUR GOAL
12.3 DEFINE YOUR TARGET CAGR
12.4 SCREEN
12.5 ANALYSE
12.6 INVEST: PORTFOLIO CONSTRUCTION
12.7 MANAGING YOUR PORTFOLIO

What follows is a step-by-step guide that provides a full and clear plan. We'll cover everything from creating your first stock screen, assessing those stocks against your *Target CAGR* at your *Target Timeframe*, identifying potential investment candidates, determining how they fit into a wider portfolio of assets, and the management of that portfolio going forward.

The first time you read through these instructions you may feel a little daunted, but the best way to improve is a little at a time. By following the process step-by-step you will quickly identify investments that move you towards your goals.

During the screening and analysis process we will use the free 'Goal Planner & Stock Screen' spreadsheet which can be downloaded from *theinvestorssolution.com* website. When writing this book and creating this tool, I did not want to make this a 'black box' solution, with all calculations and logic hidden from you, the reader. Instead I wanted to publish material that was completely transparent, enabling you to drill down into the calculations and to see how everything works.

Instead of stepping through the plan in an academic manner, we will inject some life into it, making it more realistic by stepping into the shoes of *Investor B*, who we met earlier in the book. In this way, rather than focusing on an investor at the very start of their journey, or an investor nearing retirement, we can examine a profile that sits quite nicely in the middle of the two, providing context for a wide range of possible life stages.

Principally looking for security and peace of mind, *Investor B* has a moderate salary, modest savings, and plans to retire in 20 years. As we proceed through the steps below, we'll examine *Investor B*'s thought process and decision-making, explaining any actions taken as clearly as possible.

Ultimately it is up to you to understand your own income, savings and retirement requirements and to balance all of these to create your personal goal and return targets. But this case study should make those thought processes more relatable and accessible throughout.

12.1
DEFINE YOUR DREAM

INVESTOR B

"*I am the parent of two young kids. I love spending time with them, playing and watching them grow. I want to provide a comfortable future for my family, but I don't want to sacrifice our time together or our quality of life. I would like my kids to have a wide variety of experiences, like clubs, sports, travels, and I want to be able to put them through college. I'd like to retire as soon as possible, with the aspiration that I retire 20 years from now, at age 55. I'm a little frustrated that the current low interest rates mean my pension and modest savings aren't growing. I'm not sure how big my pension pot will be when I retire or what income it will provide. I want to take more control of my investments and take my future into my own hands.*"

"*My dream is to secure financial freedom for myself and for my family so that we can live comfortably and enjoy experiences together without having to worry about money.*"

12.2
DETERMINE YOUR GOAL

Opening the '*Goal Planner & Stock Screen*' spreadsheet, and navigating to the '*Goal Planner*' tab, *Investor B* enters the following information into the yellow input cells:

ENTRY FIELDS A-K

A. Your current age: "*35.*"

B. Current gross annual income: *"My current gross income, before any tax is deducted, is 40,000. This is comfortable for me but isn't going to make me super rich."*

C. Annual inflation rate or estimated increase in your income per annum: *"I expect my salary to grow modestly over time. The annual rate of inflation is currently 2% and I expect my salary to rise slightly faster than this, by an additional 1%. This gives a total estimated increase in income of 3% per annum."*

D. Current savings balance available for investment: *"I have 20,000 already in my pension and I will use this full amount to invest and to generate returns."*

E. Additional cash installments you plan to add to investments per annum: *"I plan to set aside 10% of my salary to invest each year. In the first year that equates to an additional 4,000."*

F. Estimated increase in the size of the cash installments you will make each year: *"Since I plan to put aside 10% of my salary, my installments will automatically increase at the same 3% rate that my income does, matching the rate I entered in Field C. So, in Year 2 my installments will have grown by 3% from 4,000 to 4,120, representing 10% of my Year 2 salary of 41,200."*

G. Retirement income you know you'll receive outside of your investments: *"I don't have any other personal arrangements that will provide me with an income in retirement, but I am likely to receive government benefits of 1,000 per annum."*

H: Estimated annual increase in known retirement income: *"The 1,000 of government benefits I expect to* *receive when I retire are likely to grow a rate of 2% per annum in order to take into account inflation. So, in my second year of retirement the benefits I receive from the government should have increased to 1,020, and so on."*

I: Desired goal/retirement age: *"I would ideally like to retire at age 55."*

J: Number of years of income required: *"I plan to live to at least one hundred years old, so would require the pension to pay income for at least 45 years."*

K: Income replacement %: *"As shown in the 'Chart Details' table below the yellow input fields, in the year prior to retirement my salary should have grown from 40,000 to 70,140 (at the 3% rate estimated in Field C). In the year I retire, this will have increased a further 3%, so my final salary will be 72,244 (not shown in the table). During retirement my expenditures will be lower than at present. I will have paid off the mortgage on my house and my commute costs will be lower. As a result, I estimate that I will need only 75% of my final salary to live on without compromising my family's quality of life. This will give me a retirement income of 75% x 72,244 = 54,183 in my first year of retirement. 1,000 of this income will be fulfilled with the 1,000 of government benefits (Field G), so the remaining 53,183 will need to come out of my Investment Balance."*

GRAPHICAL OUTPUT

Investor B hasn't yet filled in *Fields L* and *M*, which are the estimated returns that need to be generated pre- and post-goal. Before doing so, *Investor B* makes a cursory examination of the chart output at the top of the *Goal Planner* tab. This is reproduced below in Figure 69. Since *Fields L* and *M* are set to 0%, the value of the *Investment Balance Pre-Goal Date* (rising blue line) reflects only the

FIGURE 69: BALANCE OF TOTAL SAVINGS AT AGE 55 (INVESTMENT

1. GOAL PLANNER
OOPS! This plan will only provide income to age 56. You'll need
Income Withdrawals
Investment Balance Pre-Goal
Blue line rising to 127,481
Out of money
35 37 39 41 43 45 47 49 51 53 55 57 59 61 63 65 67 69
ENTER AMOUNTS INTO YELLOW INP
STEP 1: NOW
A. Your current age
35
B. Current gross annual income (before tax is taken off)
40,000
C. Annual inflation rate or estimated increase in your income per annum (%)
3.0%
D. Current savings balance available for investment
20,000
E. Additional cash installments you plan add to investments per annum
4,000
F. Estimated increase in the size of the cash installments you will make each year (%)
3.0%
STEP 2: AT GOAL
G. Retirement income you receive outside of your
H. Estimated annual known retirement inco
I. Desired goal/ret
J. Number of years of income conservative and pick a long ti
K. Income replacement % (H your final salary do you want to
Years to goal/

money saved into the pension over the years.

"Between my original savings balance of 20,000 and the additional cash installments I made over time, by age 55 I will have accumulated an Investment Balance Pre-Goal Date of 127,481, shown by the rising blue line in the chart.

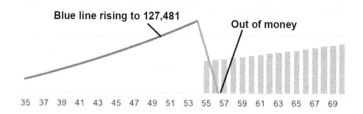

PLUS ADDITIONAL CASH INSTALLMENTS
BALANCE PRE-GOAL DATE)

to make some adjustments.

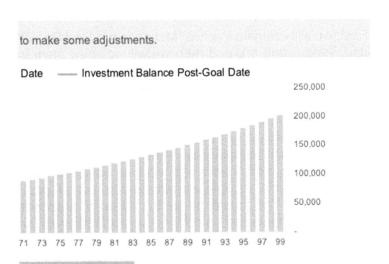

Date ----- Investment Balance Post-Goal Date

UT CELLS

/RETIREMENT STEP 3: REQUIRED RETURNS

know you'll investments	**1,000**	L. Minimum required CAGR post-goal (%)
increase in me in G (%)	**2.00%**	M. Minimum required CAGR pre-goal (%)
irement age	**55**	
required (be me horizon)	**45**	
ow much of survive on?)	**75%**	
Retirement	20	

L. Minimum required CAGR post-goal (%)	**0.00%**
M. Minimum required CAGR pre-goal (%)	**0.00%**

Since I need to take out 53,183 in my first year of retirement, 54,789 (55,809-1,020) in the second year, and 56,443 (57,483-1,040), I will run out of money in just over 2 years (falling line to "Out of money"). My investments have certainly got their work cut out for them!"

12.3
DEFINE YOUR TARGET CAGR

First, we will estimate the two "*Minimum required CAGR*" fields (*Fields L* and *M*), and then we will optimise them in order to arrive at an *Investment Balance* that is sufficiently big to satisfy all subsequent *Income Withdrawals*.

L. Minimum required CAGR post-goal: "*5%.*"

The first CAGR we will enter is the post-goal CAGR in *Field L*. The 'goal' for many is retirement, so we will be conservative in our estimation of *Field L* so as to provide a prudent and stable income stream in the period post-goal/retirement. This could be in the form of dividends received from blue-chip stocks, interest received on Treasury bonds or income from an annuity. The stock market has, on aggregate, generated an average return for investors in excess of 7% per annum over many decades, so we will use this as a benchmark. For prudence, however, we will lower our expectation to 5% per annum.

M. Minimum required CAGR pre-goal: "*20%.*"

The final field to complete is the pre-goal CAGR. Here we will experiment by entering different rates until we find **the smallest rate** that enables us to meet our objectives. There are two key areas to keep an eye on here. First, the rate you settle on must result in the *Investment Balance Pre-Goal Date* providing you with sufficient income post-goal, for sufficient time. If you plan to live to 100 years old, you cannot pick a rate that leads to you running out of money before then. Second, if you wish to have money left over at the end of your post-goal time horizon, perhaps because you might live longer than expected, or because you wish to provide your family with an inheritance, the *Investment Balance Post-Goal Date* must exceed zero at the end of your post-goal time horizon.

"I started estimating the pre-goal CAGR at the same rate as the post-goal rate, being 5%. The result significantly undershot my expectations since the projections showed that I would run out of money far too soon. I gradually increased the pre-goal rate. At 19% the projection showed that I would still run out of money too early, at 93 years of age. However, a CAGR of 20% generated an Investment Balance Pre-Goal that was big enough to fund all of my planned Income Withdrawals and provided a residual pot of money (733,793) at age 100. While I certainly experienced the temptation to enter even higher rates into Field M, which resulted in me joining Mr. Buffett among the richest in the world, I remained practical and disciplined, opting for the smallest rate that enabled me to meet my objectives."

"Under these projections, in the first year of retirement my 'Start of Year Investment Balance' will be 1,626,316, as shown in the 'Chart Details' table. In that year I would generate a post-goal return of 5% on that balance of 81,316 (5% x 1,626,316). Subtracting the 53,183 of required income calculated above, my Year End Investment Balance will increase by 81,316 - 53,183 = 28,132, ending at 1,654,449."

So, *Investor B* has determined the minimum CAGR required in order to retire at 55 years of age. A CAGR of 20% enables the *Investment Balance* to grow to sufficient size that it covers all *Income Withdrawals* and leaves enough residual money to fund retirement if *Investor B* lives longer than expected, or to provide an inheritance for the family. This is illustrated in Figure 70.

FIGURE 70: PRE- AND POST-GOAL CAGRS INVESTMENT BALANCE SUFFICIENT TO COVER PROVIDE A

1. GOAL PLANNER

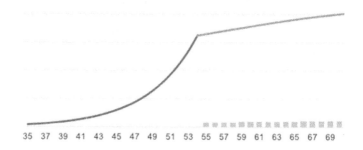

Success! Your 'Investment Balance Pre-Goal Date' covers all income Wi

▨▨▨ Income Withdrawals   ▬▬ Investment Balance Pre-Goal

35 37 39 41 43 45 47 49 51 53 55 57 59 61 63 65 67 69

ENTER AMOUNTS INTO YELLOW INP

STEP 1: NOW		STEP 2: AT GOAL
A. Your current age	35	G. Retirement income you receive outside of your
B. Current gross annual income (before tax is taken off)	40,000	H. Estimated annual known retirement inco
C. Annual inflation rate or estimated increase in your income per annum (%)	3.0%	I. Desired goal/ret
D. Current savings balance available for investment	20,000	J. Number of years of income conservative and pick a long ti
E. Additional cash installments you plan add to investments per annum	4,000	K. Income replacement % (H your final salary do you want to
F. Estimated increase in the size of the cash installments you will make each year (%)	3.0%	Years to goal/

THAT PROVIDE INVESTOR B WITH AN ALL INCOME WITHDRAWALS AND RESIDUAL POT

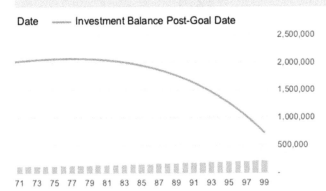

thdrawals and at age 100 you have a residual investment balance of $733,793.

Date —— Investment Balance Post-Goal Date

2,500,000
2,000,000
1,500,000
1,000,000
500,000

71 73 75 77 79 81 83 85 87 89 91 93 95 97 99

UT CELLS

/RETIREMENT STEP 3: REQUIRED RETURNS

know you'll investments	1,000	L. Minimum required CAGR post-goal (%)	5.00%
increase in me in G (%)	2.00%	M. Minimum required CAGR pre-goal (%)	20.00%
irement age	55		
required (be me horizon)	45		
ow much of survive on?)	75%		
Retirement	20		

We know that achieving a compound annual growth rate of 20% percent per annum is possible because we've seen Warren Buffett do it for an extraordinary six decades. Now we just need to find the stocks that will get us there.

12.4
SCREEN

STOCK SCREEN TOOLS/SERVICES

Stock screeners are online tools or services that enable you to create and apply multiple stock selection criteria to a market, automatically filtering an entire universe of stocks down to a handful that meet your particular requirements. It saves an awful lot of time compared to performing the analysis manually and is worth its weight in gold if you can find a good screen tool/service use. There are a number of free tools out there, including on *Yahoo Finance*, *Investing.com*, and the *Financial Times*, which has good one called "*Equity Screener.*"

In general, none of the free tools provide you with sufficient granularity to create all of the rules necessary for *The Investor's Solution*, but they can get you 90% of the way there in a quick and cost-effective manner. They are a great way to go through the motions, learn the approach and improve your understanding, before committing to a paid tool at a later date, if desired.

A great paid tool will accelerate all of the above, enabling you to save an awful lot of time and effort. Since stock screen providers, and the services they offer, are constantly changing, head to *theinvestorssolution.com* for my latest recommendations.

To take into account both circumstances I have created two toolkits for you to use within the *Goal Planner & Stock*

Screen spreadsheet.

The first set of tool tabs are labelled '*CORE*'. These incorporate the minimum level of information required to calculate the *Investor's Short-Term Return*, *Investor's Long-Term Return* and the *Target CAGR* at the *Target Timeframe*. Free stock screen tools will usually provide enough information and granularity to fulfill the *CORE* approach. The second set of tool tabs are labelled '*SUPPLEMENTARY*'. This is the preferred level of detail, taking into account the financial health of the company by incorporating our complete list of screen rules.

If you are not using a screening tool and are perhaps sourcing your information manually instead, you could use the '*CORE*' tabs as the preliminary screen to create a shortlist of prospective investment candidates, and then subsequently use the '*SUPPLEMENTARY*' tabs to add more detail for stocks of particular interest.

Bringing our entire list of stock screen rules together, let's work through each criterion step-by-step and run our first stock screen.

INSTRUCTIONS FOR USING THE 'CORE' APPROACH

NOTE: Throughout the Goal Planner & Stock Screen spreadsheet, yellow cells indicate 'input' cells, which you will be required to populate as instructed.

Turning to the *Goal Planner & Stock Screen* spreadsheet, navigate to the tab named '*Data Inputs - CORE*'.

FIGURE 71: THE DATA INPUTS – CORE TAB

DATA INPUTS - CORE (THE MINIMUM REQUIRED)

YELLOW CELL = INPUT CELL

Company Name	INVESTMENT MECHANISM 1: ROE — STOCK SCREEN RULE 1 — ROE %	INVESTMENT MECHANISM 2: PRICE — STOCK SCREEN RULE 2 — P/B (Latest)	INVESTMENT MECHANISM 3 — CAPITAL ALLOCATION — STOCK SCREEN RULE 3 (Depending on whether your screen gives you Earnings Retention Rate, or a Payout Ratio, or EPS and DPS data, only paste one set of data below...)				INVESTMENT MECHANISM 4: Calculated Earnings Retention Rate (%)	STOCK SCREEN RULE 10 — Price Pattern	STOCK SCREEN RULE 11 — Do You Understand the Business?
			Earnings Retention Rate (%) — Here...	Payout Ratio (%) — Or here...	Earnings Per Share (EPS) ($)	Dividends Per Share (DPS) ($) — Or here...			
1 Align Technology Inc	27.1%	7.3		0.0%			100.0%	YES	NO
2 Apple Inc	45.3%	19.5		24.5%			75.5%	YES	YES
3 Biogen Inc	35.8%	3.4	100.0%				100.0%	YES	YES
4 Booking Holdings Inc	38.6%	16.5					100.0%	YES	YES
5 Copart Inc	32.5%	8.2		0.0%	4.00	0.00	100.0%	YES	YES
6 Credit Acceptance	34.7%	3.7		0.0%			100.0%	YES	YES
7 Edwards Lifesciences	25.6%	10.7		0.0%			100.0%	YES	YES
8 Evertec Inc	59.7%	7.9			1.16	0.20	82.8%	YES	NO
9 Factset Research Systems	54.2%	15.7		29.6%			70.4%	YES	YES
10 Kla	74.3%	12.7		38.3%			61.7%	YES	YES
11 Lam Research	34.6%	9.7		0.0%			100.0%	NO	YES
12 Microsoft	35.4%	13.0		34.4%			65.6%	YES	YES
13 Nvidia	32.3%	17.2	88.2%				88.2%	YES	YES
14 Sei Investments Co	28.6%	4.5	77.9%				77.9%	NO	YES
15 Texas Pacific Land Trust	112.0%	10.0	83.0%				83.0%	YES	YES
16 Trex Inc	46.5%	16.3					100.0%	YES	YES
17 T. Rowe Price Inc	27.7%	4.2		39.9%			60.1%	YES	NO
18 Visa Inc	28.5%	13.8			5.46	1.00	81.7%	YES	YES

CORE SCREEN - STEP 1

INVESTMENT MECHANISM 1:
RETURN ON EQUITY
STOCK SCREEN RULE 1
ROE must consistently match or exceed the Target CAGR

We already calculated the *Target CAGR* percentage in the *Goal Planner* and will use this as our minimum ROE threshold. The stripped-down CORE approach requires that we enter a single value to represent a company's ROE. If you are using a screening service/tool you might be able to create a metric that is the 5-year average ROE. If so, this is the preferred value to use. Where this value is not available you can instead use the ROE for the previous year as a gauge. In either case you will need to check that the ROE exceeds the *Target CAGR* in each of the three preceding years to ensure that we meet our rule's requirement of consistently matching or exceeding the *Target CAGR*. When you have identified one or more companies with a sufficiently high ROE, **record the 5-year average ROE, or the prior year ROE where the 5-year average is not available, together with the company name into the yellow cells on the left-hand side of the input table**.

CORE SCREEN - STEP 2

INVESTMENT MECHANISM 2:
PRICE
STOCK SCREEN RULE 2
The P/B ratio must be 20.0 or below

Include a rule within your screen to limit results to companies that have a P/B ratio of 20.0 or below. If you are performing a manual screening process, take the companies you identified in *STEP 1* and eliminate any that have a P/B above 20.0. **Record the P/B ratios for successful companies into the table alongside their Name and ROE**.

CORE SCREEN - STEP 3

INVESTMENT MECHANISM 4:
CAPITAL ALLOCATION
STOCK SCREEN RULE 3
The Earnings Retention Rate must be consistently 60% or more, or the Payout Ratio consistently 40% or less

As described in Chapter 6, there are three methods we can use to determine the Earnings Retention Rate. Whether using a stock screen tool/service, or assessing company data manually, the data provided will take three forms:

a) In the form of the desired Earnings Retention Rate;
b) The opposite of the Earnings Retention Rate, which is the Payout Ratio;
c) Or as base metrics of Earnings per Share (EPS) and Dividend per Share (DPS) which require us to calculate the Earnings Retention Rate ourselves.

The '*Data Inputs – CORE*' table can accommodate all three types of information and there are three clearly labelled sections to show you where to provide *either* Earnings Retention Rate, *or* Payout Ratio, *or* the EPS/DPS information. **Depending on which section you populate, the table will automatically make the right calculation**

for you and create a master Earnings Retention Rate number on the right-hand side. It is important not to enter data into more than one of these sections. If you happen to have EPS and DPS data for a company, and you also have that company's Earnings Retention Rate, pick only one set of data to enter into the table so that the spreadsheet doesn't experience a calculation error. The table is pre-populated with examples to demonstrate this approach.

If you are able to do so, the ideal scenario is to create a rule in your stock screen that specifies that your stocks must have an Earnings Retention Rate of 60% or more. If your screen tool/service does not provide Earnings Retention Rate, but does provide Payout Ratio, instead create a rule that requires your stocks to have a Payout Ratio of 40% or less. If your screen tool/service has neither of these options, create two rules that require the EPS to be greater or equal to zero, and the DPS to be greater or equal to zero. This will result in the screen delivering the raw EPS and DPS data that you need to paste into the *Data Inputs – CORE* table.

If you are performing a manual screening process, take the companies remaining after *STEPS 1* and *2*, and either eliminate any with an Earnings Retention Ratio below 60% or a payout Ratio greater than 40%. If those two measures aren't readily available, you can also record the raw EPS and DPS data in the spreadsheet and allow the table to calculate the Earnings Retention Rate for you.

CORE SCREEN - STEP 4

STOCK SCREEN RULE 10
An upward-sloping share price chart over the last ten years

Once your list of stocks has been filtered down to a manageable list that meets all of the quantitative rules above, it is time to check that the stock price has demonstrated a track record of increasing over time. The stocks we buy should exhibit charts with relative linearity in their trend, rising consistently from left to right over a 10-year period or longer. We don't want stocks with a share price that has gone nowhere for prolonged periods, or stocks which swing all over the place. Eliminate stocks form the list that do not satisfy your criteria. **Record the stocks that meet your criteria with a "YES" in the 'STOCK SCREEN RULE 10' column**.

CORE SCREEN - STEP 5

STOCK SCREEN RULE 11
Ensure that you understand the business

Now take some time to familiarise yourself with the business. Make sure you understand what it does. **If you are comfortable that you understand the business, record a "YES" in the 'STOCK SCREEN RULE 11' column**.

CORE SCREEN - STEP 6

REVIEW THE LIST TO ENSURE ALL REMAINING STOCKS PASS ALL RULES

Even though you might initially paste a large number of stocks into these input tables, your key role is to ensure that you eliminate any stocks from the sheet that do not pass your required screen rules. For example, you might have been using a screen tool/service which enabled you to filter the entire market down to stocks with ROEs consistently above the *Target CAGR*, and which have P/B ratios of 20.0

or less. However, you might have been unable to get the screen tool/service to provide an Earnings Retention Rate, opting instead to request EPS and DPS greater than, or equal to zero. In this instance you will have pasted a list of stocks into the table that will have passed the ROE and P/B screens but now require you to manually check that the Earnings Retention Rate is sufficient. Your objective is to end up with a list of stocks that pass *all CORE* screen rules before moving on to the next step. So, if your minimum required ROE is 20%, ensure there are no stocks with ROEs lower than this. If a stock has a P/B above 20.0, eliminate it. If stocks have an Earnings Retention Rate below 60%, eliminate them too.

Excellent work. The data you have pasted into the *Data Inputs - CORE* table feed automatically into the sheet named '*Analysis – CORE*'.

INSTRUCTIONS FOR USING THE 'SUPPLEMENTARY' APPROACH

The steps involved in undertaking the *SUPPLEMENTARY* approach are very similar to those listed for the *CORE* approach, but with additional criteria applied. The *SUPPLEMENTARY* approach will be much easier to populate using a stock screening tool/service.

Turning to the *Goal Planner & Stock Screen* spreadsheet, navigate to the tab named '*Data Inputs - SUPPLEMENTARY*'.

FIGURE 72: THE DATA INPUTS – SUPPLEMENTARY TAB – TABLE PART A
DATA INPUTS - SUPPLEMENTARY (A MORE IDEAL, FULLER SET OF FUNDAMENTALS)

YELLOW CELL = INPUT CELL

Company Name	INVESTMENT MECHANISM 1: RETURN ON EQUITY				INVESTMENT MECHANISM 2: PRICE	INVESTMENT MECHANISM 4: CAPITAL ALLOCATION				
	STOCK SCREEN RULE 1a	STOCK SCREEN RULE 1			STOCK SCREEN RULE 2	STOCK SCREEN RULE 3 (Depending on whether your screen gives you Earnings Retention Rate, or a Payout Ratio, or EPS)				
			STOCK SCREEN RULE 1b			Here...	Or here...	Or here...		
	ROE % (5y Avg)	ROE % (3y Ago)	ROE % (2y Ago)	ROE % (Last Year)	P/B (Latest)	Earnings Retention Rate (%)	Payout Ratio (%)	Earnings Per Share (EPS) ($)	Dividends Per Share (DPS) ($)	Calculated Earnings Retention Rate (%)
1 Align Technology Inc	27.1%	29.4%	33.3%	34.1%	7.3	0.0%				100.0%
2 Apple Inc	45.3%	36.9%	50.6%	55.9%	19.5		24.5%			75.5%
3 Biogen Inc	35.8%	30.0%	34.7%	44.6%	3.4					100.0%
4 Booking Holdings Inc	38.6%	35.3%	39.4%	65.9%	16.5	100.0%		4.00		100.0%
5 Copart Inc	32.5%	42.1%	31.8%	35.3%	8.2		0.0%		0.00	100.0%
6 Credit Acceptance	34.7%	42.1%	32.6%	30.2%	3.7		0.0%			100.0%
7 Edwards Lifesciences	25.6%	31.5%	24.2%	28.8%	10.7		0.0%			100.0%
8 Evertec Inc	59.7%	44.2%	48.5%	43.2%	7.9	85.5%		1.16	0.20	82.8%
9 Factset Research Systems	54.2%	48.0%	53.9%	58.3%	15.7		29.6%			70.4%
10 Kia	74.3%	91.9%	81.0%	54.0%	12.7		38.3%			61.7%
11 Lam Research	34.6%	44.7%	39.2%	45.7%	9.7		0.0%	5.46		100.0%
12 Microsoft	35.4%	35.5%	42.6%	40.1%	13.0		34.4%			65.6%
13 Nvidia	32.3%	44.0%	32.9%	26.0%	17.2	88.2%				88.2%
14 Sei Investments Co	28.6%	28.2%	32.9%	30.0%	4.5	77.9%				77.9%
15 Texas Pacific Land Trust	112.0%	127.2%	120.0%	84.2%	10.0	83.0%				83.0%
16 Trex Inc	46.5%	53.1%	46.9%	36.5%	16.3		0.0%			100.0%
17 T. Rowe Price Inc	27.7%	28.3%	30.5%	31.4%	4.2		39.9%			60.1%
18 Visa Inc	28.5%	23.8%	35.7%	40.3%	13.8				1.00	81.7%

SUPPLEMENTARY SCREEN - STEP 1

INVESTMENT MECHANISM 1: RETURN ON EQUITY

We already calculated the *Target CAGR* percentage in the *Goal Planner* and will use this as our minimum ROE threshold. To ensure our screen is not circumvented by fluctuations in ROE over time, we add a little more rigour to the rule by splitting it further.

STOCK SCREEN RULE 1: ROE must consistently match or exceed the Target CAGR, is broken down into:

STOCK SCREEN RULE 1a
Average ROE for last five years must exceed the Target CAGR

To ensure a consistently high ROE we require that the average ROE over the last 5 years exceeds the *Target CAGR*. **Record the 5-year average in the table**.

STOCK SCREEN RULE 1b
ROE must exceed the Target CAGR in each of the three most recent years

To ensure that the ROE has not fallen below our threshold in recent years we require that the ROE exceeds the *Target CAGR* in each of the three most recent years. This will create three outputs, being the ROE 3 years ago, the ROE 2 years ago, and the ROE last year. **Record these values in the table**.

If your stock screen tool/service has been able to generate these fields, it has done the job of checking whether the ROE matches or exceeds the *Target CAGR* on a consistent basis. If not, you may still need to perform a manual check to ensure that the ROE does indeed meet the criteria required by these rules.

SUPPLEMENTARY SCREEN - STEP 2

INVESTMENT MECHANISM 2:
PRICE
STOCK SCREEN RULE 2
The P/B ratio must be 20.0 or below

As for the *CORE* approach, include a rule within your screen to limit results to companies that have a P/B ratio of 20.0 or below. **Record the P/B ratios for successful companies into the table alongside their Name and ROEs.**

SUPPLEMENTARY SCREEN - STEP 3

INVESTMENT MECHANISM 4:
CAPITAL ALLOCATION
STOCK SCREEN RULE 3
The Earnings Retention Rate must be consistently 60% or more, or the Payout Ratio consistently 40% or less

As for the *CORE* approach, there are a number of methods for calculating the Earnings Retention Rate. The data provided will take three forms:

a) In the form of the desired Earnings Retention Rate;
b) The opposite of the Earnings Retention Rate, which is the Payout Ratio;
c) Or as base metrics of Earnings per Share (EPS) and Dividend per Share (DPS) which require us to calculate the Earnings Retention Rate ourselves.

The *Data Inputs – SUPPLEMENTARY* table can accommodate all three types of information and there are three clearly labelled sections to show you where to provide *either* Earnings Retention Rate, *or* Payout Ratio, *or* the EPS/DPS information. **Depending on which section you populate, the table will automatically make the right calculation for you and create a master Earnings Retention Rate.** It is important not to enter data into more than one of these sections. If you happen to have EPS/DPS data for a company, and you also have that company's Earnings Retention Rate, pick only one to enter into the table so that the spreadsheet doesn't experience a calculation error. The table is pre-populated with examples to demonstrate this approach.

If you are able to do so, the ideal scenario is to create a rule in your stock screen that specifies that your stocks must have an Earnings Retention Rate of 60% or more. If your screen tool/service does not provide Earnings Retention Rate, but does provide Payout Ratio, instead create a rule that requires your stocks to have a Payout Ratio of 40% or lower. If your screen tool/service has neither of these options, create two rules that require the EPS to be greater or equal to zero, and the DPS to be greater or equal to zero. This will result in the screen delivering the raw EPS and DPS data that you need to paste into the *Data Inputs – SUPPLEMENTARY* table.

FIGURE 73: THE DATA INPUTS – SUPPLEMENTARY TAB – TABLE PART B

Company Name	SUPPLEMENTARY SCREEN RULES							
	Mkt Cap (USD millions) STOCK SCREEN RULE 4	Sales CAGR % STOCK SCREEN RULE 5	EPS CAGR % STOCK SCREEN RULE 6	Net Margin % STOCK SCREEN RULE 7	Assets/Equity % STOCK SCREEN RULE 8	Current Ratio STOCK SCREEN RULE 9	Price Pattern STOCK SCREEN RULE 10	Do You Understand the Business? STOCK SCREEN RULE 11
Align Technology Inc	23,324	25.9%	24.4%	17.8%	185.8	1.7	YES	NO
Apple Inc	1,667,679	7.3%	13.0%	21.8%	374.1	1.5	YES	YES
Biogen Inc	43,514	8.2%	21.5%	32.0%	204.1	1.7	YES	YES
Booking Holdings Inc	69,081	12.3%	19.5%	25.2%	360.7	1.8	YES	YES
Copart Inc	21,771	11.9%	26.3%	24.0%	143.3	2.4	YES	YES
Credit Acceptance	8,542	15.5%	22.5%	40.3%	315.2	n/a	YES	YES
Edwards Lifesciences	49,086	13.4%	28.4%	19.9%	156.4	3.3	YES	NO
Evertec Inc	2,254	6.1%	10.9%	19.2%	378.6	1.9	YES	YES
Factset Research Systems	13,135	9.3%	13.1%	23.9%	232.1	2.7	YES	NO
Kla	30,684	9.3%	16.1%	21.8%	338.8	2.4	YES	YES
Lam Research	55,014	13.8%	29.8%	20.7%	281.5	3.6	YES	NO
Microsoft	1,543,727	8.9%	20.3%	25.2%	254.7	2.5	YES	YES
Nvidia	261,104	18.5%	32.6%	25.7%	141.9	7.7	NO	NO
Sei Investments Co	7,659	5.4%	12.1%	27.3%	123.7	4.4	NO	YES
Texas Pacific Land Trust	4,301	54.8%	58.3%	64.9%	116.8	n/a	YES	YES
Trex Inc	8,091	13.7%	31.2%	16.2%	131.9	3.9	YES	YES
T. Rowe Price Inc	30,523	6.7%	13.9%	32.1%	131.4	n/a	YES	NO
Visa Inc	413,491	12.6%	15.1%	44.9%	209.2	1.6	YES	YES

SUPPLEMENTARY SCREEN - STEP 4

STOCK SCREEN RULE 4
Current Market Capitalisation must exceed $1 billion

Create a rule to include only companies that have a market capitalisation over $1 billion. **Record the current Market Capitalisation in the table**.

SUPPLEMENTARY SCREEN - STEP 5

STOCK SCREEN RULE 5
Five-year average Sales growth of 5% or more per annum

Create a rule that requires the Sales over the last 5 years to have grown by an average annual rate of 5% or more, often referred to as Sales CAGR. **Record the 5-year average growth rate in the table**.

SUPPLEMENTARY SCREEN - STEP 6

STOCK SCREEN RULE 6
Five-year average Earnings per Share (EPS) growth of 10% or more per annum

Create a rule that requires the Earnings over the last 5 years to have grown by an average annual rate of 10% or more, often referred to as Earnings CAGR or EPS CAGR. **Record the 5-year average growth rate in the table**.

SUPPLEMENTARY SCREEN - STEP 7

STOCK SCREEN RULE 7
Net Profit Margin (Net Income/Sales) consistently above 15% in each of the last 5 years

Create a rule that requires the Net Profit Margin, which is Net Income/Sales, to be 15% or above. To ensure this margin has been achieved on a consistent basis, we must examine the Net Profit Margin over the last 5 years, ensuring it exceeds our 15% threshold throughout. You may be able to create screen rules that do this for you, delivering the Net Profit Margin 5 years ago, 4 years ago, 3 years ago, 2 years ago, last year, and the 5-year average. In the table, **assuming the stock has consistently delivered a Net Profit Margin above 15% in each of the last 5 years, record the 5-year average in the table**.

SUPPLEMENTARY SCREEN - STEP 8

STOCK SCREEN RULE 8
Financial Leverage (Assets/Equity) less than 4.00 or less than 400% (currently and/or last year)

Depending on the tool/service used, Financial Leverage may be presented as a decimal, such as 4.00, or as a percentage, such as 400%. Create a rule that requires the Financial Leverage, which is Assets/Equity, to be less than 4.00 or 400% as appropriate. **Record the 'current' value as the preferred choice of metric, but you can also use the prior year number where a current value is not available**.

SUPPLEMENTARY SCREEN - STEP 9

STOCK SCREEN RULE 9
Current Ratio (Current Assets/Current Liabilities)
above 1.0 (currently and/or last year)

Create a rule that requires the Current Ratio, which is Current Assets/Current Liabilities, to be greater than 1.0. **Record the 'current' value as the preferred choice of metric, but you can also use the prior year number a current value is not available**.

SUPPLEMENTARY SCREEN - STEP 10

Run the screen

If you haven't already done so, run your stock screen and paste the output data into the applicable columns in the yellow cells of the *Data Inputs – SUPPLEMENTARY* table. Personally, I find it easier to download the screen outputs into a separate spreadsheet first, move the columns around to broadly match the layout of the *Data Inputs – SUPPLEMENTARY* table, and then paste my data into the appropriate yellow columns block by block.

SUPPLEMENTARY SCREEN - STEP 11

STOCK SCREEN RULE 10
An upward-sloping share price chart over the last ten years

Once your list of stocks has been filtered down to a manageable list that meets all of the quantitative rules above, it is time to check that the stock price has demonstrated a track record of increasing over time. The stocks we buy should exhibit charts with relative linearity in their trend, rising consistently from left to right over a 10-year period or longer. We don't want stocks with a share price that has gone nowhere for prolonged periods, or stocks which swing all over the place. Eliminate stocks form the list that do not satisfy your criteria. **Record the stocks that meet your criteria with a "YES" in the 'STOCK SCREEN RULE 10' column**.

Some screening tools will enable you to enter a '*Price CAGR*' criteria that measures the compound annualised growth of the share price over the past 5 or 10 years. Such a feature will remove the need to manually check the share charts for your stocks. Set your *Price CAGR* threshold at 10% per annum, since over long periods of time we'd expect the share price growth to exceed that limit. **If your screen tool/service does provide Price CAGR, record this percentage in the 'STOCK SCREEN RULE 10' column instead of a "YES."**

SUPPLEMENTARY SCREEN - STEP 12

STOCK SCREEN RULE 11
Ensure that you understand the business

Now take some time to familiarise yourself with the business. Make sure you understand what it does. **If you are comfortable that you understand the business, record a "YES" in the 'STOCK SCREEN RULE 11' column**.

SUPPLEMENTARY SCREEN - STEP 13

REVIEW THE LIST TO ENSURE ALL REMAINING STOCKS PASS ALL RULES

Even though you might initially paste a large number of stocks into these input tables, your key role is to ensure that you eliminate any stocks from the sheet that do not pass your required screen rules. For example, you might have been using a screen tool/service which enabled you to filter the entire market down to stocks with ROEs consistently above the *Target CAGR*, and which have P/B ratios of 20.0 or less. However, you might have been unable to get the screen tool/service to provide an Earnings Retention Rate, opting instead to request EPS and DPS greater than, or equal to zero. In this instance you will have pasted a list of stocks into the table that will have passed the ROE and P/B screens but now require you to manually check that the Earnings Retention Rate is sufficient. Your objective is to end up with a list of stocks that pass *all* supplementary screen rules before moving on to the next step.

Excellent work. The data you have pasted and curated in the *Data Inputs - SUPPLEMENTARY* table will feed automatically into the sheet named *'Analysis - SUPPLEMENTARY'*. As previously mentioned, if you used the *'CORE'* approach preceding this, the data you have pasted and curated in the *'Data Inputs – CORE'* table will feed automatically into the sheet named *'Analysis - CORE'*.

12.5
ANALYSE

Now that data gathering is complete you can move on to the assessment of your investment shortlist. Whether you have been able to screen for all rules, or just the 'CORE' elements, you should now have a relatively short list of potential investments, perhaps thirty stocks in total. You must determine whether these potential stocks are suitable investment candidates by checking whether they achieve your required short- and long-term returns and whether they achieve your *Target CAGR* at your *Target Timeframe*.

ANALYSIS - STEP 1

NAVIGATE TO TAB 'Analysis – CORE' or 'Analysis – SUPPLEMENTARY'

Depending on whether you used the 'CORE' or 'SUPPLEMENTARY' data input tables, navigate to the 'Analysis – CORE' or 'Analysis – SUPPLEMENTARY' sheet as appropriate. There you will see that your stock data has been pulled automatically into the blue cells on the left-hand side. In all respects both sheets are identical. The difference relates solely to your choice of input sheet.

At the top of either sheet you will see that your *Target Timeframe* and *Target CAGR* have been pulled through from the *Goal Planner* tab into the yellow cells. You have the option of overriding these cells manually, but I'd recommend planning your investments with your original goal firmly in mind, leaving them to pull through automatically from the *Goal Planner* wherever possible.

FIGURE 74: THE ANALYSIS–CORE and ANALYSIS–SUPLEMENTARY SCREEN ANALYSIS TABLE

ANALYSIS - CORE

YELLOW CELL = INPUT CELL

Requirement Inputs

Target Timeframe (years)	20
Target CAGR	20.0%
Minimum Investor's Short-Term Return	5.0%
Minimum CAGR at Target Timeframe	22.0%
Minimum Investor's Long-Term Return	24.0%

Feeds automatically from Goal Planner, or manually enter desired value in yellow cell
Feeds automatically from Goal Planner, or manually enter desired value in yellow cell

Screen Analysis Table

Company Name	ROE %	P/B (Latest)	Calculated Earnings Retention Rate (%)	Investor's Short-Term Return	Theoretical CAGR at Target Timeframe	Investor's Long-Term Return	Price Pattern	Do You Understand the Business?	Your Criteria Met?
				Cell turns green if return requirement is met	Cell turns green if return requirement is met	Cell turns green if return requirement is met	Cell turns green if you enetered "YES" in 'Data Inputs - CORE' page	Cell turns green if you enetered "YES" in 'Data Inputs - CORE' page	Cell turns green if stock meets the criteria you set
Aspirational Return Curve	40.0%	4.0	75.0%	10.0%	23.1%	30.0%			N/A
Align Technology Inc	27.1%	7.3	100.0%	3.7%	15.4%	27.1%	YES	NO	
Apple Inc	45.3%	19.5	75.5%	2.3%	17.5%	34.2%	YES	YES	YES
Biogen Inc	35.8%	3.4	100.0%	10.7%	27.8%	35.8%	YES	YES	
Booking Holdings Inc	38.6%	16.5	100.0%	2.3%	20.6%	38.6%	YES	YES	
Copart Inc	32.5%	8.2	100.0%	4.0%	19.4%	32.5%	YES	YES	
Credit Acceptance	34.7%	3.7	100.0%	9.4%	26.2%	34.7%	YES	NO	YES
Edwards Lifesciences	25.6%	10.7	100.0%	2.4%	12.1%	25.6%	YES	NO	
Evertec Inc	59.7%	7.9	82.8%	7.6%	36.0%	49.4%	YES	YES	YES
Factset Research Systems	54.2%	15.7	70.4%	3.5%	22.6%	38.2%	YES	NO	
Kla	74.3%	12.7	61.7%	5.9%	31.6%	45.9%	YES	YES	YES
Lam Research	34.6%	9.7	100.0%	3.6%	20.3%	34.6%	YES	NO	
Microsoft	35.4%	13.0	65.6%	2.7%	11.3%	23.2%	YES	NO	
Nvidia	32.3%	17.2	88.2%	1.9%	12.6%	28.5%	YES	NO	
Sei Investments Co	28.6%	4.5	77.9%	6.3%	15.1%	22.3%	NO	YES	
Texas Pacific Land Trust	112.0%	10.0	83.0%	11.2%	73.6%	93.0%	YES	YES	YES
Trex Inc	46.5%	16.3	100.0%	2.9%	27.5%	46.5%	YES	YES	
T. Rowe Price Inc	27.7%	4.2	60.1%	6.6%	11.7%	16.6%	YES	NO	
Visa Inc	28.5%	13.8	81.7%	2.1%	10.0%	23.3%	YES	YES	

ANALYSIS - STEP 2

IDENTIFY INVESTMENT IDEAS

The 'Screen Analysis Table' calculates the Investor's Short-Term Return, a stock's theoretical CAGR at the Target Timeframe, and the Investor's Long-Term Return. It also pulls in whether STOCK SCREEN RULES 10 and 11 were passed, indicating whether or not the price pattern is adequate and whether you understand the business. Green shading in a cell indicates that a particular stock has achieved the required criteria in that particular column. A stock only becomes an investment idea if it has achieved the requirements of all five columns and is labelled "YES" in the "Your Criteria Met?" column on the right-hand side of the table. There will likely be 10 or fewer such candidates in the market at any given time.

As I was finalising this book, I ran the CORE and the SUPPLEMENTARY screens on the U.S. market to serve as a general illustration of typical results Investor B might have generated. I ran the screen on 28th June 2020. Of the 5,794 stocks in the U.S. at that time, the screen returned 18 potential investment candidates ready for further inspection. One of them, Sei Investments Co, could be eliminated from consideration as it did not exhibit an upward-sloping share price. Of the 17 candidates remaining, 3 companies were stocks that Buffett holds in his portfolio, namely Apple, Biogen and Visa. This isn't bad going for a quick, simple, screen approach. Overall, Investor B had an understanding of 12 of the businesses, and 5 stocks ultimately emerged as investment ideas, shown in Figure 74 above.

This list of 17 stocks and 5 investment ideas is typical of the kind of results you will get at any point in time. You are likely to see the list shrink during extended stock market rallies, since stocks become too expensive to trigger buy recommendations. The list will grow during market corrections because falling stock prices lead to lower P/B ratios, raising short-term returns above our minimum short-term threshold of 5%. During corrections like these, great Buffett-owned companies like Apple and Visa will fall sufficiently to meet all of your criteria. As long as you understand the businesses involved, when such opportunities arise, fill your boots.

Theoretically, all five of the investment ideas would make great buys for *Investor B* over the long-term. However, rather than purchasing a stake in each of them, *Investor B* decided to weigh them up against each other before purchasing one or two.

ANALYSIS - STEP 3

EXAMINE THE RETURN CURVES OF EACH INVESTMENT IDEA

To compare the return characteristics of each stock, *Investor B* examined the '*Investor's Return Curves*' chart, situated to the right of the *Screen Analysis Table*. This shows the return curves of each of the investment ideas over the next thirty years. A stock will not show up in the chart unless all investor criteria are met.

Generally, the highest curve on the chart will be the most appealing investment. However, attention should be paid to the slope of the curve in the years leading up to your *Target Timeframe* - the curve which ends up the highest overall isn't necessarily the one that will deliver your required return earlier on.

Investor B scanned across the horizontal axis of the chart to the *Target Timeframe*, which was 20 years. In that year, *Investor B* scanned upwards to examine the height and trajectory of the curves leading up to that point in time, noting that they all exceeded the *Target CAGR* of 20% by a reasonable margin. If a curve only just makes it to your *Target CAGR* at your *Target Timeframe*, there is a higher risk that you will not be able to achieve your goal over the long-term. Ideally, you'd like to see return curves comfortably exceed your *Target CAGR* at your *Target Timeframe*.

ANALYSIS - STEP 4

SELECT THE STOCKS YOU MIGHT LIKE TO INCLUDE IN YOUR PORTFOLIO

For stocks that you might be interested in buying, copy the Name, ROE, P/B and Earnings Retention Rate from the blue cells in the *Screen Analysis Table* and paste them into the identically coloured blue cells in the '*Portfolio Construction*' tab.

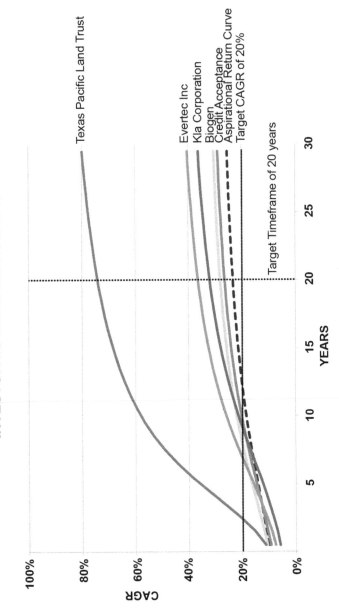

FIGURE 75: COMPARISON OF INVESTORS RETURN CURVES FOR INVESTOR Bs INVESTMENT IDEAS

12.6
INVEST: PORTFOLIO CONSTRUCTION

Your ultimate aim is to build a portfolio of businesses which, when combined with other holdings in your portfolio such as cash or ETFs, delivers your *Target CAGR* at your *Target Timeframe*. Buffett is a proponent of focus investing, holding large positions in a small number of stocks. He believes that this approach decreases the risk inherent in the portfolio since it forces you to think carefully about the economic characteristics of the companies you are buying.

You're not trying to build a portfolio of hundreds of stocks, but a small list of very high-quality businesses. For this reason, only 20 rows are provided in the Portfolio Construction table, plus an additional row for cash. Buffett regularly remarks that investors would be better off if they were given a punch card with 20 punches on it. If every big financial decision you made used up one punch, you'd get very rich because you would think through each idea properly and make good investments. And because you only have 20 punches available, you'd make big investments.[97]

> "If we want to invest in a business through the stock market, we want to put a lot of money in. We do not believe in a little of this and a little of that."[98]

> Warren Buffett – Berkshire Hathaway
> 2003 Annual Meeting

You can use the *Portfolio Construction* table to see how your current investments measure up to delivering your *Target CAGR*, and experiment with different allocations of investment ideas and cash to ensure that your overall portfolio reaches your ultimate goal.

FIGURE 76: PORTFOLIO CONSTRUCTION TABLE

PORTFOLIO CONSTRUCTION

Requirement Summary

Target Timeframe (years):	20
Target CAGR:	20.0%
Minimum Investor's Short-Term Return	5.0%
Minimum Investor's Long-Term Return	24.0%

ORANGE CELL = CASH INTEREST RATE, CASH ALLOCATION AND INPUT EXISTING HOLDINGS
BLUE CELL = INPUT INVESTMENT IDEAS
YELLOW CELL = INPUT ESTIMATED ALLOCATIONS FOR INVESTMENT IDEAS

Name or Cash Account	ROE % (5y Avg) or Interest Rate on Cash Account	P/B (At purchase date for owned investments, current value for investment ideas)	Calculated Earnings Retention Rate (%)	Percentage Allocation of Portfolio	Investor's Short-Term Return	Theoretical CAGR at Target Timeframe	Investor's Long-Term Return
Cash	0.5%	1.0	100.0%	20%	0.5%	0.5%	0.5%
1 Apple	45.3%	19.5	75.5%	15%	2.3%	17.5%	34.2%
2 Visa	28.5%	13.8	79.5%	7%	2.1%	9.7%	22.7%
3 Vanguard S&P 500 Index ETF	19.3%	3.1	69.0%	10%	6.2%	9.6%	13.3%
4 Evertec Inc	59.7%	7.9	85.5%	8%	7.6%	37.3%	51.0%
5 Holding 5							
6 Holding 6							
7 Holding 7							
8 Holding 8							
9 Holding 9							
10 Holding 10							
11 Kia	74.3%	12.7	61.7%	10%	5.9%	31.6%	45.9%
12 Texas Pacific Land Trust	112.0%	10.0	47.4%	10%	11.2%	41.7%	53.1%
13 Biogen Inc	35.8%	3.4	100.0%	10%	10.7%	27.8%	35.8%
14 Credit Acceptance	34.7%	3.7	100.0%	10%	9.4%	26.2%	34.7%
15 Stock 10							
16 Stock 11							
17 Stock 12							
18 Stock 13							
19 Stock 14							
20 Stock 15							
Total Allocation (must equal 100%)				**100%**			
					Theoretical Overall Portfolio Return:		
					5.5%	20.1%	29.2%

PORTFOLIO CONSTRUCTION STEP 1

ENTER YOUR EXISTING INVESTMENTS AND CASH BALANCE

If part of your portfolio is comprised of cash, enter the details into the first row of the *Portfolio Construction Table*. Enter the interest rate earned on the cash and the portion of your portfolio made up of cash in the orange cells in that row.

If you already have investment holdings, enter the details of these into the orange cells below cash, entering the Name and 5-Year Average ROE in the appropriate columns.

In the P/B column you would ideally enter the P/B value crystallised at the point you purchased your investments. To do so, you could look back at historical data and calculate your original P/B value as we did for Buffett's investments in Chapter 9. Alternatively, as a quick placeholder you could include the current P/B ratio instead. Next, enter the current Earnings Retention Rate. Finally, enter the percentage of the portfolio that each holding represents on the right-hand side of the orange cells in the '*Percentage Allocation of Portfolio*' column. At the bottom of that column you must check to ensure that the total of your allocations is 100%. The cell will turn red to indicate an issue if the total allocation is either above or below 100%.

On the far right-hand side of the table, at the bottom, you will also see the '*Theoretical Overall Portfolio Return*' values. These are the weighted *Investor's Short-Term Return*, CAGR at your *Target Timeframe*, and *Investor's Long-Term Return* for the portfolio overall, including any cash you hold. Because cash will normally earn only a small interest rate, 0.5% in this example, large cash balances will reduce your overall portfolio return. Your objective is to sensibly reduce cash by adding stocks to your portfolio that will help you achieve your goal, which we will discuss next.

PORTFOLIO CONSTRUCTION STEP 2

ADD INVESTMENT IDEAS

For stocks that you are interested in buying, copy the Name, ROE, P/B and Earnings Retention Rate data from the blue cells in the previous '*Analysis*' tab and paste them into the matching blue cells in the *Portfolio Construction Table*. Next, input an initial estimate of how much of your portfolio you would invest in those companies in the yellow '*Percentage Allocation of Portfolio*' cells on the right-hand side. Any portfolio allocation you set for an investment idea must reduce the cash allocation by the equivalent percentage. So, if you want to determine the impact a 10% holding of Texas Pacific Land Trust will have on your overall portfolio, you must reduce your cash holding by a corresponding 10%. The *Total Allocation* cell at the bottom of the table will alert you if your totals do not add up.

As described above, together with the details of your existing investments and cash holdings, the table will calculate the theoretical weighted *Investor's Short-Term Return*, CAGR at *Target Timeframe*, and *Investor's Long-Term Return* for your portfolio on an overall basis.

PORTFOLIO CONSTRUCTION STEP 3

EXPERIMENT WITH INVESTMENT ALLOCATIONS TO MOVE YOUR OVERALL PORTFOLIO RETURN TOWARDS YOUR TARGET RETURN

By experimenting with different investment allocations, you can influence the *Theoretical Overall Portfolio Return* and ensure that you achieve a sufficiently high return to meet your goal. The three *Theoretical Overall Portfolio Return* cells at the bottom of the table are your guides. They will automatically turn red if your portfolio has failed to achieve one or more requirements.

Use the *Percentage Allocation of Portfolio* column to vary the allocations of cash and stocks in order to alter the overall portfolio returns. For example, holding 20% of your portfolio in cash that is earning an interest rate of 0.5% per annum will contribute little to your overall return goal. Try reducing the cash balance and increasing the allocation of one of your investment ideas to increase the overall return. Or, perhaps a stock you already own exhibits great return characteristics, so you could reduce cash and increase your holding in that stock instead.

To help you visualise the impact the various stocks have on the overall portfolio return, you will find a chart showing the return curves for each stock below the portfolio table. The chart also shows the impact of Cash and a line representing the *Theoretical Overall Portfolio Return*. If your current returns are too low, look for stocks with curves that are higher than your *Target CAGR* at the *Target Timeframe* and amend your allocation percentages in favour of those companies. In Figure 76 above, *Investor B* allocated 10% of the portfolio to four investment ideas in order to elevate the overall return and achieve the *Target CAGR* of 20% at the *Target Timeframe* of 20 years.

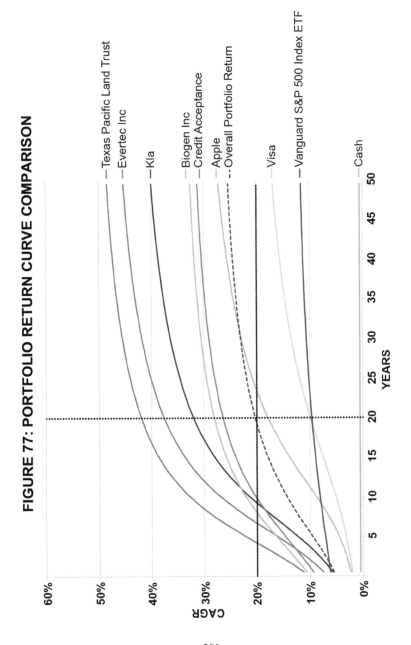

FIGURE 77: PORTFOLIO RETURN CURVE COMPARISON

You might have noticed that *Investor B*'s portfolio contains an investment in an ETF, the Vanguard S&P500 index tracker (VOO). As described in Chapter 10, it isn't always possible to screen different indices, or the ETFs which track them, but if you can find the ROE, P/B and can calculate the Earnings Retention Rate from the information on an ETF's website, it is possible to include the ETF's investment return profile within your portfolio table.

Investor B purchased VOO on 23rd March 2020, at the bottom of the 2020 COVID-19 correction. At that point the S&P500 had fallen dramatically from its highs in a very short space of time. *Investor B* recorded the ROE, P/B and calculated the Earnings Retention Rate for VOO on that date.[99] These metrics offered an *Investor's Short-Term Return* of 6.2% and an *Investor's Long-Term Return* of 13.3%, excellent return characteristics for an index comprised of 500 of the largest companies in the U.S. Furthermore, this return was significantly better than holding cash with an interest rate of 0.5%, or bonds and Treasuries paying only 1-3% of interest per annum.

FINAL THOUGHTS: DON'T CHASE RETURNS

If one or more of the *Theoretical Overall Portfolio Return* fields is below your requirements, you do not need to rush to invest the rest of your cash balance in an attempt to chase returns or make up for lost time. This is especially true if you are relatively new to investing and have not purchased many stocks previously. If you have a 15-30-year timeframe and beyond, you can take your time and add great quality stocks as and when they become available. You may even be able to take advantage of a market correction or two along the way. The objective isn't to go from zero to your required return as fast as possible, in the same way that the objective of a conductor isn't to have the orchestra finish a piece of music as quickly as possible. The most important thing is to build an intelligent, well thought out portfolio of high-quality businesses that you understand and that will serve you well for a long time to come.

12.7
MANAGING YOUR PORTFOLIO

When you have screened for stocks, identified investment ideas, and made a purchase, the hard work is done. Remember that you are buying part of a business that you plan to own for the long-term. Transient stock price movements will not sway you. In fact, price doesn't tell you anything about a business; a business's own performance figures tell you everything you need to know.

THE ANNUAL CHECK UP

"If you have to closely follow a company,
you shouldn't own it."[100]

Warren Buffett – Interview with Andy Serwer,
Yahoo Finance

I recommend checking your holdings on an annual basis, after the release of a company's annual results. While it may seem like an eternity between check-ups, I would guard against checking more frequently than this. The more we check, the more opportunity we give our minds to play tricks on us, and the greater the likelihood that we will fall victim to destructive human emotional biases. If you happen see that earnings decreased in a particular quarter, you may begin to project that decline forward into the future. You may begin to question the reason for buying the stock in the first place, especially if it has fallen in price since you bought it. Thought processes such as these completely undermine the logical and rational selection of high-quality stocks and they introduce a lot of unnecessary stress and uncertainty into your life. Keep the context of the purchase firmly in mind at all times.

"If you are in a wonderful business for a long time, even if you pay a little bit too much going in, you will get a wonderful result if you stay in a long time."[101]

Warren Buffett – Talk at The University
of Florida Business School

In Chapter 3 we noted that Buffett has zero intention of selling any of his wholly owned businesses, no matter how much he is offered. And in terms of his marketable securities, such as his stock investments, his inclination is not to sell unless he gets really discouraged with the management, or he thinks the economic characteristics of the business have changed fundamentally, such that the returns he anticipated are no longer expected to materialise.

Generally, if a company is deteriorating it will show up as a meaningful fall in the ROE. However, it may also show up in a number of other ways, which is why it is important to check a broad set of metrics. Our original screen rules provide an efficient and effective way of assessing the businesses we own in the years following purchase. For example, a company experiencing a fall in ROE could take on more leverage to prop up ROE over the short-term. In this case, we might not notice a fall in ROE itself, but we would see a corresponding increase in the Financial Leverage metric.

On an annual basis, check the screen metrics to determine whether anything has changed significantly since you bought.

- Has the ROE fallen significantly?
- Was the dividend policy changed in a significant way, reducing the Earnings Retention Rate?
- Are sales still growing on a 5-year average basis?
- Are earnings still growing on a 5-year average basis?
- Is the Net Margin still above 15%?
- Is the Financial Leverage still below 4.00 or 400% respectively?
- Is the Current Ratio still above 1.0?

It is not necessary to examine, record or update the most recent P/B ratio. It is the P/B ratio at the point you first bought which determines your returns and future performance, so subsequent changes in the P/B ratio have no impact on your portfolio.

SHOULD ANYTHING BE SOLD?

To sell a high-quality business because the price looks a little high is almost always a mistake. If you believe that the long-term economics of a business are terrific, it's rare that it makes any sense to sell it. However, the temptation to sell will almost certainly manifest itself, often amplified by market corrections and price drops.

Scenario 1: All metrics have got slightly worse

This is not a reason to sell, especially as we expect to see volatility in results year on year. So if the ROE has fallen from 30% to 25%, the Earnings Retention Rate has fallen from 75% to 73%, sales and earnings growth are down slightly, the Net Margin as dropped from 18% to 16%, Financial Leverage has increased from 3.00 to 3.50, and the Current Ratio has dropped from 2.3 to 1.8, these changes are all likely to occur within the normal range of business outcomes. If this trend continues year after year for several years you may decide to drop the investment, but generally some years will be better, and some will be worse. Your role is to stay invested for the long-term and not get thrown off the horse.

Scenario 2: One or more metrics no longer meet your screen criteria

Perhaps your *Target CAGR* was 20% and the ROE of a company has dropped since you bought it, to 19%. Simultaneously, the Net Profit Margin might have fallen below your 15% threshold. The screen rules are there to provide you with a shortlist of compelling investment opportunities *before* you initiate a position, and the failure of one or more screen rules *in subsequent years* is *not* a reason to sell a stock that you already own. The screen rules do act as a useful, annual sense check of performance for the stocks you own, but unless a metric or combination of metrics has deteriorated significantly, the long-term economics of the business will likely be just fine.

Scenario 3: One or more metrics have experienced a significant fall

You might consider selling if the economic characteristics of the business have changed in a big way. If a business has demonstrated a consistent ROE of 40% for the last five years and it subsequently falls to 35%, or even 30%, that is still an excellent return - we're not trying to be greedy, we're trying to be smart and hold for a long time. However, if a company with a consistent ROE of 40% suddenly reports a ROE of 10%, that change is worth examining further and may require action. The same is true for the other screen metrics; a significant change may require action, but it must be a significant change that will impact your ability to generate compound returns. Otherwise, leave your high-quality businesses alone to grow.

Scenario 4: The stock price has dropped significantly

If the overall market collapses 20%, this is no reason to sell. The stock you own is the same productive business that it was before the correction, and there is no reason to expect that this will change in the future. Mr. Market may be having a tantrum, but we do not listen to Mr. Market, we make our own decisions based on timeless investment principles and sound investment mechanisms. If the overall market hasn't dropped but your stock has, it is again a sign to monitor the holding periodically but is not necessarily a trigger to sell the position. As was the case in the examples above, unless there is a fundamental business change that means that you do not expect the future returns to materialise, you should continue to hold. Robust financial results will, over time, result in higher share prices, regardless of temporary fluctuations.

UPDATING COMPANY DATA IN THE PORTFOLIO CONSTRUCTION TABLE

Following the release of a company's annual results, determine the latest ROE and Earnings Retention Rate and enter these into your Portfolio Construction table, replacing those which existed at the time of purchase. Since our initial screens were based on the 5-year average ROE, it is recommended that you take the latest ROE and re-calculate the new 5-year average before updating your portfolio table, rather than using the latest number in isolation.

Do not change the P/B ratio, as this is linked to your original purchase price, not the latest market price.

Check the company's updated 'CAGR at Target Timeframe' and Investor's Long-Term Return. If the company has operated on a consistent basis versus the prior year, there should be little difference in those numbers and no action is required.

If company performance has deteriorated significantly, it is something to monitor going forward. A fall in the '*CAGR at Target Timeframe*' and the *Investor's Long-Term Return* will reduce the '*Theoretical Overall Portfolio Return*'. In this case, you will need to ensure that future stock purchases offer sufficient return to compensate for any shortfall experienced elsewhere.

UPDATING YOUR PROGRESS AND PERSONAL CIRCUMSTANCES IN THE GOAL PLANNER

As you move closer to your *Target Timeframe*, you will also need to change your personal circumstances within the *Goal Planner*. As a minimum, '*Your current age*' (*Field A*) must be updated annually. *Investor B* started at age 35 with a '*Desired goal/retirement age*' (*Field I*) of 55, yielding a '*Years to goal/Retirement*' of 20 years. A year later, the age will have changed to 36, reducing the duration to 19 years. The *Goal Planner* sheet should also be refreshed with other relevant updates. You can update the '*Current savings balance*' (*Field D*) to reflect your most recent year-end Investment Balance. Perhaps you received an unexpected pay rise, in which case update the '*Current gross annual income*' field (*Field B*). Or perhaps you decided to retire earlier than first planned. Whatever the change may be, it is important to keep the *Goal Planner* as accurate as possible.

Any changes you make in the *Goal Planner* will impact the size of your *Investment Balance Pre-Goal Date* and the size of any subsequent income withdrawals you can take. You must check that the pre-goal CAGR (*Field M*) is still sufficient to meet your needs. As you did when you originally determined your *Target CAGR*, you must tweak the pre-goal CAGR, either up or down, to find **the smallest rate** that meets your objectives. This rate must deliver an investment pot of sufficient size at your goal date that it provides you with adequate post-goal income, for sufficient time, and leaves you with enough residual *Investment Balance* to fund retirement if you live longer than expected, or to provide your family with an inheritance.

Any changes made in the *Goal Planner* will automatically flow through to the *Portfolio Construction* tab. These updates, together with the updated financial results from company annual reports, will enable you to monitor progress of your portfolio and to make course corrections as necessary.

RICHARD WORNER

CONCLUSION

At the very start of the book I wrote, "People with lots of money didn't always start out that way, and there's no reason you can't join them!" That statement is certainly true. Warren Buffett demonstrated that, through investing, you can become one of the richest people in the world. Countless others have invested their way to wealth, security and financial freedom.

Determining a way to make money in the market, however, is no easy matter. Regardless of individual circumstances, mental and emotional obstacles stand in the way of success. To become successful investors, we must adopt an approach that passes a number of crucial tests.

First, the scope of the financial markets is vast, and conditions are continuously changing. We are bombarded with new information at mind-boggling pace, so our methodology must focus on the right information and be highly effective at filtering out noise.

Once we have overcome that mental hurdle, we must protect ourselves from the influence of our emotions. Deep-rooted, evolutionary biases will invade our decision-making. To guard against these, and any counter-productive influence from our ego, we must have an approach that is clearly defined and rational.

Next, a successful methodology must not be dependent on an individual's unique knowledge, skills or resources; it must be accessible to all, providing everyone with the opportunity to achieve above-average returns. And it must stand the test of time; it must be consistently valid and relevant, despite changing market conditions. Both of these challenges require that the approach be based on simple, universal principles.

Finally, a successful investment approach must be actionable. It must be clear which stocks generate high returns, and what level of returns you can expect to receive by investing in them. Ultimately, a successful approach must secure a positive response to the question, *"Can I take action right now?"*.

THE INVESTOR'S SOLUTION

The Investor's Solution cuts through market noise, using only three simple metrics. To generate above-average returns we will seek out businesses with consistently high *Returns on Equity*, high *Earnings Retention Rates*, and we will endeavour to buy them at reasonable prices, represented by the *Price/Book Ratio*.

These metrics are used in two simple calculations, determining our theoretical *Investor's Short-* and *Long-Term Returns*. An *Investor's Return Curve* connects the two, providing our theoretical return at any point in time.

The impact of emotions is thus mitigated through the rational comparison of *Investor's Return Curves*, offering a factual basis for investment decision-making in preference to speculative activities that focus on fleeting price fluctuations.

While this list of metrics is small, and the calculations simple, their output is powerful. By varying the ROE, Earnings Retention Rate and P/B, we can identify stocks with the return curve characteristics required to achieve very particular goals.

Since only a handful of companies will pass all of our requirements, when we find one, we should buy a meaningful amount.

By putting together a portfolio of such businesses at prices that represent good value, we can secure above-average rates of return. We will hold our investments for a long time, utilising the timeless principle of compounding to accelerate our returns.

Once purchased, we need not worry about selling unless a business we own changes fundamentally. We will simply sit back and watch our aggregate portfolio returns march upwards over time.

Happy hunting!

NOTES

INTRODUCTION

1. *"There are a million ways to make money in the markets. The irony is that they are all very difficult to find."* Schwager, Jack D. *The New Market Wizards: Conversations With America's Top Traders*. New York, U.S.A: HarperCollins, 1992, xi.
2. Statista.com. "Number of regulated open-end funds worldwide from 2008 to 2019." Accessed June 4, 2020. https://www.statista.com/statistics/630524/number-of-regulated-open-end-funds-worldwide/
3. Statista.com. "Number of ETFs worldwide 2019." Accessed June 4, 2020. https://www.statista.com/statistics/278249/global-number-of-etfs/
4. *"We could never make market decisions without them, but they are also very dangerous to people who are not aware that they exist."* Tharp, Van K. *Trade Your Way to Financial Freedom*. New York, U.S.A: McGraw-Hill, 2007, P21.
5. *"I believe that uncontrolled basic emotions are the true and deadly enemy of the speculator; hope, fear and greed are always present."* Livermore, Jesse and Richard Smitten. *How to Trade in Stocks*. IA, U.S.A: Wasendorf & Associates Inc, 2001, P142.

CHAPTER 1: THE STUDENT

6.   WhichWayHome.com. "WhichWayHome Timeline." Accessed June 4, 2020. http://www.whichwayhome.com/index.php/investment/investment-track-record/time-and-money.html.

7.   WhichWayHome.com. "House Prices Track Record." Accessed June 4, 2020. http://www.whichwayhome.com/index.php/investment/investment-track-record/house-prices-record.html.

8.   WhichWayHome.com. "Stock Market Track Record." Accessed June 4, 2020. http://www.whichwayhome.com/index.php/investment/investment-track-record/stock-market-record.html.

9.   WhichWayHome.com. "Gold & Silver Track Record." Accessed June 4, 2020. http://www.whichwayhome.com/index.php/investment/investment-track-record/gold-record.html.

10.   WhichWayHome.com. "Gold & Silver Track Record." Accessed June 4, 2020. http://www.whichwayhome.com/index.php/investment/investment-track-record/gold-record.html.

11.   *Dalio*, Raymond T. *Paradigm Shifts.* https://economicprinciples.org/downloads/Paradigm-Shifts.pdf. P1.

CHAPTER 2: INVESTORS, OBSTACLES & SOLUTIONS

12.   *"By far the best investment you can make is in yourself."* Widely quoted. See: *Buffett*, Warren E. *"Warren Buffett shares advice on becoming successful."* Interview by Andy Serwer. Yahoo Finance, June 19, 2019. Video, 00:00:51. https://www.youtube.com/watch?v=Tr6MMsoWAog. See also: *Pecaut*, Daniel and Corey Wrenn. *Into the Minds of Warren Buffett and Charlie Munger: Lessons Learned from Berkshire Hathaway's Approach to Investing.* Mumbai, India: Jaico Publishing House, 2017. Introduction.

13.   *Cicero*, Marcus Tullius. *Discourse on Old Age.*

14.   *"It's a huge structural advantage not to have a lot of*

money." Bianco, Anthony. *"The Warren Buffett You Don't Know." Business Week*, July 4, 1999. See also: *Buffett*, Warren E. *"Warren Buffett on Investment Strategy."* Interview by Carol Loomis. Fortune Magazine, October 7, 2014. Video, 00:33:00.
https://www.youtube.com/watch?v=cSU3y0N60XU&

CHAPTER 3: THE MASTER

15. *Thorndike*, William N. *The Outsiders: Eight Unconventional CEOs and Their Radically Rational Blueprint for Success.* Boston, U.S.A: Harvard Business Review Press, 2012, P171.
16. Fortune.com. "Fortune 500." Accessed June 4, 2020. https://fortune.com/fortune500/
17. *Buffett*, Warren E. Berkshire Hathaway Annual Report 2019, P2.
https://www.berkshirehathaway.com/2019ar/2019ar.pdf
18. Bloomberg.com. "Bloomberg Billionaires Index." Accessed June 4, 2020. https://www.bloomberg.com/billionaires/
19. *"Becoming Warren Buffett."* HBO Documentary, HBO, 2017. Video, 00:44:43. See also: "The World's Greatest Money Maker: Evan Davis meets Warren Buffett – A Modest Man." Interview by Evan Davis. BBC, October 27, 2009. Video, 00:05:08.
https://www.bbc.co.uk/programmes/b00nn7vs
20. *Buffett*, Warren E. Berkshire Hathaway Annual Report 2019, A-1.
https://www.berkshirehathaway.com/2019ar/2019ar.pdf
21. *Gates*, William H. "Becoming Warren Buffett." HBO Documentary, HBO, 2017. Video, 01:18:34.
22. *"Business schools reward complex behavior more than simple behavior, but simple behavior is more effective."* *Bauer*, Patricia E. "The Convictions of a Long Distance Investor." *Channels*, November 1986, P28.
23. *"There seems to be some perverse human characteristic that likes to make easy things difficult."* *Buffett*, Warren E. "The Superinvestors of Graham-and-Doddsville." Columbia Business School Magazine, 1984. P15.
https://www8.gsb.columbia.edu/sites/valueinvesting/files/fil

es/Buffett1984.pdf

24. *Buffett*, Warren E. "1982 Shareholder Letter."
https://www.berkshirehathaway.com/letters/1982.html

25. *Buffett*, Warren E. "2014 Shareholder Letter."
https://www.berkshirehathaway.com/letters/2014.html

26. "The David Rubenstein Show: Warren Buffett on His Early
Career in Finance." Interview by David Rubenstein.
Bloomberg QuickTake. November 3, 2016. Video,
00:18:40.
https://www.youtube.com/watch?v=u8ANHNU0Fng

27. "*I think, partly, because it is so simple,*" *Buffett*, Warren E.
"Adam Smith's Money World: Episode #112: Money
Managers: Meet The Man Who Bats 1000." Interview by
George J. W. Goodman. WNET, PBS, 1985. Video,
00:06:30. https://licensing.wnet.org/content/adam-smiths-
money-world-112-money-managers-meet-the-man-who-
bats-1000/.

28. "Warren Buffett reveals his investment strategy and
mastering the market." Interview by Andy Serwer. Yahoo
Finance, May 2, 2019. Video, 00:02:50.
https://www.youtube.com/watch?v=SEZwkbliJr8&t=381s.
See also: "Warren Buffett on Investment Strategy."
Interview by Carol Loomis. Fortune Magazine, October 7,
2014. Video, 00:22:00.
https://www.youtube.com/watch?v=cSU3y0N60XU

29. "Nightline with Warren Buffett." Interview by Ted Koppel,
Nightline, ABC News. March 2, 1999. Video, 00:07:09
https://www.youtube.com/watch?v=wHub2E5deSs

30. "*I can understand Gillette, I can understand Coca-Cola
and I can understand Wrigley's Chewing Gum…and I have
a pretty good idea of what they're going to look like 10-15
years from now.*" *Buffett*, Warren E. "Nightline with Warren
Buffett." Interview by Ted Koppel, Nightline, ABC News.
March 2, 1999. Video, 00:14:36
https://www.youtube.com/watch?v=wHub2E5deSs. See
also: "Warren Buffett Talks Business." The University of
North Carolina Center for Public Television, distributed by
PBS Home Video. 1996. Video, 00:17:03.
https://www.youtube.com/watch?v=zRM5b9zLmQE&t=113
8s.

31. *"Take Wrigley's chewing gum. I don't think the Internet is going to change how people are going to chew gum."* Schlender, Brent. "Bill & Warren." *Fortune*, July 1998. P55.

32. *"We have to deal in things that we're capable of understanding. And then, once we're over that filter we have to have a business with some intrinsic characteristics that give it a durable competitive advantage. And then, of course, we vastly prefer a management in place with a lot of integrity and talent. And finally, no matter how wonderful it is, it's not worth an infinite price, so we have to have a price that makes sense. It's a very simple set of ideas."* Munger, Charles T. "The World's Greatest Money Maker: Evan Davis meets Warren Buffett – A Modest Man." Interview by Evan Davis. BBC, October 27, 2009. Video, 00:12:50. https://www.bbc.co.uk/programmes/b00nn7vs

33. *"You don't need to be a rocket scientist. Investing is not a game where the guy with the 160 IQ guy beats the guy with the 130 IQ."* Widely quoted. See: *Loomis*, Carol J. *Tap Dancing to Work: Warren Buffett on Practically Everything, 1966-2012*. Penguin Books Ltd. 2012. P101. See also: *Lowe*, Janet. *Warren Buffett Speaks: Wit and Wisdom from the World's Greatest Investor*. New Jersey, U.S.A: John Wiley & Sons. 2007. P56.

34. *"What we do is not beyond anyone else's competence...it is just not necessary to do extraordinary things to get extraordinary results."* Loomis, Carol J. "The Inside Story of Warren Buffett." *Fortune*, April 11, 1988.

35. *"It's a temperamental quality not an intellectual quality. You don't need tonnes of IQ in this business...you do not have to be able to play three-dimensional chess."* Buffett, Warren E. "Adam Smith's Money World: Episode #112: Money Managers: Meet The Man Who Bats 1000." Interview by George J. W. Goodman. WNET, PBS, 1985. Video, 00:01:17. https://licensing.wnet.org/content/adam-smiths-money-world-112-money-managers-meet-the-man-who-bats-1000/.

36. "The World's Greatest Money Maker: Evan Davis meets Warren Buffett – A Modest Man." Interview by Evan Davis. BBC, October 27, 2009. Video, 00:05:22. https://www.bbc.co.uk/programmes/b00nn7vs. See also:

Bauer, Patricia E. "The Convictions of a Long Distance Investor." *Channels*, November 1986, P22.

37. *Buffett*, Warren E. Berkshire Hathaway Annual Report 2019, P10.
https://www.berkshirehathaway.com/2019ar/2019ar.pdf

38. *"We own [5.7%] of Apple and it's probably the best business I know in the world…I don't think of Apple as a stock, I think it's our third largest business."* Buffett, Warren E. "Watch CNBC's full interview with Berkshire Hathaway CEO Warren Buffett." Interview by Becky Quick. CNBC, February 24, 2020. Video, 01:13:13 and 01:25:24.
https://www.youtube.com/watch?v=JvEas_zZ4fM

39. "Nightline with Warren Buffett." Interview by Ted Koppel, Nightline, ABC News. March 2, 1999. Video, 00:14:10
https://www.youtube.com/watch?v=wHub2E5deSs

40. *"Wall Street makes its money on activity. You make your money on inactivity."* Widely quoted. See: *Andrews*, David. *The Oracle Speaks: Warren Buffett In His Own Words.* Chicago, U.S.A: Agate Publishing, Inc, 2012, P28. See also: *Warren Buffett Talks to MBA Students*. CA, U.S.A: BN Publishing, 2009, E-book location 363.

41. *"In the short run, the market is a voting machine but in the long run it is a weighing machine."* Widely quoted. See: *Hagstrom*, Robert G. *The Warren Buffett Way: Investment Strategies of the World's Greatest Investor*. New York, U.S.A: John Wiley & Sons, 1994, P99.

42. "Watch CNBC's full interview with Berkshire Hathaway CEO Warren Buffett." Interview by Becky Quick. CNBC, February 24, 2020. Video, 00:01:50.
https://www.youtube.com/watch?v=JvEas_zZ4fM

43. *Buffett*, Warren E. "Adam Smith's Money World: Episode #112: Money Managers: Meet The Man Who Bats 1000." Interview by George J. W. Goodman. WNET, PBS, 1985. Video, 00:02:20. https://licensing.wnet.org/content/adam-smiths-money-world-112-money-managers-meet-the-man-who-bats-1000/.

44. "University of Georgia Terry College of Business Presents Warren Buffett." Terry Leadership Speaker Series, July 18, 2001. Video, 00:34:00.
https://www.youtube.com/watch?v=2a9Lx9J8uSs

45. "University of Georgia Terry College of Business Presents Warren Buffett." Terry Leadership Speaker Series, July 18, 2001. Video, 00:35:00.
https://www.youtube.com/watch?v=2a9Lx9J8uSs

46. *"We expect to hold these securities for a long time. In fact, when we own portions of outstanding businesses with outstanding managements, our favorite holding period is forever." Buffett,* Warren E. *"1988 Shareholder Letter."*
https://www.berkshirehathaway.com/letters/1988.html

47. *"If a business does well, the stock eventually follows."* Widely quoted. See: *Bloch,* Robert L. *My Warren Buffett Bible: A Short and Simple Guide to Rational Investing: 284 Quotes from the World's Most Successful Investor.* London, U.K: Piatkus, Litte, Brown Book Group, 2015, P31. See also: *Buffett,* Mary and David Clark. *The Tao of Warren Buffett: Warren Buffett's Words of Wisdom.* London, U.K: Simon & Schuster UK, 2007, P31.

48. *"consistently earn above-average returns on capital." Buffett,* Warren E. Berkshire Hathaway Owner Related Share Principles, P1, Principle 4.
https://www.berkshirehathaway.com/ownman.pdf

49. *"I would rather have a $10 million business making 15% than a $100 million business making 4%." Lowenstein,* Roger. *Buffett: The Making of an American Capitalist.* New York, U.S.A: Random House, 1996, P111.

50. *"Price is what you pay; value is what you get."* Widely quoted.

51. *"It's far better to buy a wonderful company at a fair price than a fair company at a wonderful price."* Widely quoted. See: *Pecaut,* Daniel and Corey Wrenn. *University of Berkshire Hathaway: 30 Years of Lessons Learned from Warren Buffett & Charlie Munger at the Annual Shareholders Meeting.* IA, U.S.A: Pecaut & Company, 2018, P20.

52. "The World's Greatest Money Maker: Evan Davis meets Warren Buffett – A Modest Man." Interview by Evan Davis. BBC, October 27, 2009. Video, 00:21:30.
https://www.bbc.co.uk/programmes/b00nn7vs

53. *"Our system ought to be more copied than it is." Matthews,* Jeff. *Pilgrimage to Warren Buffett's Omaha: A Hedge Fund*

Manager's Dispatches from Inside the Berkshire Hathaway Annual Meeting. New York, U.S.A: McGraw Hill, 2009, P233.

CHAPTER 6: THE INVESTOR'S LONG-TERM RETURN

54.   *"We don't get rich on our dividends that we receive…we get rich on fact that the retained earnings are used to build new earning power."* Buffett, Warren E. "Watch CNBC's full interview with Berkshire Hathaway CEO Warren Buffett." Interview by Becky Quick. CNBC, February 24, 2020. Video, 00:06:40.
https://www.youtube.com/watch?v=JvEas_zZ4fM&t=3223s

55.   *"…on their retained earnings, investors could earn [the full] 12%…The right to reinvest automatically a portion of the equity coupon at 12% was of enormous value."* Buffett, Warren E. "How Inflation Swindles the Equity Investor." *Fortune*, May 1977.

56.   *Buffett*, Warren E. Berkshire Hathaway Annual Report 2019, The Power of Retained Earnings, P3.
https://www.berkshirehathaway.com/2019ar/2019ar.pdf

CHAPTER 9: BUFFETT'S INVESTMENTS

57.   *"That which goes up doesn't necessarily have to come down." Buffett*, Mary and David Clark. *The Tao of Warren Buffett: Warren Buffett's Words of Wisdom.* London, U.K: Simon & Schuster UK, 2007, P136.

58.   Berkshire Hathaway Annual Report 2019, P10.
https://www.berkshirehathaway.com/2019ar/2019ar.pdf

59.   The Coca-Cola Company Annual Report, 1987.

60.   *Buffett*, Warren E. *"1989 Shareholder Letter."*
https://www.berkshirehathaway.com/letters/1989.html

61.   The Coca-Cola Company Annual Report, 1988.

62.   Yahoo Finance. The Coca-Cola Company > Historical Data. Accessed June 4, 2020.
https://uk.finance.yahoo.com/quote/KO/history?p=KO

63.   The Coca-Cola Company Annual Report, 1994, 10-Year

Summary.

64. Wells Fargo & Company Annual Report, 1989, Highlights section before Page 1.
https://www.wellsfargohistory.com/assets/pdf/annual-reports/1989-annual-report.pdf

65. Wells Fargo & Company Annual Report, 1989, P6. Calculated from Table 2: Six-Year Summary of Selected Financial Data.
https://www.wellsfargohistory.com/assets/pdf/annual-reports/1989-annual-report.pdf

66. *Buffett*, Warren E. "*1990 Shareholder Letter.*"
https://www.berkshirehathaway.com/letters/1990.html

67. Wells Fargo & Company Annual Report, 1990, P26, Consolidated Balance Sheet.
https://www.wellsfargohistory.com/assets/pdf/annual-reports/1990-annual-report.pdf

68. Yahoo Finance. Wells Fargo & Company > Historical Data. Accessed June 4, 2020.
https://uk.finance.yahoo.com/quote/WFC/history?p=WFC

69. Berkshire Hathaway Annual Report 2016, P48, Note 4.
https://www.berkshirehathaway.com/2016ar/2016ar.pdf

70. *Buffett*, Warren E. "*2011 Shareholder Letter.*" Page 7.
https://www.berkshirehathaway.com/letters/2011ltr.pdf

71. International Business Machines Corporation Annual Report, 2010, P131, Five-Year Comparison of Selected Financial Data.
https://www.ibm.com/investor/att/pdf/IBM_Annual_Report_2010.pdf

72. *Buffett*, Warren E. "*2011 Shareholder Letter.*" Page 16.
https://www.berkshirehathaway.com/letters/2011ltr.pdf

73. International Business Machines Corporation Annual Report, 2010, P63, Consolidated Statement of Financial Position.
https://www.ibm.com/investor/att/pdf/IBM_Annual_Report_2010.pdf

74. International Business Machines Corporation Annual Report, 2010, P108, Note R.
https://www.ibm.com/investor/att/pdf/IBM_Annual_Report_2010.pdf

75. Yahoo Finance. International Business Machines

Corporation > Historical Data. Accessed June 4, 2020.
https://uk.finance.yahoo.com/quote/IBM/history?p=IBM

76. *Buffett*, Warren E. Berkshire Hathaway 2017 Annual Meeting. "Apple is in, IBM is out." CNBC. Video, 00:00:28. https://buffett.cnbc.com/video/2017/05/06/apple-is-in-ibm-is-out.html

77. *Buffett*, Warren E. "2011 Shareholder Letter." Page 7. https://www.berkshirehathaway.com/letters/2011ltr.pdf

78. Berkshire Hathaway Annual Report 2016, P19. https://www.berkshirehathaway.com/2016ar/2016ar.pdf

79. *Buffett*, Warren E. "*2019 Shareholder Letter.*" Page 10. https://www.berkshirehathaway.com/letters/2019ltr.pdf

80. Calculated from Apple Inc, Annual Report, 2015 (and earlier reports where necessary). https://www.sec.gov/Archives/edgar/data/320193/0001193 12515356351/d17062d10k.htm

81. *Buffett*, Warren E. "*2016 Shareholder Letter.*" Page 19. https://www.berkshirehathaway.com/letters/2016ltr.pdf

82. Apple Inc, Annual Report, 2016, P41. https://www.sec.gov/Archives/edgar/data/320193/0001628 28016020309/a201610-k9242016.htm

83. Apple Inc, Annual Report, 2016, P48. https://www.sec.gov/Archives/edgar/data/320193/0001628 28016020309/a201610-k9242016.htm

84. Apple Inc, Annual Report, 2019, P48. https://www.sec.gov/ix?doc=/Archives/edgar/data/320193/ 000032019319000119/a10-k20199282019.htm

85. *Lowe*, Janet. *Damn Right! Behind The Scenes with Berkshire Hathaway Billionaire Charlie Munger.* New York, U.S.A: John Wiley & Sons, 2000, Appendix D. Charles T. Munger's Speeches. Multidisciplinary Skills: Educational Implications, P257.

86. Apple Inc, 10-Q Quarterly Report, for quarter ended March 26, 2016, P5. https://www.sec.gov/Archives/edgar/data/320193/0001193 12516559625/d165350d10q.htm

87. Biogen Inc, Annual Report, 2018 (and earlier reports where required). https://investors.biogen.com/static-files/30ea6b55-6a57-48ae-840d-96ac58ddf031

88. Biogen Inc, Quarterly Report, for quarter ended June 30,

2019, P7. https://investors.biogen.com/static-files/e6da9439-f776-43d5-8257-24123c53dd25

89.   Biogen Inc, Quarterly Report, for quarter ended June 30, 2019, P37. https://investors.biogen.com/static-files/e6da9439-f776-43d5-8257-24123c53dd25

CHAPTER 10: OTHER INVESTMENT CONSIDERATIONS

90.   "In the securities business, you literally, every day, have thousands of the major American corporations offered to you, at a price that changes daily, and you don't have to make any decisions…nothing is forced upon you." Buffett, Warren E. "Adam Smith's Money World: Episode #112: Money Managers: Meet The Man Who Bats 1000." Interview by George J. W. Goodman. WNET, PBS, 1985. Video, 00:05:22. https://licensing.wnet.org/content/adam-smiths-money-world-112-money-managers-meet-the-man-who-bats-1000/.

91.   Investor.Vanguard.com. "Vanguard S&P 500 ETF (VOO)." Accessed March 23, 2020. https://investor.vanguard.com/etf/profile/portfolio/voo

92.   Investor.Vanguard.com. "Vanguard S&P 500 ETF (VOO)." Accessed March 23, 2020. https://investor.vanguard.com/etf/profile/performance/voo

93.   Warren Buffett Talks to MBA Students. CA, U.S.A: BN Publishing, 2009, E-book location 930. See also: Buffett, Warren E. "1996 Shareholder Letter." https://www.berkshirehathaway.com/letters/1996.html. See also: Footage from the 2002 Berkshire Hathaway Annual Meeting: https://www.youtube.com/watch?v=Clj-r1Pzu0w&feature=youtu.be. See also: Buffett, Warren E. "Nightline with Warren Buffett." Interview by Ted Koppel, Nightline, ABC News. March 2, 1999. Video, 00:18:02 https://www.youtube.com/watch?v=wHub2E5deSs

94.   Apple Inc, Annual Report, 2019, P31. https://www.sec.gov/ix?doc=/Archives/edgar/data/320193/000032019319000119/a10-k20199282019.htm

95.   Apple Inc, Annual Report, 2016, P41.

https://www.sec.gov/Archives/edgar/data/320193/0001628
28016020309/a201610-k9242016.htm

96.   Biogen Inc, Annual Report, 2019. F-4.
      https://investors.biogen.com/static-files/f86236ee-b489-
      461e-bb28-b7b4ccc4aeea

CHAPTER 12: TAKING ACTION

97.   Widely quoted. See: *Buffett*, Warren E. "University of
      Georgia Terry College of Business Presents Warren
      Buffett." Terry Leadership Speaker Series, July 18, 2001.
      Video, 00:31:28.
      https://www.youtube.com/watch?v=2a9Lx9J8uSs. See
      also: *Hagstrom*, Robert G. *The Warren Buffett Way:
      Investment Strategies of the World's Greatest Investor.*
      New York, U.S.A: John Wiley & Sons, 1994, P180.

98.   "*If we want to invest in a business through the stock
      market, we want to put a lot of money in. We do not
      believe in a little of this and a little of that.*" *Buffett*, Warren
      E. Berkshire Hathaway Annual Shareholder Meeting,
      2003. Video: 00:00:23.
      https://www.youtube.com/watch?v=IpwWzrPfa9M&feature
      =youtu.be

99.   Investor.Vanguard.com. "Vanguard S&P 500 ETF (VOO)."
      Accessed March 23, 2020.
      https://investor.vanguard.com/etf/profile/portfolio/voo

100. "*If you have to closely follow a company, you shouldn't
      own it.*" *Buffett*, Warren E. "Warren Buffett reveals his
      investment strategy and mastering the market." Interview
      by Andy Serwer. Yahoo Finance, May 2, 2019. Video,
      00:06:37. https://www.youtube.com/watch?v=SEZwkbliJr8

101. "*If you are in a wonderful business for a long time, even if
      you pay a little bit too much going in, you will get a
      wonderful result if you stay in a long time.*" *Buffett*, Warren
      E. "Warren Buffet speaks with Florida University."
      University of Florida Business School, October 15, 1998.
      Video, 00:12:15.
      https://www.youtube.com/watch?v=2MHIcabnjrA

ABOUT THE AUTHOR

Richard Worner started investing while at university in London. His timing appeared perfect, stepping into the markets just as the Dot-com boom sent stock prices soaring. Despite making every amateur mistake in the book, Richard amassed a lot of money in a short space of time – the tide was rising in his favour, buoyed by rampant speculation.

His fortunes reversed in March 2000 when the Dot-com bubble burst, causing markets to collapse around the world. His new-found wealth disappeared faster than you can say "*rookie error*".

More fascinated than disappointed, Richard embarked on an extensive study of the markets and trading strategies, determined to work out what had happened and why. By forming an understanding of market boom and bust characteristics he intended to exploit future price anomalies and profit from them. After five years of study, pieces of the financial market puzzle finally clicked into place.

Sensing the emergence of a new global bubble, in 2006 Richard decided to share his knowledge and investment opinions with the public for free. *WhichWayHome.com* was launched at the start of 2007, becoming one of the few publications worldwide to predict successfully the 2008 Credit Crisis and the accompanying collapse in stock markets and house prices worldwide. His success continued to grow, with subsequent predictions of powerful moves in gold and silver coming to fruition in the years that followed.

A decade later, after taking a well-earned break from active investing to reflect on market dynamics, he's back with a mission to make above-average investment returns accessible to all. Seeking to simplify the complex world of investing into a simple, effective approach, he created *The Investor's Solution*, a powerful investment methodology with simplicity at its heart.

Lightning Source UK Ltd.
Milton Keynes UK
UKHW021824200122
397476UK00005B/812